# GANDHI in BOMBAY

# GANDHI in BOMBAY

## towards swaraj

Usha Thakkar
Sandhya Mehta

OXFORD
UNIVERSITY PRESS

# OXFORD
UNIVERSITY PRESS

Oxford University Press is a department of the University of Oxford.
It furthers the University's objective of excellence in research, scholarship,
and education by publishing worldwide. Oxford is a registered trademark of
Oxford University Press in the UK and in certain other countries.

Published in India by
Oxford University Press
YMCA Library Building, 1 Jai Singh Road, New Delhi 110001, India

© Oxford University Press 2017

The moral rights of the authors have been asserted.

First Edition published in 2017

ISBN-13: 978-0-19-947070-9
ISBN-10: 0-19-947070-7

Typeset in Trump Mediaeval LT Std 9.5/16
by Tranistics Data Technologies, New Delhi 110044
Printed in India by Replika Press Pvt. Ltd

# CONTENTS

# LIST OF PHOTOGRAPHS

# FOREWORD

GANDHI CALLED BOMBAY THE 'FIRST CITY OF INDIA', BY WHICH HE meant, among other things, that it had a highly developed, public-spirited civic culture not found in other Indian cities. That civic culture was marked by a willingness to contribute generously to worthwhile public causes, the reason why Gandhi also called it 'Bombay the Beautiful'. As he put it, 'Bombay is beautiful not for its big buildings for most of them hide squalid poverty and dirt, nor for its wealth for most of it is derived from the blood of the masses, but for its world renowned generosity.' Gandhi spoke from personal experiences. Bombay contributed generously to the Tilak Swaraj Fund as well as to the Deenbandhu (C.F. Andrews) Memorial Fund. Andrews was not a household name in a way that Tilak was, nor was his impact on popular consciousness as great.

Yet Bombay contributed handsomely to the Deenbandhu Fund, enabling Gandhi to collect Rs 500,000 in just eight days. 'Bombay has never disappointed me whenever I have gone there for collection,' he said. For Gandhi, 'Bombay the Beautiful' served as the idealized norm against which he judged the city's responses to his various demands, and rebuked it when it failed to comply with them.

Gandhi thought that the Parsi contribution to the development of Bombay's civic culture was considerable, even decisive. He said, 'If Bombay was beautiful, if Bombay was noted for its generosity, if Bombay was noted for its public spirit, it was due to the Parsi contribution. If it were not for the Parsis, Bombay would be like any other city in India.' Gandhi was exaggerating because Bombay's culture was also shaped by Gopal Krishna Gokhale, Bal Gangadhar Tilak, and others. However, he was not entirely wrong because individuals such as Dadabhai Naoroji, Pherozeshah Mehta, and Cowasji Jehangir had also shaped and dominated Bombay's public life and 'set its tone'. Thanks to its civic culture, the 'great Parsi community' exercised self-restraint and did not engage in massive protests even when Bombay enforced the policy of prohibition in 1939 that damaged their economic interests.

The civic culture of Bombay shared some ideas with Gandhi's philosophy of satyagraha, and he made full use of them to attain his objectives. He mounted the Non-Cooperation Movement in the 1920s, mobilized the masses, staged hartals and boycotts, and gave political salience to the hitherto neglected areas of the city. He gave a call to 'Do or Die' as part of his Quit India Movement, and Bombay responded with its characteristic verve. Gandhi energized its citizens, gave them the courage to stand up to their colonial masters, and restored their sense of power and dignity. He tapped into their sense of social concern and urged them to care for the poor. When he heard of a proposal to build his statue, he successfully urged the organizers to use the money instead to improve the sanitary and housing conditions of the poor and grow more food crops. He even persuaded the middle classes, especially the women, of Bombay to follow him in making bonfires of foreign cloth as a 'sacrament', and thereby help in removing what he called a source of the country's moral 'pollution'. He was both criticized and applauded for this, but he was not a man to give in on issues he felt strongly about or on his stand regarding which he had no doubts.

Bombay's liberal civic culture, which was also partly Gandhi's, had its limitations, and explains the weaknesses of his movement. Gandhi did not take up the cause of the city's textile and other workers who preferred a more radical and confrontational approach. Although sympathetic to the cause of the Dalits, his approach to their condition tended to be patronizing, even paternalistic, and alienated some of their activists. At a different level, right-wing Hindus and those committed to a strong and militarist India remained hostile to him and some even threatened his life. Thanks to the influence of modernity, of which the Parsis were one of the major carriers, Gandhi's views on prohibition, castes, moral puritanism, and social conservatism in general found only limited support among the city's middle classes. Even as Gandhi accepted some aspects of Bombay's culture and rejected others, the city did the same with him.

The story of Gandhi's association with Bombay from the time he first visited the city on his way to London to train as a lawyer, to his last visit in July 1946 has not yet been told. This book fills that gap and is an invaluable source of information. The authors detail Gandhi's visits with great care, discuss who he met and in what context, and examine with considerable erudition the various campaigns and activities he conducted in the city. As they ably show, Bombay was largely his political *karmabhumi*, a place where he undertook a wide range of political and social activities, some of which were locally relevant, though most of them had a national significance. Bombay had not shaped him, made him one of its own, and to some extent he remained a relative outsider. For his part, he tried to mould it in his image with some notable successes and some equally notable failures. This rich and well-researched book is indispensable for a student of Gandhi, Bombay, and the Indian struggle for independence in general, and is to be warmly welcomed.

Bhikhu Parekh
Emeritus Professor, University of Hull
and University of Westminster, UK,
and Member, House of Lords, UK

# ᏙᎢ

# ACKNOWLEDGEMENTS

—◦—

THE JOURNEY FOR THIS BOOK, SPANNING OVER YEARS, HAS BEEN AT times difficult, but on the whole exciting. There were times when we were concerned about the scarcity of information regarding certain matters and there were also times when we felt overwhelmed with the huge mass of data available. It was not easy to find the way amidst this plethora of data and information. In addition, there were many lanes and bylanes—alluring but deviating from the main track; the temptation to explore them had to be resisted. Many friends and well-wishers have helped us in our journey to reach the completion of the book. We are grateful to them.

Intertwining of Gandhi's life with Bombay unfolded various intersections of India's freedom movement, bringing in focus various people and places, some well-known and some veiled in

ACKNOWLEDGEMENTS

anonymity. We discovered many inspiring facets of the history of the city during our journey. The names of places came alive with the scenes of meetings and processions and the pages of history vibrated with the presence of leaders and lovers of freedom. Our informal discussions with Professor Usha Mehta, Professor Aloo Dastur, and Vasant Pradhan over the years at Mani Bhavan enriched us with important information and insight. Unfortunately, today they are not with us to see this book. We owe a huge debt to them.

Engaging conversations with Professor Bhikhu Parekh have always been a great learning experience. These have helped enrich our understanding of Gandhi and sharpened the focus of the book. We are very grateful to him for sparing his time for such conversations and writing the foreword to the book amidst various demands on his time.

Dr Aroon Tikekar was always available as a storehouse of knowledge about Bombay and also as a sounding board for arguments. We acknowledge his help in enhancing our knowledge and understanding of Bombay and his encouragement throughout the project. He passed away suddenly in January 2016. We sadly miss his presence.

Our special thanks to Yogesh Kamdar, who extended his unstinting support at every stage of the book. We have benefited immensely by his incisive comments and valuable suggestions on the drafts and his administrative acumen. His accessibility and readiness to help have been a great source of encouragement to us.

We thank the staff of the Mani Bhavan Gandhi Sangrahalaya who have been with us from the beginning of this book. M.T. Ajgaonkar wholeheartedly provided administrative support and often talked about the times when many freedom fighters visited Mani Bhavan. Sajeev Rajan was always helpful. Ranjan Bharuchi promptly found the relevant books and never disappointed us in locating the important books. Rajesh Shinde readily provided crucial technical assistance whenever needed.

The Maharashtra State Archives have been an important source where we could get a lot of data. The director, the archivist, the librarian, and the staff have all been efficient and helpful. We thank them all.

We thank David Wilson for sharing a document of G.S. Wilson and permitting us to use an extract from it.

We found some important books and the files of the *Bombay Chronicle* at the Asiatic Society of Mumbai. We thank the Asiatic Society of Mumbai, its office-bearers, and staff for their willing cooperation.

We thank the Mani Bhavan Gandhi Sangrahalaya, the Asiatic Society of Mumbai, Pratap M.B. Velkar, and Jagdish Agarwal for giving permission to publish visuals from their collections in this book.

Our thanks are due to Professor J.V. Naik for reading the manuscript and making suggestions. Our discussions with Satish Sahney, Dr Aneesh Pradhan, Professor Geraldine Forbes, Professor Mridula Ramanna, Professor Thomas Pantham, and Professor Mangala Sirdeshpande have been rewarding, and we are thankful to them. We appreciate the quiet and firm support provided by Rohil Mehta, Jyotsna Tanna, Archisha Mehan, Shardul Mehta, and Kuber Mehta.

Lastly, the team at Oxford University Press has been efficient and cooperative in seeing the book through the various stages of publishing. Our sincere thanks to them all.

# INTRODUCTION

GANDHI CONTINUES TO INSPIRE GENERATIONS TO THINK AND WORK for the good of all. While the main arenas of his activities were India, England, and South Africa, his ultimate focus was the entire humanity. At the young age of 19, he left the protected atmosphere of his home in Porbandar to study in England. While some years of his youth—1888 to 1891—were spent in England pursuing studies and widening his horizons, the years from 1892 to 1915 (with occasional visits to India and England) were spent in South Africa exploring the efficacy and new avenues of experimenting with satyagraha. After his return to India, he left the country only once, briefly in 1931, to go to England to attend the Round Table Conference and thereafter to travel to Europe. The period from 1915 until his assassination on 30 January 1948 was dedicated to his motherland. He launched satyagrahas against the colonial rule, mobilized Indians, addressed meetings, established ashrams in Ahmedabad and Wardha, engaged in constructive work, travelled widely to the different corners of India from remote villages to glittering cities, opened channels of communication with those in power, and touched the hearts of his countrymen. Amidst this entire conundrum, Bombay[1] remained important for him; it was here that his voice found an echo, his activities got an encouraging response, many of his strategies were formed, and a large number of his colleagues and followers assembled. Bombay took to him as one of its own.

Gandhi and Bombay shared a symbiotic relationship that spanned over decades and strengthened over the years. The city welcomed him warmly on his return from South Africa on 9 January 1915, and this warmth never faded away. For years, Bombay became the site of his political activities and agitations; processions and protest meetings organized under his name drew people from all sections of society. If Gandhi's leadership was magnetic, the city's response was overwhelming. Gandhi's important nationwide movements were intertwined with the life of this city and its people. Gandhi was full of energy and the city brimming with vibrancy. This amalgam resulted in a powerful synergy that made history.

This book attempts to present an overview of the relationship between Gandhi and Bombay during the period from his arrival from South Africa in 1915 to the time of his assassination. It is fascinating to explore when Gandhi visited the city, what he said, whom he met, which meetings he organized or attended and where, what movements he launched and why, who he worked with, and so on. These small and large snippets of information put together create a rainbow collage that presents the story of the remarkable relationship between the leader and the city. The methods by which he set the tone and tenor of his movements in the city, the manner in which he energized and mobilized the local people, the obstacles he faced, and also the ways in which the city supported and nurtured him are fascinating. The subject is overwhelming, because the leader is exceptional and the city dynamic.

———

The introduction is divided into three parts. The first part presents a brief sketch of Bombay, and the second part provides glimpses of Gandhi's links with the city before 1915. The third part outlines Gandhi's presence and work in Bombay from 1915 until the time of his assassination. It also mentions some important studies and presents the chapter scheme of the book.

Bombay has existed in many layers—of time, space, and cultures. The wholesome blend of various communities of the city such as Kolis and Agris, Parsis and Muslims, Khojas and Bohras, Hindus and Christians, Memons and Jews, Gujaratis and Marwaris has manifested in myriad ways encompassing all these layers. This ever-changing city has witnessed stories of wealth creation and its decline, unplanned growth of one area after another, and the resultant civic problems. Chawls and *wadi*s are tucked in the heart of the city with colonial structures looking on. Small lanes and dilapidated buildings bear mute testimony to the tales of bygone days, while the wide roads and matchbox-like buildings stare blankly at visitors. Bombay's small shops and bazaars are not embarrassed in the company of huge skyscrapers and swanky malls. The remnants of colonial rule have survived the onslaught of 'modernity'. The city has assimilated the old and the new, the traditional and the modern, mosques and temples, churches and lecture halls with a remarkable ability.

By the time of Gandhi's arrival, Bombay was already a centre of commerce, finance, and textile industry, and a hub of diverse intellectual and social reform activities. It is often said that the

British wanted to develop Bombay as the 'London of the East', just as the Portuguese tried to develop Goa as the 'Rome of the Tropics'. Editor Robert Knight, who promptly noticed the quick financial growth of the city, changed in 1861 the title of his newspaper from the *Bombay Times* to the *Times of India* and, announcing the change, he remarked in the very first editorial that the city had already become the financial capital of India.[2] A meeting point of the East and the West, this port city has developed a strong cosmopolitan identity.

This city originally consisted of seven islands and formed an outlying portion of the dominions of various dynasties in western India such as the Mauryas, the Satavahanas, the Chalukyas, and the Rashtrakutas. Being the far-flung portion of these successive kingdoms, Bombay generally remained in a state of neglect. Over the centuries, the rulers of the place changed. The rule of the Hindu kings over the island of Bombay and its dependencies ended around the mid-fourteenth century, when it passed into the hands of the Muslim rulers. It remained so until AD 1534, when the islands were ceded to the Portuguese by Sultan Bahadur of Gujarat. Thereafter, Bombay was handed over to the British crown by the Portuguese in 1661 as part of the royal dowry to Charles II when he married Infanta Catherine Braganza. The Portuguese and the British periods saw rapid development of Bombay. Mahim enjoyed more importance during the Portuguese period, while it lost its position of privilege under the British, with Bombay Island gaining importance.[3]

The early decades of the nineteenth century witnessed the consolidation of the British authority in this area, which brought accelerated economic, political, and social changes. The growth of the opium trade involving India, China, and Britain increased the importance of Bombay. The city began attracting people, and migrants started coming in. British governors such as Mountstuart Elphinstone and Sir John Malcolm contributed to the city's development. Bombay became a major centre of cotton trade consequent to the American Civil War in 1861. When the American cotton could not reach the Lancashire cotton mills, Bombay gained prominence, for it began to send cotton to England. The first cotton textile mill in Bombay was established in 1854, and soon the number of cotton mills grew. The city overflowed with wealth and affluence. The end of the American Civil War in 1865, however, brought an unprecedented financial crash, washing away the fortunes of the ordinary people and millionaires in the city. But Bombay survived the setback and continued its journey on the path of progress. The opening of the Suez Canal in 1869 increased its importance as a port, since its distance to London was reduced.

The development of the means of communication helped the growth of Bombay. The railways linked the city port with the hinterland. The first Indian train started in 1853, and it ran from Bombay to Thane. Horse-drawn trams were introduced in the city in 1874 (however, the first electric tram service was inaugurated much later in 1907). The orders to remove the obsolete fortifications and old ramparts in the city were given by Sir Bartle Frere in 1862. Impressive houses were built, public works were undertaken, and new areas reclaimed. The 1870s and 1880s witnessed the construction of majestic colonial buildings such as the telegraph office, the general post office, the high court, and the university library and convocation hall. The building of the Victoria Terminus (now Chhatrapati Shivaji Terminus), the headquarters of the GIP (Great Indian Peninsula) railways, was started in 1878 and completed 10 years later; the construction of the Bombay Municipal Corporation (BMC) building began in 1884 and was completed by 1893.

With the growth of industries, people from the hinterland continued to pour into Bombay. This led to the evolution of the machinery for civic matters. The Act of 1865 created the office of a single municipal commissioner and also a body corporate of justices of the peace with powers to impose rates and taxes. The subsequent Act of 1888 was a major landmark in the history of the BMC. It recognized the corporation as the supreme governing body of the city and the municipal commissioner as its chief executive authority. The franchise qualification was lowered to include more houseowners, and university graduates were granted the right to vote in the municipal elections. Efforts to improve sanitation in the city were also started. The Bombay City Improvement Trust was created in 1898 after the ravage of plague.

The new discoveries and technology did not take long to reach the city. The first exhibition of electric light was made before Lord and Lady Falkland in the Town Hall in 1847. In 1883, electricity illuminated the high court followed by the university and the adjacent public buildings. The first motor car in Bombay was seen around 1898 and taxis in 1911. The telephone system was introduced in 1882. Theatres and clubs came up to enrich the social life of people; the first film screenings happened in 1896 at Watson's Hotel (now known as Esplanade Mansion) and games such as football and cricket began to gain popularity. Photography became a popular hobby by the end of the nineteenth century. The arrival of new means of communication with the development of roads, trains, port facilities, and infrastructure made such a growth possible and widened the horizons of the Bombay society.

Civic and educational institutions and various associations and organizations had started coming up by the mid-nineteenth century; some based on caste or religion or profession and some inspired by liberal nationalistic and progressive ideas, intellectual quest, and enthusiasm for social reform. The Literary Society (that later developed as the Asiatic Society of Mumbai) was established in 1804, Elphinstone College and the Bombay Medical and Physical Society in 1835, the Bombay Chamber of Commerce in 1836, the Paramhansa Mandali in 1847, the Students' Literary and Scientific Society in 1848, the Bombay Association in 1852, and the Gujarati Sabha (now Forbes Gujarati Sabha) in 1865. The establishment of the University of Bombay (now University of Mumbai) in 1857 was a milestone in the city's history. The Prarthana Samaj was established in 1867, the Bombay Mill Owners' Association in 1875, the Bombay Natural History Society in 1883, and the Bombay Presidency Association in 1885. The Indian Merchants' Chamber was established in 1907 and the Seva Sadan Society in 1908. Many schools, libraries, and educational institutions started blooming from the beginning of the nineteenth century. Newspapers such as the *Times of India* started in 1838, the *Mumbai Samachar* (Gujarati) in 1822, the *Bombay Darpan* (Marathi) in 1832 along with many others, opening up the gates of information. Started in 1913, the *Bombay Chronicle* remained nationalist to the core and became the vanguard of the nationalist movement. The educated people of the city were drawn into the process of their establishment and sustenance. With the spread of Western education, ideas of liberalism and later the spirit of nationalism got integrated into the elite section of society. The education system introduced by the British brought some of the finest teachers from Britain, Scotland, and other parts of Europe such as Sir Alexander Grant and Professor William Wordsworth. George Birdwood was a doctor who not only taught at the Grant Medical College but also contributed to the sociocultural activities of the city. The Reverend Dr John Wilson arrived as a missionary who contributed to educational activities, including the establishment of the Wilson College.

Bombay has benefited immensely from the contribution of eminent leaders of different Indian communities, such as Jagannath Shankarshet, Sir Jamsetji Jeejeebhoy, Sir Cowasji Jehangir, Gokuldas Tejpal, Premchand Roychand, Balashastri Jambhekar, Dr Bhau Daji, R.G. Bhandarkar, Atmaram Pandurang Tarkhadkar, Naoroji Furdoonji, Dinshaw Edulji Wacha, Badruddin Tyabji, K.T. Telang, Morarji Gokuldas, and J.N. Tata. When Gandhi arrived in Bombay, the city already had established leaders such as Bal Gangadhar Tilak (1856–1920), Sir Pherozeshah Mehta (1845–1915), Dadabhai Naoroji (1825–1917), and Gopal Krishna Gokhale (1866–1915) whom the entire nation respected.

The establishment of the Indian National Congress (INC) in 1885 in Bombay, its 1904 session there, and the Bombay High Court's sentence of six-years' imprisonment to Tilak in 1908 for fermenting sedition through his writings generated political fervour in the city. Increasing aspirations gave rise to the demand of right of representation in the representative bodies and participation in the political process. Gradually, the Indians in Bombay, as in other cities, started entering the citadels of power.

The years from the last quarter of the nineteenth century to the early decades of the twentieth century witnessed many developments in Bombay. Booming commerce and flourishing textile mills and overseas trade had cemented the city's position as a powerful business hub. The spread of education and strengthening of civic and educational institutions had opened new vistas for the people of the city. The cosmopolitan and cultural fabric of the metropolis was strengthened by individuals determined to see the city progress. All these forces were charting a new course for the city. Epidemics, communal riots, and labour unrest could not suppress the energy of the city to move forward. Bombay, slowly and surely, was reaching its iconic status as the centre of adventure and enterprise, hopes and dreams. It was truly the 'Urbs Prima in Indis' (the premier city in India).

———————

Bombay can claim connection with Gandhi since before 1915, although that association was of a different nature. Gandhi mentions glimpses of such association in his autobiography. When he passed his matriculation examination in 1887, the examination used to be held at two centres: Ahmedabad and Bombay. Like him, students from Kathiawad preferred to go to the nearer and cheaper centre, Ahmedabad. A little later when he had to choose a college between Bhavnagar and Bombay, he decided to go to Bhavnagar since it was cheaper. He joined the Samaldas College but found himself at sea.[4] Soon thereafter, he was set to go to England but there was a hurdle before him in Bombay. The headman of his caste group (Modh Bania) threatened to declare him an outcaste if he travelled across the seas. A general meeting of the caste members was called, and Gandhi was summoned to appear before them. A young Gandhi remained firm in his resolve; he was then declared to be an outcaste. He boarded a steamship, *Clyde*, for London on 4 September 1888. He discovered the new world and began to question the established principles. He learnt about vegetarianism and his own culture in England and returned to India in 1891. However, he was not confident at all to practise at the bar. He realized that he had read the laws but not learnt how to practise law. He had learnt absolutely nothing about the Indian law, and did not have the slightest idea about the Hindu and Muslim laws. He did not even know how to draft a plaint.[5] On his return journey the sea was rough in Bombay harbour; in his words, 'the outer storm was to me a symbol of the inner'.[6]

When Gandhi landed in Bombay from *S.S. Assam* on 5 July
1891, he still had to find his moorings in India by establishing
his legal practice. His elder brother had come to see him at the
dock and informed him of his mother's death. Gandhi was greatly
shocked. His brother did not inform him about it earlier to spare
Gandhi the blow in a foreign land. Dr Pranjivan Mehta insisted
that Gandhi should stay at his house. Dr Mehta introduced
Gandhi to his brother Revashankar Jagjivan, 'with whom there
grew up a lifelong friendship'.[7] Gandhi also met Raychand
or Rajchandra, known for his phenomenal memory and deep
knowledge of religion, and found that 'no one else has ever made
on me the impression that Raychandbhai did'.[8] Before going to
Rajkot, Gandhi's brother took him to Nasik on 7 July for the rite
of purification for readmission to their caste and, on reaching
Rajkot, he gave a caste dinner. Gandhi did not like it but gave in
to his brother's wish out of devotion for him.

After reaching Rajkot he realized the urgency of earning his
living and decided to start his legal practice. His friends advised
him to go to Bombay to get some experience at the high court and
to study the Indian law. Gandhi came to Bombay in November
1891 to start his legal practice. He started a household in
Girgaum, with an incompetent cook. But he found it difficult to
establish his legal practice. Consequently, he found it impossible
to survive in Bombay for more than a few months—there being
no income to square with the ever-increasing expenditure. In his
words, 'I found the barrister's profession a bad job—much show
and little knowledge.'[9]

Gandhi's friend Virchand Gandhi told him stories about the
legal prowess of stalwarts such as Sir Pherozeshah and Badruddin
Tyabji. He also said that it was not unusual for a barrister to
'vegetate for five or seven years' before establishing their practice.
While trying to understand the complexities of law, Gandhi

found the study of Indian law tedious and could not get on with the Civil Procedure Code. However, he developed some liking for the Evidence Act and read J.D. Mayne's Hindu Law with deep interest. But he had 'no courage to conduct a case': 'I was helpless beyond words, even as the bride come fresh to her father-in-law's house!'[10] He refused to pay commission to the touts to get a case. In spite of that he got the case of a woman client Mamibai. It was an easy case, and he charged Rs 30 as his fees. It was his debut in the Small Causes Courts. He appeared for the defendant and had to cross-examine the plaintiff's witnesses. But he could not argue at all.

He left the court feeling ashamed. He decided not to take up any more cases until he had enough courage to conduct them.[11] And he did not go to the court again until he went to South Africa. However, before leaving Bombay he drafted a memorial for a poor Muslim whose land was confiscated in Porbandar. Gandhi read it to his friends, and they approved of it. This, to some extent, made him feel confident that he was qualified enough to draft a memorial.

He had even tried to get a job as a part-time teacher in Bombay. He applied to a school after seeing the following advertisement by a famous high school in the newspaper: 'Wanted, an English teacher to teach one hour daily. Salary Rs. 75.' He applied and was called for an interview. When the principal found out that Gandhi was not a graduate, he regretted. Gandhi's education in London was of no help. He used to go to the high court while in Bombay but admitted: 'I cannot say that I learnt anything there. I had not sufficient knowledge to learn much.'[12] Often he did not follow the cases and dozed off. The fact that there were others, too, like him lightened his burden of shame. After a time, he even lost the sense of shame, as he 'learnt to think that it was fashionable to doze in the High Court'. During this period he used to walk to the High Court from Girgaum where he lived; it took him 45 minutes, and he also came back on foot. He hardly took a carriage or a tram car. This walk, though exposed him to the heat of the sun, helped him save money and stay healthy.[13]

His little establishment in Bombay was closed after a few months, and he went back to Rajkot. Life in Rajkot also did not favour him much. So he grabbed the opportunity to go to South Africa and left Bombay on 24 April 1893. There he grew in stature and metamorphosed into a leader.

In 1896, three years after his stay there, he felt that he had established a fairly good practice. So he decided to return home to fetch his wife and children. He also thought that he might be able to do some public work in India by educating public opinion and generating more interest in the Indians of South Africa.[14] He made a short visit to India in 1896. He left Durban by the steamer *Pangola* on 5 June 1896. Thereafter, he went to Rajkot and wrote a pamphlet 'The Grievances of the British Indians in South Africa: An Appeal to the Indian Public'. This was published in Rajkot on 14 August 1896. It was known as 'Green Pamphlet' since its cover was green. Gandhi was 26 years old at that time. He came to Bombay and met some leading legal luminaries such as Justice Ranade, Badruddin Tyabji, and Sir Pherozeshah Mehta, the uncrowned king of the Bombay Presidency.[15] He wanted to educate public opinion in cities on the situation in South Africa by organizing meetings, and Bombay was the first city he chose. Sir Pherozeshah Mehta agreed to organize a meeting and asked Gandhi to meet him a day before the meeting. Gandhi, thereafter, was busy nursing his ailing brother-in-law in Rajkot, who ultimately could not be saved. He came to Bombay for the public meeting the day after his brother-in-law's death. When an exhausted Gandhi reached Bombay and went to see Sir Pherozeshah Mehta, the latter wanted a copy of Gandhi's speech. Gandhi had none. Mehta told him 'that will not do in Bombay'. He insisted on the written speech to benefit from the meeting and wanted it to be printed by the next morning. Gandhi worked hard to complete it.[16]

The meeting was held under the auspices of the Bombay Presidency Association at the Framji Cowasji Institute on 26 September 1896. Pherozeshah Mehta presided over it.[17] Being soft-spoken, Gandhi was not audible at the meeting. So the audience desired that Wacha read the speech. The speech was well received, and Sir Pherozeshah Mehta liked it too. This made Gandhi 'supremely happy'.[18]

Gandhi left Bombay with his wife Kasturba, sons Harilal and Manilal, and nephew Gokaldas and set sail for South Africa on 30 November 1896 by *Courland* that belonged to Dada Abdulla & Co. By 1901, Gandhi realized that his work was required more in India than South Africa. His friends back home were also pressing him to return. His co-workers in South Africa accepted it reluctantly, but only on the condition that Gandhi should return to South Africa if, within a year, the Indian community would need him. He accepted this condition out of love for them.[19] On 28 November 1901, he reached Bombay.

Upon his return, he decided to spend some time going around the country, including attending the Congress session in Calcutta (now Kolkata), staying with Gokhale for a month, and a quick trip to Benares. Gokhale was keen that Gandhi should settle in Bombay, practise at the bar, and help him with public work. Gandhi liked Gokhale's advice but was not very confident of succeeding as a barrister due to the unpleasant memories of his past failure. Additionally, he was averse to using flattery for getting briefs. So he decided to work at Rajkot and did well in practice. However, his well-wisher Kevalram Mavji Dave persuaded him to go to Bombay, since he felt that Gandhi was destined to do public work and could not stay buried in Kathiawad.

After receiving a remittance from Natal, Gandhi went to Bombay to start his practice and took chambers in Payne, Gilbert, and Sayani's offices.[20] His chamber was situated in the Aga Khan building, opposite the high court. He came to Bombay on 11 July 1902 and rented a portion of the bungalow of Keshavji Tulsidas on Girgaum Back Road. When Manilal, his second son, fell seriously ill, Gandhi did not accept the doctor's advice to give eggs and chicken broth to the child. He treated Manilal with a hydropathic treatment, a careful diet, and nursing. Manilal's recovery reconfirmed Gandhi's faith in God. Thereafter, he left the damp and ill-lit house in Girgaum. In consultation with Revashankar Jhaveri, he shifted to a well-ventilated bungalow in Santacruz, since it was the best from the point of view of sanitation.

Gandhi used to take a first-class season ticket from Santacruz to Churchgate and frequently felt a certain pride in being the only passenger in his compartment. Often he walked to Bandra to take the fast train directly to Churchgate. He had not yet succeeded in securing any work in the high court but attended the 'moot' that used to be held in those days. Although he never took part in it, he recalled Jamiatram Nanabhai taking a prominent part. Like other barristers, he attended the hearing of cases in the high court more 'for enjoying the soporific breeze coming straight from the sea than for adding to my knowledge'.[21] This practice 'seemed to be the fashion and therefore nothing to be ashamed of'.[22] However, he had started making use of the high court library and developing new contacts. He had begun to feel somewhat at ease about his profession. He even took an insurance policy of Rs 10,000 on Kasturba's name from an American insurance agent. Gokhale also used to peep in his chambers twice or thrice every week. Gandhi's South African clients often entrusted him with some work, and D.B. Shukla, his barrister friend in Rajkot, also sent some drafting work to him. At this juncture, he was able to earn enough to meet his expenses.[23] Just when he seemed to be settling down in Bombay, he received an unexpected cable from South Africa. In November 1902, his countrymen in South Africa urged him to return immediately, since the visit of Joseph Chamberlain, the secretary of state for the colonies, demanded his presence. Gandhi remembered his promise and started preparations to go there. He gave up his chambers, but not the bungalow, and left Kasturba and the children thinking that the work in South Africa would keep him engaged for a year or so and then he would return.[24] He left Bombay for South Africa on 25 November 1902 and planned to stay there for a short period, but destiny had a different plan. His work in South Africa was to make history.

———

Gandhi was accorded a rousing welcome by the people of Bombay on his return from South Africa on 9 January 1915. From that time, a special relationship between the leader and the city began to be forged. By the beginning of the twentieth century, Bombay got increasingly enmeshed in the terrain of democratic urges and nationalist aspirations of the people. In 1919, Gandhi's first nationwide protest, the satyagraha against the unjust Rowlatt Act in Bombay, propelled him to the position of an undisputed leader. His sincere efforts to bring the Hindus and Muslims together by his involvement in the Khilafat issue made an impact. Soon thereafter, the launch of the Non-Cooperation Movement on 1 August 1920 opened a new chapter in the history of India, and again Bombay was the site for this powerful movement. Three bonfires of foreign cloth in the city attracted the attention of the nation, and the charkha became the symbol of the swadeshi movement. The city became an important site for political action and new allies.

Gandhi's Salt March in March 1930 evoked a spontaneous and enthusiastic response in Bombay, making places such as Wadala and Vile Parle in the city the centres of protest. The women of Bombay responded to Gandhi's call in an unprecedented manner. With great enthusiasm and energy, the Desh Sevikas, in their orange saris, picketed the shops selling liquor and foreign cloth. In 1931, before his departure to London to attend the Round Table Conference, Gandhi gave an important speech at Azad Maidan. Massive crowds had gathered to hear him and see him off as he boarded *M.S. Rajputana* on 29 August 1931. Bombay welcomed him enthusiastically on his return from London in December 1931. Very soon thereafter, in the early morning hours of 4 January 1932, he was arrested from the terrace of Mani Bhavan. Shortly before that he had written to Tagore, 'I am stretching my tired limbs.'[25]

Bombay was the nerve centre of the Quit India Movement. It was at the Congress session on 7 and 8 August 1942 at the Gowalia Tank Maidan (now known as the August Kranti Maidan) in Bombay that Gandhi gave the historic mantra of 'Do or Die'. The youth of Bombay took the lead in organizing meetings, distributing nationalist leaflets, and taking up activities that disrupted the administration.

Bombay was again the city where the important Gandhi–Jinnah meetings took place in September 1944. Gandhi used to walk a short distance from Birla House to Jinnah's bungalow at Mount Pleasant Road. On his release in 1944, he spent a month at Shanti Kumar Morarji's bungalow in Juhu to recuperate. He was not a frequent visitor to Bombay during the last years of his life. However, he did visit the city in 1945 and 1946 to attend the meetings of the Kasturba Memorial Trust. Gandhi's last visit to Bombay was presumably on 31 March 1946. During this visit, Gandhi stayed at the Harijan colony in Worli where some miscreant made an unsuccessful attempt to burn his hut.

Bombay was also an important site for Gandhi's propagation of swadeshi and khadi work. The first *khadi bhandar* (khadi store) in the country was opened by Gandhi in January 1920 in Morarji Gokuldas Market. Vithaldas Jerajani was appointed the manager, and Sheth Narayandas Parasotamdas donated Rs 10,000 to start it.[26] Soon khadi bhandars started becoming popular. The women of Bombay were very active in the movements and work initiated by Gandhi. Many elite women discarded their foreign clothes and adopted khadi willingly. Women cared deeply for Gandhi and his causes. Whenever Gandhi was in Bombay, he also worked for the cause of the Harijans. He visited the Harijan colonies of Walpakhadi, Mahalaxmi, and Tadwadi and collected the Harijan Fund for their upliftment.

**Figure I.1** An advertisement in the *Bombay Chronicle* dated 18 June 1919, announcing the opening of Shoodh Swadeshi Bhandar in Kalbadevi, Bombay.

*Source*: The Asiatic Society of Mumbai.

**Figure I.2**  Gandhi receiving donation for the Harijan Fund in Bombay in September 1945.
*Source*: Vithalbhai Jhaveri Collection/Dinodia Photos.

Bombay had witnessed Gandhi the fundraiser at his best. The city was the single-largest contributor towards the Tilak Swaraj Fund. It also contributed generously to Gandhi's call for the Harijan Fund and the fund for the Kasturba Memorial Trust.

Bombay has earned a special place in the history of the freedom struggle under Gandhi's leadership. It was in Bombay that Gandhi devised various political strategies and found many trusted colleagues and followers. His allies often came from diverse backgrounds and ideologies. In 1919, he had colleagues such as Benjamin Guy Horniman, Umar Sobani, and Shankarlal Banker who were with the Home Rule League. In the early 1920s, he had support from people such as Vithalbhai Patel and others of the Swaraj Party who thought that participating in representative institutions would be helpful, and in 1942, socialist leaders such as

Ram Manohar Lohia extended support to the national movement. Over the years Gandhi had made inroads into business networks. The cotton merchants, grain merchants, and shopkeepers were, by and large, with him during his movements and constructive activities. Merchants, shopkeepers, and inhabitants from areas such as Girgaum, Bhuleshwar, Kalbadevi, Vile Parle, and Borivali backed him. The women of Bombay always remained a loyal and strong constituency for Gandhi.

The protest inspired by Gandhi against the British rule opened new dimensions of politics in Bombay as in other places. Political discourse and political action changed under his leadership. Bhikhu Parekh has perceptively observed:

Thanks to his passionate commitment to a non-violent vision of human life, Gandhi challenged conventional wisdom, broke through traditional categories of thought, stretched the boundaries of imagination in all areas of life, and opened up new philosophical and practical possibilities. Gandhi's questions demand answers. And if we reject his answers, as we are bound to do in several cases, we need to provide alternative answers. He requires us to think afresh about things we have long taken for granted, and therein lies his greatest contribution and true originality.[27]

Gandhi inspired the people of Bombay to think afresh about the British rule and question the prevailing injustice and denial of freedom. His insistence on truth as the end and non-violence as the means, his advocacy of non-violent ways of protest, and his persistence of constructive work made an impact on the people of Bombay as in the rest of the country. They became active and visible in the city—from residential parts to business centres, from the heart of the city to suburbs, from areas such as Bhuleshwar, Kalbadevi, and Girgaum with strong presence of the Gujarati and Maharashtrian communities to the European-dominated parts of the city such as the Fort area, and from open areas of the Esplanade ground to the Chowpatty sands. Marches, processions, meetings, picketing, flag-hoisting, and strikes organized by them claimed the city's space as their own places for the display of nationalism. Their display was spectacular and presented a firm challenge to the colonial rule. The spontaneous coming out of thousands of men and women for meetings or demonstrations in streets signalled the shedding of fear of the government authorities and asserted their new identity as aspirants to freedom.

**Figure I.3** Gandhi walking with a group of volunteers for the prayer meeting at the Rungta House compound, Bombay, in April 1945.
*Source*: Vithalbhai Jhaveri Collection/Dinodia Photos.

Gandhi spoke mostly in Hindustani or Gujarati, the languages that connected him easily with the people. His meetings went beyond the concrete confines of halls such as the Congress House, the Morarji Gokuldas Hall, the Royal Opera House, the Muzaffarabad Hall, and the Jinnah Hall. Open grounds such as the Chowpatty sands or the space near Shantaram Chawl or the French Bridge or Juhu Beach could be effortlessly converted into sites for huge meetings. Gandhi could bring people of all strata and communities together. He wove together threads of different colours and textures in a pattern where the 'different' did not mean the jarring opposite.

The Gothic structures and markets as well as the roads and lanes of the city witnessed many processions and people's protests against the unjust British rule. Gandhi explained, whenever possible, to the people of Bombay the logic of satyagraha, the power of prayer and the effectiveness of fasts, the importance of constructive work, and the collective strength of people. His ideas and movements brought subtle changes in the lifestyles of people. Khadi became a symbol of self-sufficiency and khadi caps symbols of assertion of a common identity in the nationalist struggle against the colonial rule. Insistence on a simple way of living and use of symbols rooted in the Indian ethos such as salt and the spinning wheel were silent yet powerful protests against the British rule; sharing a common historical experience heralded the coming of freedom.

National consciousness had penetrated deep into the lives of people. The opposition against British drinks such as tea called for the popularization of certain indigenous Indian drinks in some corners of Bombay. Around 1926, a shop in Girgaum called Tambe Arogya Bhavan propagated buttermilk against tea. The shop owners had started selling a drink called Piyush prepared with buttermilk, saffron, nutmeg, and sugar. Likewise, they

also prepared a hot drink, coffee of barley (*gavhachi* coffee), and
named it Vitogen.[28]

Bombay has always been an important place for commercial films. Films reflect as well as mould the consciousness of people. Many films during the time of nationalist movements propagated nationalist feelings. *Bhakt Vidur*, a film made in the silent era of 1921, showed Vidur, the central protagonist, with makeup and dress like Gandhi's. *Brahmachari* made in 1938 showed an ashram like Gandhi's Wardha ashram and gave the message of spinning. There were some historical and stunt films like those by Sohrab Modi or Homi Wadia that gave the message of freedom. Individuals such as Dadasaheb Phalke, Himanshu Roy, Devika Rani, and V. Shantaram, companies such as Bombay Talkies, and Prabhat and Prithvi theatres conveyed nationalist messages through their work. As pointed out by Prem Chowdhry, it is interesting that in the late 1930s, the marketability of nationalism and its viability were visible not merely in the films produced by Indians—most of which became popular hits—but also in the way producers, distributors, and exhibitors advertised their products.[29] Gandhi, for example, was a favourite for advertising the films. Large photographs of Gandhi adorned film advertisements along with much smaller photographs of the lead hero or heroine. Yet other films were advertised as 'helper to the cause of Mahatma Gandhi', or viewers were invited to see films advertised as portraying 'the ideals of Mahatma Gandhi', or it was claimed that 'Mahatma Gandhi's immortal words inspire a picture'. So much so that the distributors and exhibitors of a Hollywood film also felt it commercially prudent to put in a sponsored advertisement claiming 'Mahatma Gandhi sees the first talking picture *Mission to Moscow*'.[30]

People loved the patriotic songs, and there emerged a market for them. Anonymous poets rode the wave of the swadeshi movement of the early 1920s on the efforts of patriotic businessmen who financed the recording of such patriotic songs on sound discs and got them into public circulation. These songs exhorted listeners to boycott foreign goods and purchase exclusively Indian ones. T.S. Ramchander & Co., a firm in Bombay, recorded a number of such songs by local artists, penned by unknown poets, and had them pressed into discs from abroad.[31] There was also an indigenous effort in 1938. A new recording company called the National Gramophone Record Company had 'Young India' as its trademark with the emblem of the national flag.[32]

The Gandhian era witnessed the proliferation of patriotic songs that were sung by the people. Using different folk forms such as *rasda*s, *garba*s, and bhajans, many songs with patriotic fervour were composed in Gujarati. They were not always written by well-known poets but were often composed by anonymous patriots, literate and illiterate, who were inspired by Gandhi and the struggle for freedom. Some collections contained militant songs that overtly criticized the British government and displayed hatred for the British rule. A series of such collections was published by Shivdas Kesaria (probably a pen name) in 1930 from Bombay, entitled *Sarkarnu Uthamnu* (Condolence Meeting of the Government), *Nar Yagna* (Human Sacrifice), and *Dagmagti Satta* (Tottering Power). These collections were priced at one, two, or three paise and sold in large numbers. Militancy in tone as well as in content increased during the Quit India Movement, leading to the confiscation by the government of many such collections of aggressive songs. One such confiscated collection was entitled *Ranchandi* (The War Goddess), published in 1942 by Kunvarji Shah, the owner of a printing press in Kalbadevi. Many poets wrote garba songs invoking fierce goddesses such as Chandika, Kali, Durga, and Ambika to destroy the British empire in India.[33]

Artists and singers were drawn to Gandhi's life and often gave expression to it through their art. Pandit Vishnu Digambar Paluskar often sang at the Congress sessions. Manji Khan composed and sang 'Charkhe ke karaamat se lenge swarajya lenge' at the Blavatsky Lodge in 1930 in support of the ongoing swadeshi movement and taught this song to children participating in prabhat pheris. Musicians also contributed to the nationalist cause by participating in Marathi theatre productions that used mythological themes as metaphors to depict the contemporary political climate. In 1921, Bombay witnessed an exceptional theatrical event. This was a joint performance of the popular play Maanapamaan (Honour and Insult) by Bal Gandharva's Gandharva Natak Mandali and Keshavrao Bhosale's Lalitkaladarsh Natak Mandali, both of which were well-known and competing theatre companies. The performance was held to raise funds for the Tilak Swaraj Fund.[34] Pandit Omkarnath and his party sang 'Vande Mataram' on 26 October 1934 at the 48th session of the Congress in Bombay.[35]

Literature in Bombay did not remain untouched by the nationalist wave. Gujarati writers such as Ramnarain Pathak, K.M. Munshi, Karsandas Manek, Mansukhlal Jhaveri, Gunvantrai Acharya, Sunderji Betai, and Gulabdas Broker; Marathi writers such as Mama Varerkar, Durgabai Bhagwat, Mrinalini Desai, and Prema Kantak; and Hindi writers such as Dharmavir Bharati, Pradeep, and Narendra Sharma expressed ideas of nationalism and patriotism in their literary works.

The city of Bombay showered affection and respect on Gandhi, its charismatic leader. It was with him in processions and meetings as well as in demonstrations and strikes. The municipal corporation of Bombay honoured him twice by presenting an address. People had devised their own rituals and celebrations for political events. Prayers, flag-hoisting, and shouting slogans such as *'Mahatma Gandhi ki Jai'* (hail Mahatma Gandhi) often preceded or followed the meetings. A particular day or week was often celebrated as 'Gandhi Day' or 'Gandhi Week' to mark its association with Gandhi and his activities. For example, when Gandhi was arrested in 1930, a procession of spindles, a *takli sargha*s, was taken out in the C Ward of Bhuleshwar that moved peacefully in the city on 5 June. Later, many processions of spindles were organized on the fifth of every month for some time.[36]

The study of the Indian nationalist movement continues to attract scholars with its rich area resplendent with ideologies and action, stories and papers, larger-than-life leaders and unsung heroes. There have been different perspectives including the nationalist view offered by the scholars. The works of early historians such as Pattabhi Sitaramayya,[37] Tara Chand,[38] and R.C. Majumdar[39] are important. B.R. Nanda[40] has remained a prominent writer with his first book on Gandhi, followed by others in subsequent years.

The well-known researchers of the Cambridge school such as Anil Seal,[41] Judith Brown,[42] and David Washbrook[43] view the nationalist movement mainly in terms of the British and colonial elites. Scholars such as A.R. Desai, writing from the Marxist viewpoint, fathom the nationalist movement with the perspective of class struggle.[44] Bipan Chandra has made notable contributions to the study of the nationalist movement.[45] Subaltern scholars have developed a different perspective, emphasizing the role of the marginal groups and viewing the Indian nationalist movement and Gandhi's role from that perspective.[46]

There have been excellent works on the various aspects of Gandhi's life, work, philosophy, political ideas, and movements. Eminent scholars such as Bhikhu Parekh, B.R. Nanda, D.G. Tendulkar, Louis Fisher, Rajmohan Gandhi, Ramchandra Guha,

Ronald Terchek, Denise Dalton, Judith Brown, Thomas Weber, Narayan Desai, David Hardiman, Douglas Allen, and Faisal Devji have made valuable contribution to the area. Gandhi's close associates such as Mahadev Desai and Pyarelal have provided substantial primary material on Gandhi. There are recent noticeable comparative studies by Richard Sorabji and Bidyut Chakraborty. Gandhi had travelled across three continents and established close connections with some places. There are some interesting studies such as by James D. Hunt on Gandhi and London and by Gopal Gandhi on Gandhi and Kolkata. There is also a pictorial book on Gandhi in Ahmedabad. K. Gopalaswami has written a detailed account of Gandhi in Bombay, yet much remains to be explored on the subject.

Several interesting books have been written on the history of Bombay by many writers such as Gerson da Cunha, Samuel Sheppard, S.M. Edwardes, and James Douglas in earlier times and later by Aroon Tikekar, Prashant Kidambi, Mariam Dossal, Gillian Tindall, K.K. Chaudhari, Sharada Dwivedi, and Rahul Mehrotra. The history of some institutions in Bombay such as the high court, the University of Mumbai, and the neighbourhoods such as Bhuleshwar and the mill area is also written.

Gandhi and Bombay shared a special relationship. This book is an attempt to explore and understand that relationship. It is a story of an extraordinary leader and an extraordinary city. It is a story of drama and passion for nationalism and national liberation. The story contains powerful moments of unfolding nationalism. When the sweep of the national movement overtook the city, the intricate heterogeneity of ideological, social, and political diversity merged with the larger reality of the national struggle and Gandhian vision of a unified movement.

The time spent by Gandhi in the city was anchored in meetings, events, political protests, processions, agitations, consultations with his colleagues and followers, and constructive activities. Gandhi's voice calling for liberation from a colonized mindset and discourse was unequivocal in meetings, mass mobilizations, and gatherings that took place in the halls and open places of the city. There was a distinct local colour to the nationalist activities in the city. There was a ferment of nationalism among the people of the city, and the energy unleashed against the oppressive colonial rule was unprecedented. During the freedom struggle, the people of Bombay discovered new avenues to channelize their vigour and vitality under Gandhi's charismatic leadership. This book attempts to glance at some of these moments of the events and the happenings.

This book does not claim to be an analytical treatise or a critical inquiry. It is a descriptive historical narrative. It is a modest attempt to catch glimpses of the exciting past when Gandhi visited the city and when its people responded to his call with all their patriotism and enthusiasm.

The chapters in the book are arranged in a chronological order. The introduction presents a broad outline of the subject. Chapter 1 delineates important meetings Gandhi attended and the people he met in Bombay during the period from 1915 to 1918. Chapter 2 describes the genesis and course of the satyagraha against the unjust Rowlatt Act in 1919 and the impressive scene at Chowpatty in Bombay. Chapter 3 explores the subjects of Khilafat, the first National Week, and the launch of the Non-Cooperation Movement in 1920. Chapter 4 focuses on the collection of the Tilak Swaraj Fund and bonfires of foreign cloth at Parel in 1921. Chapter 5 takes note of the important developments that occurred during the intervening years from 1922 to 1929. Chapter 6 covers the years 1930–1 and highlights the activities in Bombay at places such as Vile Parle, Wadala, and the Congress House in Girgaum after Gandhi picked up salt at Dandi. It also covers Gandhi's return from the Round Table Conference, London, and his arrest from Mani Bhavan. Chapter 7 traces the developments between 1932 and 1941. Chapter 8 narrates the details of the historic Congress session at the Gowalia Tank Maidan as well as the genesis and course of the Quit India Movement in 1942. Chapter 9 covers the years from 1943 to 1946 and sketches an outline of Bombay's tribute to Kasturba Gandhi and Gandhi–Jinnah talks. The book ends with a concluding chapter.

This book is an endeavour to present the relationship between Gandhi and Bombay, a rather understudied subject. It draws from primary source materials taken mostly from the Maharashtra State Archives, archival materials and photographs, and Gandhi's writings—mainly *Collected Works of Mahatma Gandhi* (*CWMG*). Works of other scholars from various libraries have also been consulted. A relook at the relationship between Gandhi and Bombay, hopefully, would be both engaging and enriching for the readers.

## Notes and References

1. Bombay's name was officially changed to Mumbai in 1995.
2. *The Times of India* dated 28 September 1861 cited in Aroon Tikekar, *Mumbai De-Intellectualised: Rise and Decline of a Culture of Thinking* (New Delhi and Chicago: Promilla & Co. in association with Bibliophile South Asia, 2009), p. 31.
3. Details for this section are drawn from Aroon Tikekar, *The Cloister's Pale: A Biography of the University of Bombay* (Bombay: Somaiya Publications, 1984); *The Gazetteer of Bombay, City and Island*, Vol. II, compiled under government order (Bombay: The Times Press, 1900); Prashant Kidambi, *The Making of an Indian Metropolis:*

*Colonial Governance and Public Culture in Bombay, 1890–1920* (Hampshire: Ashgate Publishing, 2007). Additionally, discussions with Aroon Tikekar on the subject have been very helpful.

4. M.K. Gandhi, *An Autobiography or the Story of My Experiments with Truth*, Mahadev Desai (tr.), (Ahmedabad: Navajivan Publishing House, 1948), p. 52.

5. Gandhi, *An Autobiography*, p. 106.

6. Gandhi, *An Autobiography*, p. 111.

7. Gandhi, *An Autobiography*, p. 112.

8. Gandhi, *An Autobiography*, p. 113.

9. Gandhi, *An Autobiography*, p. 118.

10. Gandhi, *An Autobiography*, p. 119.

11. Gandhi, *An Autobiography*, p. 120.

12. Gandhi, *An Autobiography*, p. 122.

13. Gandhi, *An Autobiography*, p. 122.

14. Gandhi, *An Autobiography*, p. 205.

15. Gandhi, *An Autobiography*, p. 214.

16. Gandhi, *An Autobiography*, p. 216.

17. *Collected Works of Mahatma Gandhi (CWMG)*, Vol. 2 (Delhi: Publications Division, Ministry of Information and Broadcasting, Government of India, 1959), p. 70.

18. Gandhi, *An Autobiography*, p. 217.

19. Gandhi, *An Autobiography*, p. 269.

20. Gandhi, *An Autobiography*, p. 301.

21. Gandhi, *An Autobiography*, p. 306.

22. Gandhi, *An Autobiography*, p. 306.

23. *CWMG*, Vol. 3 (Delhi: Publications Division, Ministry of Information and Broadcasting, Government of India, 1960), p. 50.

24. Gandhi, *An Autobiography*, p. 307.

25. *CWMG*, Vol. 48 (New Delhi: Publications Division, Ministry of Information and Broadcasting, Government of India, 1971), p. 489.

26. *Mahasabha Suvarna Mahotsava: Bhuleshwar Zilla Mahasabha Samiti, Pandar Varshani Pravritti (1921–1935)* (in Gujarati) [The Congress Golden Jubilee Celebrations: Report of the Activities of

the Bhuleshwar District Congress Committee for Fifteen Years] (Bombay: Bhuleshwar Zilla Mahasabha Suvarna Mahotsava Samiti, n.d.), p. 4.

27. Bhikhu Parekh, *Gandhi: A Very Short Introduction* (Oxford: Oxford University Press, 2001), p. 115.

28. Kakasaheb Tambe, '*Nirvyasani*' [Free from Bad Habits or Addiction], in Aroon Tikekar (ed.), *Mussafir* (in Marathi) [Traveller] (Bombay: Shri R. Tikekar Amrit Mahotsava Samiti-Prakashan, 1976), pp. 96–7.

29. Prem Chowdhry, *Colonial India and the Making of Empire Cinema: Images, Ideology and Identity* (New Delhi: Vistar Publications, 2000), p. 155.

30. Chowdhry, *Colonial India*, pp. 155–6.

31. Gautam Kaul, *Cinema and the Indian Freedom Struggle* (New Delhi: Sterling Publishers, 1999), p. 108.

32. Kaul, *Cinema*, p. 111.

33. Kunjlata Shah, 'Patriotic Songs in Gujarat (1921–1947): The Gandhian Inspiration', in R. Srinivasan, Usha Thakkar, and Pam Rajput (eds), *Pushpanjali: Essays on Gandhian Themes in Honour of Dr. Usha Mehta* (Delhi: Devika Publications, 1999), pp. 217–31.

34. Aneesh Pradhan, *Hindustani Music in Colonial Bombay* (Gurgaon: Three Essays Collective, 2014), p. 164.

35. A.M. Zaidi and S.G. Zaidi, *The Encyclopaedia of the Indian National Congress, 1930–1935: The Battle for Swaraj*, Vol. 10 (New Delhi: S. Chand & Company, 1980), p. 310.

36. *Mahasabha Suvarna Mahotsava*, p. 13.

37. Bhogaraju Pattabhi Sitaramayya, *The History of the Indian National Congress: 1885–1935*, Vol. I (Bombay: Padma Publications, 1946). Vol. II (1935–1947) published in 1947.

38. Tara Chand, *History of Freedom Movement in India*, Vol. 111 (New Delhi: Publications Division, Ministry of Information and Broadcasting, Government of India, 1972).

39. R.C. Majumdar, *History of the Freedom Movement in India* (Calcutta: Firma K.L. Mukhopadhyay, 1971).

40. B.R. Nanda, *Mahatma Gandhi: A Biography* (London: George Allen & Unwin, 1958); Nanda, *Pan-Islamism, Imperialism and Nationalism in India* (Bombay: Oxford University Press, 1989); Nanda, *In Search of Gandhi: Essays and Reflections* (New Delhi: Oxford University Press, 2002).

41. Anil Seal, *The Emergence of Indian Nationalism: Competition and Collaboration in the Later Nineteenth Century* (Cambridge: Cambridge University Press, 1968).

42. Judith Brown, *Gandhi's Rise to Power: Indian Politics, 1915–1922* (London: Cambridge University Press, 1972); Brown, *Gandhi and Civil Disobedience: The Mahatma in Indian Politics, 1928–1934* (Cambridge: Cambridge University Press, 1977).

43. D.A. Washbrook, *The Emergence of Provincial Politics: Madras Presidency, 1870–1920* (Cambridge: Cambridge University Press, 1976).

44. A.R. Desai, *Social Background of Indian Nationalism* (Bombay: Popular Prakashan, 1948).

45. Bipan Chandra, *Rise and Growth of Economic Nationalism in India: Economic Policies of Indian National Leadership, 1880–1905* (New Delhi: Har-Anand Publications, 2010, revised edition); Chandra, *Indian National Movement: The Long-term Dynamics* (New Delhi: Vikas Publishing House, 1988).

46. Shahid Amin, 'Gandhi as Mahatma: Gorakhpur District, Eastern UP, 1921–2', in Ranajit Guha (ed.), *Subaltern Studies III: Writings on South Asian History and Politics* (New Delhi: Oxford University Press, 1984), pp. 1–61; Amin, *Event, Metaphor, Memory: Chauri Chaura, 1922–1992* (New Delhi: Oxford University Press, 1995); Partha Chatterjee, 'The Moment of Manoeuvre: Gandhi and the Critique of Civil Society', in *Nationalist Thought and the Colonial World: A Derivative Discourse* (Minneapolis: University of Minnesota Press, 1993, second impression), pp. 85–130. First published in 1986 by Zed Books on behalf of the United Nations University, Tokyo.

# I

# Back to 'Dear Old Motherland': 1915–18

9 January 1915 appeared to be like any other winter day on Bombay docks; the weather was pleasant and the place was bustling with the presence of passengers, visitors, and the people working there. The day, however, was to go down in the annals of history as a special day, because around 7.30 am, Mohandas Karamchand Gandhi returned to India with his wife Kasturba, on the steamer *S.S. Arabia* from South Africa through London. From that day the destiny of this man was to be closely intertwined with that of the country; his words were to make an impact on the people of his country; and his deeds were to change the course of history.

In 1889, at the age of 19, Gandhi had left the shores of India from Bombay, to go to England to qualify as a barrister and had hoped that the qualification would bring him fame and fortune. On his return in 1891, his unsuccessful attempts to establish legal practice in his homeland in Rajkot and Bombay forced him to find an alternate way to earn and sustain the family. His experience in the Small Causes Court in Bombay in November 1891 was dismal. He had to cross-examine the witnesses of the plaintiff. However, in his own words, 'I stood up, but my heart sank into my boots. My head was reeling, and I felt as though the whole court was doing likewise. I could think of no question to ask.'[1] After this experience, he set up his office at Rajkot and did moderately well, but petty intrigues for power and haughty behaviour of the British officials dampened him.

Gandhi found an opportunity to get away from this situation when his brother introduced him to Abdul Karim Jhaveri, a partner of Dada Abdulla & Co. The firm wanted a qualified lawyer who knew English as well as Gujarati (Gandhi's mother tongue) to go to South Africa to take care of the legal cases of the company. Gandhi accepted the offer and reached South Africa. There he suffered racial discrimination and made a resolve to fight against the injustice. He examined his inner self, explored new ways of non-violent protest, coined a new word 'satyagraha', took the cause of the indentured labourers, tried community living by establishing Phoenix and Tolstoy ashrams, widened his social circle, established a lucrative practice to leave it later, and set on a journey that was to take him from 'Mohandas' to 'Mahatma'. He had searched for the essence of the Hindu religion and the scriptures in England and South Africa, and his interaction with his Christian friends had widened his understanding of religion. To men and women in South Africa, he had shown a way to find their dignity and rights, to challenge their destinies and chart new paths. His journey in search of truth by means of non-violence was to find a wider scope in India that would involve millions of his countrymen.

When he decided to return to India after completing his work in South Africa, the Indians were already aware of his mettle and achievements in South Africa. The Indian National Congress (INC) had heard of his persuasive arguments voicing the miseries of indentured labourers, the political leaders and social reformers had known his achievements, and people had read and heard about his unusual ways of protest. Gandhi, who had left the shores of India in a Western dress and who was keen to adopt the changes in lifestyle, had returned home dressed in a Kathiawadi attire (dhoti, coat, and turban) with a determination to settle in India. The elite of Bombay were eager to welcome him. His landing took place by permission of the authorities at the Apollo Bunder—an honour India's most distinguished sons shared with the royalty and viceroys.[2] Narottam Morarji, J.B. Petit, Sir Bhalchandra Krishna, B.G. Horniman, Bahadurji, and others went to the steamer in a steam launch to welcome him. Narandas Gandhi and Revashanker Jagjivan Jhaveri also took a launch to meet them on board the ship.[3] At the quay he was received by hundreds of people. It was proposed that there should be a public reception at Apollo Bunder and that, subsequently, Gandhi and Kasturba should be taken in procession. But the authorities did not look with favour on this proposal, and arrangements for the reception had to be modified accordingly.[4]

I was filled with tears of joy when, nearing Bombay, I sighted the coast. I am still beside myself with joy. I don't like Bombay though. It looks as if it were the scum of London. I see here all the shortcomings of London but find none of its amenities; this is also one of the benefits of living in India. It would seem that Lady India had resolved to exhibit nothing but the scum of London lest we should be thrown off our balance by the amenities.[5]

Already there were discussions about the place of his stay in Bombay. Sir Pherozeshah Mehta suggested that he could stay in the palace of Sayajirao Gaekwad (the maharaja of Baroda State), but there was not enough time to make such an arrangement. Then it was decided to take him to Shantibhavan at Pedder Road, the home of Narottam Morarji. He was there for a few hours, and thereafter, he was taken to Revashankar Jagjivan's home at Santacruz. Shantikumar, Narottam Morarji's son, fondly remembers the Saturday when Gandhi visited them in their home. When Shantikumar, at that time 13 years old, reached home, it was time for Gandhi to leave. The young boy wanted to change, but his father took him to Gandhi to pay respects. He also remembers that Gandhi's eldest son Harilal had come to his home to explain Gandhi's food habits, as at that time the latter did not have grains, ghee, and milk. Gandhi's dietary experiments were becoming well known.[6]

Soon Gandhi was overwhelmed by invitations for receptions and meetings. People from diverse sections and backgrounds wanted to meet him: some to claim familiarity with him and many to establish contact that might spark off political action. A number of receptions, political meetings, and civic functions were organized, drawing him into the vortex of activities and many social and political networks. He had yet to gauge people and their aspirations and abilities, yet to find his own moorings, yet to locate a mission and find new allies and supporters. History had reserved the year 1919 as an eventful year for him and the country, when the first wave of protest was to create a nationwide upheaval. He spent the years from 1915 to 1918 understanding the situation, exploring the available avenues, and finding the best way to serve the motherland. In his interview with the *Bombay Chronicle* on the day of his arrival, he said, 'I need hardly say that having been out of India for practically [a] quarter of a century, and without interruption for over 13 years, both my wife and I were exceedingly glad to see again the dear old Motherland, and the kind and hearty reception which the public gave us has added to the joy, and overwhelmed us.'[7] He also said that Gopal Krishna Gokhale had rightly pointed out that since Gandhi was out of India for a long time he had 'no business to form any definite conclusions about matters essentially Indian' and he should pass some time in India 'as an observer and a student'. Gandhi promised to follow this advice.[8] He was determined to serve the motherland. In an interview with the *Times of India*, he said that he intended to devote his time to study the problems in India during the remainder of his life.[9]

The accounts of the various meetings and functions attended by Gandhi in Bombay give us an insight into the political intricacies and dynamics of power relations then prevailing in the city and the nation. Bombay at that time was already an established nucleus of commerce, a nurturing place for social and educational activities, and a regular site for political meetings. It had attracted various communities in its fold, and its youth was exposed to Western education and technology. This cluster of seven islands had by then developed as the powerful and prosperous city of Bombay with a distinct cosmopolitan climate.

The society in Bombay was changing in the decades of late-nineteenth and early-twentieth centuries.[10] Associations of diverse character based on economic, social, cultural, intellectual, and political issues had sprung up in the city. Some of them consisted of liberal nationalist elite and some were formed on the basis of caste or religion. The proliferation of associational life had a profound impact on the evolving public culture of the city. The emergence of the print media as well as the establishment of civic and educational institutions in those years generated new ideas and energy in the city. According to a report, by the early 1890s, no less than 51 Indian newspapers were published in Bombay alone, catering to the educated stratum within the city's diverse castes and communities.[11]

The city was naturally affected by contemporary political currents. It was also touched by the uneasiness created by the partition of Bengal in 1905 and a move to boycott the British goods. The sentence passed on 22 July 1908, imposing six-years' imprisonment on Bal Gangadhar Tilak, a leader of national stature and an ardent supporter of nationalism, for fomenting sedition through his writings in *Kesari* led to huge protests in the city. Tilak's release in 1914, after an internment of six years at Mandalay, was celebrated as much in Bombay as all over India. Disturbances caused by the First World War, aspirations for constitutional reforms, and the demand for democratization of municipal governance activated many. The INC, established in 1885, experienced the stress and strains of different ideologies over the years. Gopal Krishna Gokhale, who became the president of the INC in 1905, was the leader of the moderates, and Tilak was an acknowledged leader of the so-called extremists. Their ideologies and ways of working differed. The INC, under this tension, was split into two groups in 1907 that patched up only in 1916.

The public life of Bombay at the time of Gandhi's arrival was dominated by leaders such as Dadabhai Naoroji, Sir Pherozeshah Mehta, Bal Gangadhar Tilak, and Gopal Krishna Gokhale. Gandhi respected them and acknowledged their experience and wisdom. After returning from South Africa, he, too, was slowly drawn into the arena of political excitement and activities. This city of economic buoyancy, intellectual vitality, as well as social and cultural diversity seemed to promise him a site for action and new allies.

# Meetings and Receptions

On Gandhi's arrival in Bombay, political meetings were naturally high on his agenda and that of the city as well. January 1915 was hectic for Gandhi and Kasturba. Various meetings were held for them: some low-key and small gatherings and a few formal and elegant ones. The day of arrival itself was hectic, a precursor of events to come, when an assiduous Gandhi would remain constantly engrossed in work and interacting and communicating with people. He met Gokhale at Narottam Morarji's home; he also met Srinivas Sastri there. On 10 January 1915, he visited some relatives in Bazargate Street. There he met Swami Anand, who was to become a close associate later. There were receptions for him, such as one by the residents of the Fort area at Prabhudas Jiwanji Kothari's wadi and another by the Modh caste members at Jiwandas Pitambaradas's bunglow in the Fort area. He also visited the Modh boarding. He was also given a reception by Mulji Asharam when the play *Buddhadeo* was being staged by his troupe.[12] The name and fame earned in South Africa did not make Gandhi insulate himself from the people; in fact, he wanted to understand their life, mingle with them, and be a part of them.

Gandhi, however, was not an impressive speaker. There were some such as Indulal Yagnik who had expected a lot of verve and vigour in Gandhi's speeches. In this context, Yagnik narrated an interesting experience in his autobiography. He had gone to a function arranged in Gandhi's honour at Santacruz on 10 January. He had seen in Gandhi the new leader of Gujarat and India and thought of him as a new Aurobindo Ghose. He had expected Gandhi to issue a challenge to the British rule and give an outline of a new struggle. But he was disappointed after listening to Gandhi's speech as it contained nothing like that. [13]

The *Bombay Chronicle* records an engaging account of a reception organized for Gandhi and Kasturba on 11 January at Ghatkopar. It was presided over by Rao Bahadur Vassanji Khimji. Gandhi was presented with an address enclosed in a silver casket with fetters made of gold. In response Gandhi thanked and described the silver casket and the fetters as somewhat unsuitable for someone who neither had a roof over his head nor locked doors to his house.[14] He was uncomfortable with special attention and honours showered on him. In his letter dated 11 January 1915, he wrote to Maganlal (son of Gandhi's cousin Khushalchand Gandhi): 'I feel suffocated by all this public honouring. I have not known a moment's peace. There is an endless stream of visitors. Neither they nor I gain anything.'[15]

Another grand reception was organized at Mount Petit, the residence of J.B. Petit at Pedder Road, for Gandhi and Kasturba on 12 January 1915 where the elite of Bombay—around 600 prominent citizens, both Indians and Europeans—assembled. Sir Pherozeshah Mehta presided over it, and the list of guests included notable persons of the times such as Sir Richard Lamb, Sir Claude Hill, Sir Dorabji Tata, M.A. Jinnah, and Sir Dinshaw Wacha.[16] Gandhi expressed his gratitude but again felt uneasy amidst the pomp and glitter. He said candidly that during the three days passed in Bombay he and his wife had felt that they were much more at home among the indentured Indians, who were the truest heroes of India. He had done nothing beyond his duty. He also mentioned that Kasturba could tell them more about the sufferings of women who had rushed with babies to the jail. He paid rich tributes to Sir Pherozeshah Mehta, who had cheered him up from disappointments when he was a young briefless barrister; Dadabhai Naoroji, the Grand Old Man of India (whom he had met that morning); as well as his guide and political leader Gokhale. On behalf of his wife and himself, he expressed thanks for the great honour done to them that afternoon and hoped to receive the blessings of the whole country in their endeavour to serve the motherland.[17] While thanking the organizers, Gandhi made it clear on both the occasions that he wanted to render service to the people and could not receive costly presents. On the morning of 12 January, he went to see Dadabhai Naoroji, and in the afternoon, he saw Dr Daji Barjorji, who had attended to his wounds after he was attacked by the whites in Durban on 13 January 1897.[18]

A meeting was convened by the Bombay National Union on 13 January 1915 at Hira Baug to honour Gandhi and Kasturba. The meeting was attended by about 250 people. Bal Gangadhar Tilak attended the meeting without any formal invitation. Addressing the gathering, he said that they were only doing their duty in honouring Gandhi and his wife, as they had fought for the honour of India in a distant land. He further said that India ought to produce more men and women with the self-sacrificing spirit of the honoured guests, and impressed upon the audience that this was the lesson they had to learn from Gandhi.[19] At this meeting presided over by Chintaman Vinayak Vaidya, also present, among others, were Joseph Baptista, Ali Muhammad Bhimji, Dr Moreshwar Gopal Deshmukh, Dr D.D. Sathaye, Yeshwant Vishnu Nene, and Sitaram Vishnu Lalit.[20]

A noteworthy function was the garden party hosted on 14 January 1915 by Gurjar Sabha in honour of Gandhi and Kasturba at Mangaldas House, Girgaum. The meeting was presided over by M.A. Jinnah, the chairman of the sabha. This meeting was important as it brought Gandhi and Jinnah together on a public platform, and there seemed convergence between their ideas. In introducing the guests, K.M. Munshi said that Gandhi embodied in him the highest spirit of self-sacrifice and honour and had set a splendid example of personal service to the Indian communities. In his speech, Jinnah praised Gandhi for his arduous efforts in the causes of the indentured Indians and the motherland. He also praised Kasturba for her magnificent stand by the side of her husband in his great fight.[21]

Gandhi, in turn, thanked for the honour bestowed upon him and his wife and reiterated that they had done nothing beyond their duty. They first intended to study all the Indian questions and then to undertake the cause of serving the country; he was confident that under the guidance of Gokhale, he would adopt the right course. He said that the compromise arrived at in South Africa was satisfactory and trusted that what had remained to be gained would be gained. He was frank to admit that he had a lot to learn about the Hindu–Muslim issue but he would keep before his eyes his experience of 21 years in South Africa. He still remembered the profound sentence of Sir Syed Ahmed that Hindus and Muslims were the two eyes of Mother India. If either looked at a different end than the other, neither would be able to see anything; and if one was gone, the other would be able to see only to a limited extent. In future, both the communities should bear this in mind. Gandhi candidly admitted that while he was in South Africa, anything said about the Gujaratis was understood to have reference only to the Hindu community while the Parsis and Muslims were not thought of. He was, therefore, glad to find a Muslim as a member of the Gurjar Sabha and the chairman of that function.[22]

Gandhi reminisced in his autobiography about the receptions in Bombay that gave him 'an occasion for offering what might be called a little Satyagraha'. He wrote:

At the party given in my honour at Mr. Jehangir Petit's place, I did not dare to speak in Gujarati. In those palatial surroundings of dazzling splendor, I who had lived my best life among indentured labourers, felt myself a complete rustic. With my *Kathiawadi* cloak, turban and dhoti, I looked somewhat more civilized than I do today, but the pomp and splendour of Mr. Petit's mansion made me feel absolutely out of my element. However, I acquitted myself tolerably well, having taken shelter under Sir Pherozeshah's protecting wing. Then there was the Gujarati function. The Gujaratis would not let me go without a reception, which was organized by the late Uttamlal Trivedi. I had acquainted myself with the programme beforehand. Mr. Jinnah was present, being a Gujarati, I forget whether as president or as the principal speaker. He made a short and sweet little speech in English. As far as I remember most of the other speeches were also in English. When my turn came, I expressed my thanks in Gujarati explaining my partiality for Gujarati and Hindustani, and entering my humble protest against the use of English in a Gujarati gathering.[23]

He was glad to note that everyone seemed reconciled to his protest. He wrote: 'The meeting thus emboldened me to think that I should not find it difficult to place my new-fangled notions before my countrymen.'[24]

Gandhi and Kasturba were welcomed on the premises of the Servants of India Society's Home on 14 January 1915 by the members and supporters of the Bombay branch of the society. G.K. Devdhar spoke on behalf of those who assembled. Among those present were Sir Bhalchandra Krishna, Sir Vithaldas Thackersey, Sir Jagmohandas, Shet Dani, Shet Hansraj Pragjee, Devdhar, Ramabai Ranade, Lady Jagmohandas, Sonabai Jayakar, and Mrs Bahadurjee. Sir Bhalchandra garlanded Gandhi, and Ramabai garlanded Kasturba. Gandhi referred to Gokhale as his political leader and guide. He also announced that he would tour the country for a year, and after evaluating things for himself, he would decide his line of work.[25] At this meeting, he met Amritlal Thakkar (Thakkar Bapa), who was later to be a renowned social worker with strong Gandhian values. At night, he was honoured by the Modh community at Gulalwadi in Bhuleshwar. On 15 January 1915, he met Gokhale again, who had just arrived in Bombay.[26]

Years of principled and disciplined living had equipped him with the energy and inclination to meet people and know them. He had no hesitation in going from one meeting to another, one conclave to another, one group to another, a trait that was to continue until the end. He made a special trip from Ahmedabad to Bombay on 20 September 1915 to receive Andrews and Pearson, and on that day, he also visited the Harijan localities.[27] He met Dr Sumant Mehta and Shankarlal Banker for the first time on 22 December 1915.[28]

## Issues and Avenues

Gandhi was exploring the political atmosphere to find his own course of action in India in general and in Bombay in particular. He continued to share his experiences in South Africa and clearly expressed his concern for development of the underprivileged classes and urged for the participation of women. He welcomed opportunities to meet people from all communities and classes and accepted Gokhale's advice to tour India for a year before plunging into action. His attire of a Kathiawadi coat, a turban, and a dhoti worn with confidence and a simple way of talking without oratorical power shocked, amused, and impressed many. No platform was insignificant for him, as he tried to widen his network of relations in political as well as social spheres.

Gandhi had known the importance of the INC as the national forum. He had been to its session at Calcutta (now Kolkata) and had moved a resolution on 27 December 1901 on the status of the British Indians in South Africa.[29] Among the elite he could voice his concern for the poor and the oppressed and, at the same time, retained his traits of social grace and courtesy. He went to the railway station in Bombay to receive the Congress president-elect S.P. Sinha on 25 December 1915.[30] On 28 December 1915,

at the 30th session of the INC held at Bombay, he moved a
resolution regarding India and the colonies. He drew attention
to the unjust administration of the then existing laws on the
Indians in South Africa and Canada and made a strong case for
extending to the Indian immigrants rights equal to those of the
European immigrants.[31] Gandhi, not eligible for election to the
subjects committee, was nominated by the president.[32] Gandhi
had known Maulana Mazharul Haque earlier. In his words: 'I
knew Maulana Mazharul Haq in London when he was studying
for the bar, and when I met him at the Bombay Congress in 1915—
the year in which he was President of the Muslim League—he
had renewed the acquaintance, and extended me an invitation
to stay with him whenever I happened to go to Patna.'[33] On 30
December 1915, he attended a meeting of the Muslim League and
Social Conference.[34] This might be because of his warm personal
relations with Maulana Mazharul Haq. His openness of mind,
gentle manners, and understanding of the British as well as the
Indian ways made him comfortable in all situations. However, the
prevailing political environment did dampen his spirits at times.
He wrote to Hermann Kallenbach on 25 December 1915 that 'I
have come to Bombay for the Congress week. There is no sincerity
about anything. "Much cry and little work" proverb applies most
appropriately. What I should have done I do not know.' [35]

It was interesting to see him not only going for political
meetings but also visiting educational and social organizations.
On 7 February 1915, he visited a boarding school for the depressed
classes and also a mission school for the low-caste Hindus
without any formal invitation. He said, 'This function today has
given me greater pleasure than any grand reception ever did.'[36]
He presided over the prize distribution function of Sanatan
Dharma Nitishikshana Pravartaka Samiti on 14 February 1915
and advised the students to speak in the mother tongue, work for

success, cultivate character, and serve one's family and country.[37] On 15 February 1915, he visited the Varjivandas Madhavdas Kapol boarding school.[38] He also attended the All India Bhatia Conference on 25 December 1915 at Empire Theatre.[39]

His work in South Africa had already made him famous in India. His work on the indentured labour and his passionate fight to abolish it had created inquisitiveness and admiration for him among the citizens of Bombay. In his speech on the indentured Indian labour at a meeting organized under the auspices of the District Congress Committee and presided over by Sir Ibrahim Rahimtullah at Empire Theatre on 28 October 1915, he said that he wanted to remove the cause of ill-treatment of Indians in the colonies. It was the first of a series of lectures on indentured labour, a system under which Indian labour was sent out to colonies under an unfair agreement.[40] The Gujarati newspaper *Prajabandhu*, dated 7 November 1915, states that Gandhi inspired the founding of the Imperial Indian Citizenship Association in Bombay for guarding Indian interests abroad.[41]

On 24 December 1915, he attended the Industrial Conference presided over by Sir Dorabji Tata. He supported the resolution that thanked Lord Hardinge, the viceroy of India, for his work for the indentured Indian labour outside India and for recommending its abolition to the secretary of state. The resolution further submitted that in the highest interest of the country, the system of Indian indentured labour was undesirable and urged for its abolition looking at its highly injurious and immoral effects.[42]

A public meeting was organized at Excelsior Theatre on 9 February 1917, presided over by Sir Jamsetjee Jeejeebhoy. A resolution moved by Sir N.G. Chandavarkar demanding the immediate abolition of indentured labour was unanimously passed. Yielding to the demand from his friends on the platform, Gandhi spoke in English and strongly supported the resolution.

31 May 1917 was fixed as the last date on which this remnant of
slavery should end.[43]

Gandhi, himself an able editor of the *Indian Opinion* in South
Africa, supported the freedom of the press. There was a growing
realization about the curbs on the press. A public meeting of the
citizens of Bombay was held under the auspices of the Indian
Press Association in Empire Theatre on the evening of Saturday,
24 June 1916, 'to uphold the liberty of the Press and protest
against the Press Act of 1910'.[44] The meeting was presided over
by B.G. Horniman, the editor of the *Bombay Chronicle*, who
supported the nationalist cause and later Gandhi's movement.
Gandhi, Horniman, and Jamnadas D. Dharamsey were received
with loud cheers. Gandhi spoke in Gujarati, urging that it was
the true way of being faithful to his motherland. In this meeting
attended by many, a number of women were present including
the wife of Chimanlal Setalvad and her daughters and daughters-
in-law. Emphasizing the need for press freedom, Gandhi said,
'Whenever we are face to face with a political catastrophe, we
should never hesitate to say in as clear terms as possible what we
feel and desire to say.'[45]

Always concerned about the downtrodden and the ill-treated,
Gandhi made sincere efforts to understand their sufferings. On
11 February 1917, he attended a meeting of the untouchables at
the Servants of India Society and also presided over a meeting at
Shantaram Chawl where abolition of the system of indentured
labour was demanded.[46] On 3 January 1918, he held discussions
with 200 representatives of the untouchables (Meghwal
community) at the Servants of India Society about conversion
and certain grievances.[47] In those days, caste prejudice against
the depressed classes was very strong. Kanji Dwarkadas has
narrated an incident: in 1918, Gandhi had to go to open a temple
in Walpakhadi, the municipal sweepers' colony near Mazagaon.

Kanji noticed that no rich friend of Gandhi would give him his car for this visit, and so he drove Gandhi in his car.[48]

While Gandhi's innate sincerity and new ways of working were attracting people to him, the Home Rule was also making its presence felt. The news of the order of the internment of Annie Besant on 16 June 1917 resulted in a huge protest in Bombay. The order was lifted on 17 September 1917. Individuals such as Kanji Dwarkadas and Shankarlal Banker, who were very active with the Home Rule in Bombay, were also close to Gandhi. On 24 June 1917, Gandhi attended the opening of United Jain Students' Home in Princess Street by Sir Bhawanisinhji Bahadur, the maharaja of Jhalawar. He also met Kanji Dwarkadas for the first time that day.[49] His natural affection and amity towards people around him won him many admirers and followers. His ways of bonding with people were spontaneous and unpretentious; no gathering was too small or parochial for him. He was ever accessible to the people. He always had time to meet them and say a few friendly words. He came to Bombay from Ahmedabad to see off Polak when the latter left India on 31 August 1917, and on 31 August, and 1, 2, and 3 September 1917, he saw Polak's wife who was keeping unwell.[50]

After returning from South Africa, Gandhi was earning respect and admiration from the people all over India and was using his time and energy to convey his views to the people and take them along. The Kheda satyagraha in 1918 had attracted the attention of the nation. Gandhi explored opportunities to talk about it in Bombay. On 4 February 1918, he spoke about the plight of the agriculturists of Kheda district at a public meeting at the Mulji Jetha Market, presided over by Jamnadas Dwarkadas, which was largely attended by merchants and traders. He said that the people who did not fight for their rights were like slaves.[51] Thereafter, he wrote a letter to the editor of the *Bombay Chronicle* on the condition of the cultivators in Kheda, emphasizing that it was the sacred duty of every loyal citizen to fight unto death against the spirit of vindictiveness and tyranny.[52] He also gave a speech at a public meeting presided over by Vithalbhai Patel on 23 April 1918 at Shantaram Chawl. The proceedings were mostly in Gujarati and Marathi. The purpose of the meeting was to acquaint the citizens with the situation at Kheda and express sympathy with the satyagraha struggle.[53] Gandhi said that his experience in Kheda and Champaran taught him the crucial lesson that 'if leaders move among the people, live with them, eat and drink with them, a momentous change will come about in two years'.[54] He attended many important meetings. Gandhi was present at a meeting of the All India Congress Committee (A.I.C.C.) held on 3 May 1918 in the rooms of the Bombay Presidency Association, with Annie Besant, the president of the INC, as the chair. Other eminent individuals present included Tilak, Shastri, Khaparde, Dr Munje, Jamnadas Dwarkadas, C.P. Ramaswami Aiyar, and B.P. Wadia.[55]

The First World War had brought the realization that India could not remain untouched by the tremors and after-effects of the war. Some nationalist leaders extended unconditional support to the British government, while some such as Tilak favoured conditional support. Gandhi had placed his services at the disposal of the British authorities since the outbreak of the First World War. However, living under the protection of the navy and armed forces made him feel uneasy ever since the beginning of the war when he was in London, as it meant supporting the war indirectly. He felt that as a satyagrahi he should have gone to a place where he would not need such protection and could do without the food so procured. But he realized that he was not ready for this manner of living. As he was preparing to leave for India, he wrote to Pragji Desai from London on 15 November 1914, 'I could not summon the necessary courage. It is for cultivating such courage that I am going to India, where the circumstances are favourable. They are not so here, and to create them here one must have an *atman* a hundred thousand times stronger than mine.'[56] He did cultivate such courage and, that too, in abundance. However, it did take some time. Immediately after coming to India, he remained an advocate of the government's policy of recruiting Indians in the army and was awarded 'Kaisar-e-Hind' in 1915.

The Montagu–Chelmsford Reforms aimed at pacifying the demand of the leaders from the moderate section and the Home Rule League. They promised gradual development of self-governing institutions, with a view to the progressive realization of a responsible government in India as an integral part of the British empire. But this did not stop the British authorities from curbing the activities of the extremist leaders such as Tilak. The government convened the Imperial War Conference at Delhi and the Provincial War Conference at Bombay in early 1918 to ensure the support of varied sections, princely states, and leaders including Gandhi, Horniman, and Tilak.

The Provincial War Conference at Bombay was held on 10 June 1918 and was presided over by Lord Willingdon. It sought cooperation of the people in measures considered necessary by the government in the Bombay Presidency. When Lord Willingdon stopped Tilak and N.C. Kelkar from speaking on the resolutions there, the two, along with Gandhi, Jinnah, Horniman, and R.P. Karandikar, left the conference hall in protest.[57] A huge meeting of about 12,000 people, presided over by Gandhi, was held in the evening of 16 June 1918 at Shantaram Chawl in Girgaum in the heart of the city as an anti-Willingdon demonstration to protest against the governor's provocative statements at the Bombay Provincial War Conference regarding the Home Rule League leaders. The day was observed as 'Home Rule Day'.[58] Despite his

**Figure 1.1** The public meeting at Shantaram Chawl held on June 1918 in protest against Governor Lord Willingdon. Seen here are Tilak and Jinnah.
*Source*: Pratap M.B. Velkar.

ideological differences with Tilak, Gandhi clearly expressed that in his ruling Lord Willingdon committed 'a grave blunder' and offered a gratuitous insult to Tilak and Kelkar.[59] By this time, Gandhi was very much a part of the political developments in the city and was in constant touch with the people and the government. His association with the city and Mani Bhavan, Revashankar Jagjivan's home where he stayed, grew stronger. In his letter to L. Robertson, the chief secretary of the Political Department, Government of Bombay, dated 9 June 1918, he gave his address as 'care of Mr. Rewashankar Jagjiwan, Laburnum Road, Chowpati'.[60]

Gandhi's passion for khadi—hand-spun cloth—increased as the time passed. Around 1917, he was still trying to grasp the nitty-gritty of spinning. In the latter half of December 1918, he was not well and came to Mani Bhavan to recuperate. He wrote:

I was laid up in bed at Bombay. But I was fit enough to make searches for the wheel there. At last I chanced upon two spinners. They charged one rupee for a *seer* of yarn, i.e., 28 *tolas* or nearly three quarters of a pound. I was then ignorant of the economics of Khadi. I considered no price too high for securing handspun yarn. On comparing the rates paid by me with those paid in Vijapur, I found that I was being cheated. The spinners refused to agree to any reduction in their rates. So I had to dispense with their service. But they served their purpose. They taught spinning to Shrimatis Avantikabai, Ramibai Kamdar, the widowed mother of Sjt. Shankarlal Banker and Shrimati Vasumatibehn. The wheel began merrily to hum in my room, and I may say without exaggeration that its hum had no small share in restoring me to health.... In Bombay, again, the same old problem of obtaining a supply of hand-made slivers presented itself. A carder twanging his bow used to pass daily by Sjt. Revashankar's residence. I sent for him and learnt that he carded cotton from stuffing mattresses. He agreed to card cotton for slivers, but demanded a stiff price for it, which, however, I paid. The yarn thus prepared I disposed of to some Vaishnav friends for making from it garlands for the *pavitra ekadashi*. Sjt. Shivji started a spinning class in Bombay. All these experiments involved considerable expenditure. But it was willingly defrayed by patriotic friends, lovers of the motherland, who had faith in *khadi*. The money thus spent, in my humble opinion, was not wasted. It brought us a rich store of experience, and revealed to us the possibilities of the spinning wheel. I now grew impatient for the exclusive adoption of khadi for my dress. My *dhoti* was still of Indian mill-cloth. The coarse khadi manufactured in the Ashram and at Vijapur was only 30 inches in width. I gave notice to Gangabehn that, unless she provided me with a *khadi dhoti* of 45 inches width within a month, I would do with coarse, short *khadi dhoti*. The ultimatum came upon her as a shock. But she proved equal to the demand made upon her. Well within the month she sent me a pair of *khadi dhotis* of 45 inches width, and thus relieved me from what would then have been a difficult situation for me.[61]

Since his days in South Africa, Gandhi had a special rapport with women and great faith in their capacity to work and their commitment to non-violence. The women of India strengthened

his faith. He encouraged women to choose a mode of life that was above selfish interests and had to be pursued with fearlessness and inner strength in the service of society and the nation. Women, in turn, did not disappoint him. They acquired confidence and a sense of self-esteem as they participated in the activities initiated by Gandhi. They realized that they could also handle spinning and social work along with their family responsibilities. Gandhi had made a public appeal for voluntary teachers to work in Champaran and, as he noted, 'it received ready response'. Women such as Avantikabai Gokhale from Bombay, Anandibai Vaishampayan from Poona, Durga Desai, Maniben Parikh, and Kasturba came forward. Gandhi explained to them that they were expected to teach the children not the grammar and the three R's so much as cleanliness and good manners; the teaching of the rudiments of the alphabets and numerals was not a difficult matter. The result was that the classes taken by these women 'were found to be most successful. The experience inspired them with confidence and interest in their work. Avantikabai's became a model school. She threw herself heart and soul into her work. She brought her exceptional gifts to bear on it.'[62]

On 20 February 1918, Gandhi was invited by the Bhagini Samaj of Bombay (founded in 1916 in the memory of Gokhale) to preside over its annual meeting at the Morarji Gokuldas Hall. Gandhi stirred feelings of patriotism, service, and sacrifice among the women present. In his long speech, he said that woman is the companion of man, gifted with equal mental capacities. She has the right to participate in the very minutest detail in the activities of man and she has an equal right of freedom and liberty with him. Man and woman are of equal rank, but they are not identical. They are a peerless pair, being supplementary to each other; one helped the other so that without one the existence of the other could not be conceived.[63]

Kasturba, the quiet companion of Gandhi and his partner in all the hardships, was recognized in Bombay. She was given an address on 15 January 1915 by women at a gathering presided over by Lady Pherozeshah Mehta at Madhav Baug.[64] Tributes were paid by the speakers such as Lady Pherozeshah Mehta, Lady Cowasji Jehangir, Mrs Ranade, and Mrs Tyabji to the courage and sacrifice of Kasturba and her utter disregard of personal comfort in going to jail with her illustrious husband.[65]

———

Gandhi's experiences in South Africa had prepared him for a bigger role on the Indian soil. They had also helped him develop a perspective wide enough to appreciate the elements of various cultures and groups. Ramachandra Guha comments:

For most people, South Africa in the early 1900s was a crucible of social inequality, where individuals of one race or class learned very quickly to separate themselves from people of other races and classes. For this Indian, however, South Africa became a crucible of human togetherness, allowing him to forge bonds of affiliation with compatriots with whom, had he remained at home, he would have had absolutely no contact whatsoever.[66]

Gandhi's unusual ways of thinking and working as well as his noble qualities were recognized in India much before his return to India. It is important to note that Pranjivandas Jagjivandas Mehta, in his letter dated 8 November 1909 to Gopal Krishna Gokhale, had already referred to Gandhi as 'a great Mahatma'.[67] Prominent citizens of Jetpur (Gujarat) in their commemoration/scroll of honour presented to Gandhi on 21 January 1915, had also addressed him as 'Shriman Mahatma Mohandas Karamchand Gandhi'.[68]

After returning to India, Gandhi had thought of joining the Servants of India Society founded by Gokhale, his political guru. Gokhale was keen, and Gandhi was willing. But Gokhale died soon after Gandhi's arrival in India in 1915, and many members of the society had reservations on certain issues such as Gandhi's views on satyagraha and his religious expressions. Ultimately, Gandhi gave up the idea of joining the society.

Gandhi and Tilak respected each other despite their different political views. Tilak did not approve of Gandhi's unconditional support to the British war effort, nor was he sure of the efficacy of satyagraha, non-violence, and abstract principles in politics. Differences between the two leaders have been demonstrated in the oft-quoted passages of *Young India*. Soon after the INC session in December 1919 at Amritsar, Gandhi wrote that Tilak 'considers that everything is fair in politics'. Tilak replied stating that 'politics is a game of worldly people and not of Sadhus'. However, Gandhi's view was its opposite, and his rejoinder was: 'With deference to the Lokmanya I venture to say that it betrays mental laziness to think that the world is not for Sadhus.'[69] Differences in political views, however, did not diminish their respect for each other's qualities and work. In his preface to the biography of Gandhi written by Avantikabai Gokhale, Tilak paid rich tributes to Gandhi's character, his moral stature, his sense of duty to the nation, his work in South Africa, and his selfless efforts for the betterment of the nation. He recognized the importance of satyagraha but maintained that it would be difficult to say whether it would be fruitful at all times on all occasions.[70]

By the end of 1918, Gandhi had a fair understanding of the scenario in India. People had started rallying round him, and the leaders had taken a note of him. His enthusiasm for recruitment faded, and he started realizing the hollowness of the promises of the British government. He studied the attitude of the British government and its policies; he still had to decide about the protest—its feasibility, timing, and befitting cause. At that time, the vacuum in public life created by the demise of Sir Pherozeshah Mehta and Gokhale in 1915 and of Dadabhai Naoroji in 1917 was also being felt.

Gandhi's advent around that time was welcome and his presence was felt by 1918. He had already launched satyagraha in Champaran in 1917 and in Kheda in 1918 that had attracted the country's attention. He was also actively propagating his ideas on swadeshi, press freedom, and the betterment of society. His understanding of the situation, his novel method of protest, his humility, his preference for the mother tongue, and his ways of communicating and conducting himself vis-à-vis the rulers and the poor had evoked a range of responses—from awe to admiration, criticism to praise. Unfazed by such responses and remaining firmly rooted in the soil, he was ready to face new challenges and determined to weave together different strands of politics and moral principles.

## Notes and References

1. Gandhi, *An Autobiography*, p. 120.
2. D.G. Tendulkar, *Mahatma: Life of Mohandas Karamchand Gandhi*, illustrations collected and arranged by Vithalbhai K. Jhaveri, Vol. I (Bombay: Vithalbhai K. Jhaveri and D. G. Tendulkar, 1951), p. 193.
3. K. Gopalaswami, *Gandhi and Bombay* (Bombay: Gandhi Smarak Nidhi, Bharatiya Vidya Bhavan, 1969), p. 20.
4. Tendulkar, *Mahatma*, Vol. I, p. 193.
5. Gandhi's letter to Maganlal Gandhi, dated 11 January 1915, quoted in *CWMG*, Vol. 13 (Delhi: Publications Division, Ministry of Information and Broadcasting, Government of India, 1964), p. 4.

6. Shantikumar, *Gandhiji na Sansmarano (ane bija netao)* (in Gujarati) [Reminiscences of Gandhiji (and Other Leaders)], Swami Anand (ed.) (Bombay: N.M. Tripathi Pvt. Ltd., 1963), p. 4. Reprinted in 1985.

7. *The Bombay Chronicle* dated 11 January 1915 cited in *CWMG*, Vol. 13, p. 1.

8. *The Bombay Chronicle* dated 11 January 1915 cited in *CWMG*, Vol. 13, p. 2.

9. *The Times of India* dated 11 January 1915 cited in *CWMG*, Vol. 13, pp. 2–3.

10. Kidambi, *The Making of an Indian Metropolis*, pp. 157–233.

11. Confidential Report, GOB, Judicial, Vol. 140, Compilation no. 32, 1893, pp. 1–3, Maharashtra State Archives, quoted in Kidambi, *The Making of an Indian Metropolis*, p. 165.

12. C.B. Dalal, *Gandhi, 1915–1948: A Detailed Chronology* (New Delhi: Gandhi Peace Foundation; Bombay: Bharatiya Vidya Bhavan, 1971), p. 1.

13. *The Autobiography of Indulal Yagnik*, Vol. I, Devavrat Pathak, Howard Spodek, John R. Wood (trs), (New Delhi: Gujarat Vidyapith and Manohar, 2011), p. 207.

14. *The Bombay Chronicle* dated 15 January 1915 cited in *CWMG*, Vol. 13, p. 3.

15. *CWMG*, Vol. 13, p. 4.

16. Gopalaswami, *Gandhi and Bombay*, p. 22.

17. *The Bombay Chronicle* dated 13 January 1915 cited in *CWMG*, Vol. 13, pp. 5–7.

18. Dalal, *Gandhi*, p. 1.

19. 'Bombay Government Police Abstracts', 1915, p. 40, para 60 cited in *CWMG*, Vol. 13, pp. 7–8.

20. N.R. Phatak (ed.), *Source Material for a History of the Freedom Movement in India, Mahatma Gandhi*, Vol. III, Part I: 1915–1922 (Bombay: Directorate of Printing and Stationery, State of Maharashtra, 1965), p. 1.

21. Gopalaswami, *Gandhi and Bombay*, pp. 23–4.

22. *The Bombay Chronicle* dated 15 January 1915 cited in *CWMG*, Vol. 13, pp. 9–10.

23. Gandhi, *An Autobiography*, p. 456.

24. Gandhi, *An Autobiography*, p. 456.

25. *Indian Opinion* dated 10 March 1915 cited in *CWMG*, Vol. 13, p. 8.

26. C.B. Dalal (compiler), *Gandhijini Dinwari* (in Gujarati) [The Detailed Day-to-day Chronology of Gandhiji] (Gandhinagar: Information Department, Government of Gujarat, 1990), p. 2.

27. Dalal, *Gandhi*, p. 17.

28. Dalal, *Gandhijini Dinwari*, p. 23.

29. *CWMG*, Vol. 3, pp. 252–5.

30. Dalal, *Gandhi*, p. 7.

31. 'Report of the Thirtieth Indian National Congress', Bombay, cited in *CWMG*, Vol. 13, pp. 153–5.

32. *CWMG*, Vol. 13, p. 612.

33. Gandhi, *An Autobiography*, p. 497.

34. Dalal, *Gandhi*, p. 7.

35. *CWMG*, Vol. 96 (Supplementary volume 6) (New Delhi: Publications Division, Ministry of Information and Broadcasting, Government of India, 1994), p. 231.

36. *Gujarati* dated 14 February 1915 cited in *CWMG*, Vol. 13, p. 17.

37. *Gujarati* dated 21 February 1915 cited in *CWMG*, Vol. 13, pp. 22–3.

38. Dalal, *Gandhi*, p. 2.

39. Dalal, *Gandhi*, p. 7.

40. *The Bombay Chronicle* dated 29 October 1915 cited in *CWMG*, Vol. 13, pp. 130–4. The first batch of indentured labour reached Natal on 16 November 1860. See Dalal, *Gandhi*, p. 6, footnote 3.

41. Dalal, *Gandhi*, p. 6, footnote 2.

42. *The Hindu* dated 25 December 1915 cited in *CWMG*, Vol. 13, p. 153. He met Kishorilal Mashruwala for the first time in Bombay. See Dalal, *Gandhi*, p. 11, footnote 7.

43. *The Bombay Chronicle* dated 10 February 1917 cited in *CWMG*, Vol. 13, p. 342. The system of indentured labour was abolished in 1920.

44. 'Bombay Secret Abstracts', 1916, p. 506 cited in *CWMG*, Vol. 13, pp. 280–3.

45. 'Bombay Secret Abstracts', 1916, p. 506 cited in *CWMG*, Vol. 13, pp. 280–3.

46. Dalal, *Gandhi*, p. 12.

47. Dalal, *Gandhi*, p. 16.

48. Kanji Dwarkadas, *India's Fight for Freedom, 1913–1937: An Eyewitness Story* (Bombay: Popular Prakashan, 1966), p. 90.

49. Dalal, *Gandhijini Dinwari*, p. 44, footnote 5.

50. Dalal, *Gandhijini Dinwari*, p. 47.

51. *The Bombay Chronicle* dated 5 February 1918 cited in *CWMG*, Vol. 14 (Delhi: Publications Division, Ministry of Information and Broadcasting, Government of India, 1965), pp.182–4.

52. *The Bombay Chronicle* dated 17 April 1918 cited in *CWMG*, Vol. 14, pp. 338–41.

53. *CWMG*, Vol. 14, pp. 369–71.

54. *CWMG*, Vol. 14, p. 371.

55. 'Bombay Secret Abstract', 1918, p. 399, para 577(d) and the *Bombay Chronicle* dated 4 May 1918 cited in Phatak, *Source Material for a History of the Freedom Movement in India*, Vol. III, Part I, p. 88.

56. *CWMG*, Vol. 12 (Delhi: Publications Division, Ministry of Information and Broadcasting, Government of India, 1964), p. 554. For details of the British policy of recruitment to the army and responses of Tilak and Gandhi, see Aravind Ganachari, 2005, 'First World War: Purchasing Indian Loyalties, Imperial Policy of Recruitment and "Rewards"', *Economic & Political Weekly*, 40(8): 779–88. For the relationship of Gandhi's war service with the principle of non-violence, see Peter Brock, 1981, 'Gandhi's Non-violence and His War Service', *Gandhi Marg*, 2(11): 601–16.

57. *CWMG*, Vol. 14, p. 427. However, according to Dalal, neither Jinnah nor Gandhi left the meeting. See Dalal, *Gandhi*, p. 19.

58. *CWMG*, Vol. 14, p. 425.

59. *The Bombay Chronicle* dated 17 June 1918 cited in *CWMG*, Vol. 14, p. 427.

60. *CWMG*, Vol. 14, pp. 421–2.

61. Gandhi, *An Autobiography*, pp. 603–4.

62. Gandhi, *An Autobiography*, p. 514.

63. *The Hindu* dated 26 February 1918 and *Mahatma Gandhini Vicharsrishti* cited in *CWMG*, Vol. 14, pp. 202–9. According to Dalal, Gandhi was not in Bombay on this day. See Dalal, *Gandhi*, p. 17.

64. Dalal, *Gandhi*, p. 1, footnote 5.

65. Gopalaswami, *Gandhi and Bombay*, pp. 25–6.

66. Ramachandra Guha, *Gandhi before India* (New Delhi: Penguin, 2013), p. 537.

67. S.R. Mehrotra, *Gurudev and Mahatma* (Bombay: Vakils, Feffer & Simons, 2015), p. 6.

68. Mani Bhavan Gandhi Sangrahalaya collection, Bombay.

69. *Young India*, 28 January 1920.

70. Avantikabai Gokhale, 'Preface', *Mahatma Gandhi Yanche Charitra, Vishesh Parichay, Lekh va Vyakhyane* (in Marathi) [The Biography of Mahatma Gandhi: A Special Introduction, Essays and Speeches] (Bombay: Mumbai Vaibhav Press, 1918), pp. 7–16.

# 2

# FACING NEW CHALLENGES: 1919

THE POLITICAL SCENE IN 1919 BROUGHT NEW ISSUES AND CHALLENGES to the fore. The people, adversely affected by the war, were feeling sombre and unhappy. The announcement of the Montagu–Chelmsford Reforms in July 1918 could not satisfy the demand of the principle of self-determination for India. Gandhi's trust in the promises made by the British government had crumbled. Concerned about the violence unleashed by the revolutionary groups, the British government decided to arm itself with extraordinary powers to suppress the rights of the people. Fearing political unrest and agitation, it appointed a committee under Justice Sidney Rowlatt in December 1917 to investigate revolutionary crime in the country and to suggest legislative measures for its eradication. The committee recommended emergency powers for the government to deal with subversion and political agitation. In the light of these recommendations, the government drafted two bills that were presented in the Imperial Legislative Council in February 1919 and one of the bills was passed despite stiff opposition from all the Indian members.

The bill received the assent of the viceroy on 21 March 1919. The act, known as the Rowlatt Act or 'Black Act' in India, gave the government sweeping coercive powers, including the power to try political offenders without a jury, to detain and arrest a person suspected of subversive activities, and to control the press. This shattered the hopes of a sympathetic approach from the British government that claimed to fight the First World War to defend democracy. This act of the government, meant to tighten its hold on the Indian people, stirred anger and protest. The agitation against the Rowlatt Act brought Gandhi in the forefront, and Bombay became the centre stage. The city's politics in 1919 was in ferment.[1]

## The Rowlatt Satyagraha

### Genesis

Before 1919, Gandhi had chosen places such as Champaran, Kheda, and Bardoli as the sites of satyagraha. Strongly rooted in the soil and highly critical of modern civilization, he disliked big cities; he had described Bombay, Calcutta, and the other chief cities of India as the 'real plague spots'.[2] In 1917, however, it was Ahmedabad that was the stage of his satyagraha, and in 1919, he chose Bombay, the metropolitan city buzzing with commercial and industrial activities, to launch his first nationwide satyagraha. The coalescence of the local and larger issues of the years of the First World War had instigated social, economic, and political ferment in the city and had unleashed a diverse range of forces—some colliding and some converging. Some factors adversely affected the city; important amongst them were the increasing cost of living, shortage of consumer goods, labour unrest and workers' strikes, difficulties faced by the traders, increasing population density, and the complex composition of the city. The outbreak of epidemics such as influenza was an aggravating factor.

However, the scenario was not absolutely bleak. Around this time, the city also experienced new energy with the emergence of the young and educated elite leaders, the rising political aspirations for self-government, advent of newspapers and journals, spread of education, and the affluence of certain sections such as the mill owners, rich merchants, and industrialists. When Annie Besant established the Home Rule League in Madras in September 1916, Tilak had already formed the Home Rule League in Belgaum in April 1916 and its members were very active. The efforts of the Home Rule movement in Bombay with leaders such as Jinnah, Umar Sobani, Kanji and Jamnadas Dwarkadas, and Shankarlal Banker successfully aroused political consciousness in certain sections of the people. Jinnah, Horniman, Sobani, and others organized an effective protest in a public meeting convened by the sheriff of Bombay in honour of Lord Willingdon at the Town Hall on 12 December 1918. Started on the eve of the war, the *Bombay Chronicle* was established by 1917 as a newspaper with a large circulation and a force that could not be ignored in the political discourse of the city. Its editor Horniman sent a special reporter to Kheda for constant coverage of the satyagraha.

The city was throbbing with diverse opinions and views. There was, however, no common platform where all these could be brought together. The protest against the Rowlatt bills provided such an opportunity. Gandhi held that the proposed Rowlatt legislation was a severe blow to the freedom and rights of the people, and resolutely opposed its content as well as the manner in which it was sought to be imposed. For Gandhi, a moral protest against this unjust colonial measure was a must. He believed that satyagraha was the exercise of the purest soul force against injustice and oppression. Horniman had already argued that such a mass protest against the measure abrogating the civil rights of people was intrinsic.

When the nation was seething with anger against the harsh and repressive measures of the Rowlatt legislation, Gandhi was recuperating at Mani Bhavan from the surgery on piles performed by Dr Dalal on 20 January 1919.[3] Kasturba was extremely worried due to his ill health and his resolve not to take cow or buffalo milk. She found a way out and convinced him to take goat's milk instead.

Gandhi left for Ahmedabad on 10 February 1919. In between addressing several anti-Rowlatt protest meetings, Horniman led a Bombay delegation to meet Gandhi and Vallabhbhai Patel at the Ahmedabad ashram on 22 February. The delegates included Umar Sobani and Shankarlal Banker, who were among the *Bombay Chronicle's* board of directors, and Sarojini Naidu. Horniman issued an invitation to Gandhi to launch and lead from Bombay city an all-India 'passive resistance' campaign against the Rowlatt bills. After much hesitation and discussion that lasted two full days and nights, Gandhi finally agreed. The text of a 'Satyagraha Vow' was collectively drafted, with a view to obtain as many signatures as possible, pledging to disobey the Rowlatt laws as well as 'such other laws as a Committee to be hereafter appointed may think fit'.[4] Gandhi, along with Vallabhbhai Patel, Chandulal Manilal Desai, Kesariprasad Manilal Thakoor, Anasuya Sarabhai, and others signed the satyagraha pledge at Ahmedabad and sent a telegram to the viceroy calling the Rowlatt bills 'symptom of [a] deep-seated disease among the ruling class' and informing him about the decision to offer satyagraha. The pledge was drafted on 24 February 1919 and also signed by those present in a meeting held at Sabarmati Ashram.[5] Thereafter, Bombay became the centre of public protests against the attempt to curb the liberties and rights of people. The *Bombay Chronicle* continued to provide relevant information about the Rowlatt bills to the concerned readers.

Gandhi's previous campaigns in Champaran and Kheda focused on local issues in which the viceroy and the government of India could finally intervene. In opposing the Rowlatt bills, however, Gandhi was risking a head-on collision with the imperial government itself.[6] A campaign like the Rowlatt Satyagraha, which was designed to embrace the entire Indian

THE BOMBAY CHRONICLE, SATURDAY, FEBRUARY 22, 1919.

## AGAINST THE BLACK BILLS.

### COME TO THE GREAT PROTEST MEETING
#### AT FRENCH BRIDGE
##### TO-MORROW AT 6 P.M.

*President* :—SIR DINSHAH PETIT.

JOIN THE PROCESSION OF HOME RULE VOLUNTEERS AND MEMBERS
*starting from Dhobi Talao at 4 p.m.*

### ROUTE :—
Kalbadevi, Bhuleshwar, Girgaon Back Road, Sandhurst Road,
TO
## FRENCH BRIDGE.

**Figure 2.1** A notice of protest meeting against the Rowlatt bills organized by the volunteers and members of the Home Rule League.
*Source*: The Asiatic Society of Mumbai.

subcontinent, presented to Gandhi new problems such as those of organization, communication of ideas, mobilization of social groups, and exercise of restraint over groups that were mobilized under conditions of excitement or repression. Gandhi formed his team and devised his strategies. His lieutenants were active and effective in Bombay.[7]

When Gandhi came to Bombay on 1 March, the commissioner of police had him unobtrusively watched. Gandhi was constantly visited by the Home Rule leaders of Bombay. The Home Rulers were collecting signatures on the vow. On 2 March, a notice written with a pencil was put up at the Mulji Jetha market inviting people to sign the vow at S.G. Banker's residence. About 40 men went to do so. It was noticed that the younger generation of Bombay was responding very enthusiastically and cloth merchants were determined to follow Gandhi.[8] Attempts were made to disseminate information through posters. Posters put in many places in Nadiad Town were printed by the Gnan Sagar Litho Press, Girgaum Road, Bombay.[9]

The Satyagraha Sabha was established with its head office in Bombay. Its well-formulated rules, presumably drafted by Gandhi, were publicized. The objective of the organization was to oppose the bills by resorting to satyagraha until they were withdrawn.[10] The satyagraha pledge was also sent to the press. According to Gandhi, 'The step taken is probably the most momentous in the history of India. I give my assurance that it has not been hastily taken. Personally I have passed many a sleepless night over it. I have weighed the consequences of the act.'[11] Since the bills were an 'unmistakable symptom of a deep-seated disease in the governing body', they needed 'to be drastically treated'.[12] Precise instructions were given to the satyagraha volunteers seeking signatures from the people.[13] Thousands of men and women took the satyagraha pledge against this oppressive law.

Gandhi's main lieutenants—Sobani, Banker, Horniman, and Dwarkadas brothers—were from the Home Rule in Bombay. However, Annie Besant did not approve of Gandhi's plan of launching mass disobedience. Despite their differences on political issues, Gandhi and Besant had mutual respect for each other. Kanji Dwarkadas has written about one of their meetings in an appealing way.[14] After reaching Bombay from Madras, Annie Besant sent Kanji to Gandhi to arrange a meeting with him. Kanji saw Gandhi at 9 am and realized that the latter was not well and was seething with pain. When informed about the purpose, Gandhi said that he was sorry that he was too ill to go and see Besant. Kanji informed him that she had suggested to come to see him on the second floor of his house on Laburnum Road. Gandhi was reluctant, as he did not want Besant to take the trouble of walking up to the second floor. But on Kanji's insistence, he gave in and fixed up the time to meet at 3 pm despite his pain. Besant told him about the dangers of a mass civil disobedience movement. Gandhi, however, expressed his intention to go ahead with his plan.[15]

In March, the atmosphere of Bombay was charged with the excitement of protesting against the oppressive act. Gandhi was in Bombay in January 1919 too. He left the city twice in February and March. He again returned to Bombay on 13 March and stayed at Revashankar Jhaveri's house. He was received by Jamnadas Dwarkadas at Victoria Terminus. He was interviewed the same evening by Horniman, Kanji Dwarkadas, and a few others of the Satyagraha Sabha. On 14 March 1919, Gandhi presided over a public meeting held at French Bridge to protest against the Rowlatt bills.[16] As he was indisposed, this speech in Gujarati was read out at a Bombay meeting against the Rowlatt bills. He was clear that '[s]atyagraha is not a threat, it is a fact' and '[w]e may no longer believe in the doctrine of tit for tat; we may not meet hatred by hatred, violence by violence, evil by evil; but we have to make a continuous and persistent effort to return good for evil'.[17] Most of the merchants of the Mulji Jetha cloth market, the Lakshmidas Khimji Market, and the Morarji Goculdas Market were with Gandhi in opposing the oppressive act.

## Course of the Satyagraha

Gandhi toured various parts of the country for propagating his ideas and discussing the political scene. He came to Bombay on 3 April and made the city his headquarters for the satyagraha against the Rowlatt legislation. In his letter to the editor of the *Bombay Chronicle*, Gandhi wrote on 3 April 1919 that in opposing the Rowlatt legislation, the satyagrahis were resisting the spirit of terrorism that lay behind it and of which it was the most glaring symptom.[18] In a telegram from Bombay to S. Kasturi Ranga Iyengar on the same day, he emphasized his faith in satyagraha and hoped that 'speeches Sunday [6 April] will be free from anger or unworthy passion. Cause too great and sacred to be damaged by exhibition passion. We have no right cry out against sufferings self invited.'[19]

It was initially decided to start the satyagraha on 30 March 1919, but later the date was changed to 6 April. But the news did not reach Delhi in time and the satyagraha was launched. A procession and a meeting were organized under the leadership of Swami Shraddhananda, and there was police firing.[20] 6 April was called 'the Black Day'. On 4 April 1919, the poster of 'the Black Sunday' appeared in the *Bombay Chronicle*. Directions (and the poster, both presumably drafted by Gandhi) were also given to the demonstrators to observe 6 April as 'a day of humiliation and prayer and also of mourning by reason of the Delhi tragedy'.[21]

The day of 6 April was momentous for Bombay. The *Bombay Chronicle* carried a vivid account of the mass meeting and Gandhi's speech on 7 April 1919. It reported in detail the scene at Chowpatty. Bombay presented the sight of a city in mourning on the occasion of national humiliation, prayers, and sorrow at the passing of the Rowlatt bills, and observed a twenty-four-hour fast. Long before the sun had risen, the Back Bay foreshore was humming and throbbing with people. From early morning, people had come to Chowpatty to bathe in the sea. It was 'the Black Sunday', and the day's programme began with a sea bath. Gandhi was one of the first to arrive at Chowpatty with several volunteers, and before 6.30 am, he had taken his seat on one of the stone benches with about a hundred satyagrahis around him. As the day advanced, people kept pouring in on the seashore. Every new arrival first took bath in the sea and then came and sat around Gandhi. The crowd kept on swelling into a huge mass of people. As the time for the meeting on the Chowpatty sands neared, Gandhi moved in that direction joined by Sarojini Naidu, Jamnadas Dwarkadas, Horniman, and others. There were nearly twenty-five women. The whole Sandhurst Bridge swarmed with approximately 0.15 million people. All communities were represented there: Muslims, Hindus, Parsis, and so forth, and even one Englishman. Since Gandhi was unwell, his speech was read out by Jamnadas. He exhorted people to take the swadeshi vow and said, 'No country has ever risen, no nation has ever been made without sacrifice, and we are trying an experiment of building up ourselves by self-sacrifice without resorting to violence in any shape or form.'[22] Two resolutions were passed. First, the meeting of the inhabitants of Bombay tendered congratulations to the people of Delhi for showing self-restraint under trying circumstances and to Swami Shraddhananda and Hakim Ajmal Khan for their admirable leadership. It also offered condolences to the families of the innocent people killed in the firing ordered by the local authorities. Second, the meeting requested the secretary of state for India to advise the emperor to veto the Anarchical and Revolutionary Crimes Act of 1919; it also requested the viceroy to withdraw the Criminal Law Amendments Bill No. 1 of 1919. After the meeting, the people proceeded to Madhav Baug. From the seashore to Madhav Baug, it was a solid mass of humanity, gathering strength on its way. The houses on both sides were crowded with women and children. At Madhav Baug, the compound was completely filled up. The crowd dispersed after offering prayers.[23]

At French Bridge, 'the crowd was so great that the speakers could not make themselves heard' and two overflow meetings became necessary. For the first time, a representative of the British Labour Party, John Scurr, was among the crowd, suggesting wider ramifications of the event.[24]

After the gathering at Madhav Baug, a meeting was arranged at Grant Road in an open space in front of a mosque where no less than 5,000 Muslims had assembled. Gandhi appealed them to join the satyagraha and said that Hindus and Muslims should treat each other like brothers.[25] The same day, he also addressed a women's meeting presided over by Mrs Jayakar and appealed the Indian women to cooperate with the men in the constitutional fight they were waging against the Rowlatt legislation and to join the satyagraha movement in large numbers.[26]

To print and sell the proscribed publications openly seemed to be a direct way of offering civil disobedience. According to a statement issued by the Satyagraha Sabha, Bombay, and published in the *Bombay Chronicle* dated 8 April 1919, the following proscribed publications were selected for dissemination: *Hind Swaraj*, the Gujarati paraphrase of Ruskin's *Unto This Last*, the Gujarati paraphrase of *Defence of Socrates* by M.K. Gandhi, and *The Life and Address of Mustafa Kamal Pasha*.[27]

**Figure 2.2**   Gandhi and Umar Sobani coming down from the balcony of the Grant Road mosque after addressing a meeting on 6 April 1919.
*Source*: Vithalbhai Jhaveri Collection/Dinodia Photos.

Gandhi, as the president of the Satyagraha Sabha, and D.D. Sathaye, Umar Sobani, and Shankarlal Banker, as its secretaries, had appealed people to make copies of the prohibited literature themselves and also make them freely available.[28] Gandhi's book *Hind Swarajya*, published by him in South Africa and later proscribed by the government, was published in the form of a pamphlet bearing the names of Umar Sobani and Shankarlal Banker as publishers.[29]

The day of protest was filled with excitement. Approximately 80 per cent of shops and businesses in the city remained closed, including the cloth, fish, and vegetable markets. Apart from merchants and small traders, those who abstained from work on a large scale also included peons and clerks, taxi and hackney Victoria drivers, hawkers and various street vendors, and barbers and dhobis.[30]

Gandhi mused later that the hartal in Bombay was a complete success. All the necessary preparations had been made for starting civil disobedience. A number of copies of the proscribed books were printed for sale at the large meeting held on the evening of 6 April at the end of the day's fast. Sarojini Naidu and Gandhi went out in cars. All the copies were soon sold out. The proceeds of the sale were to be utilized for furthering the civil disobedience campaign. Although priced at four annas, they fetched much more. Five- and ten-rupee notes would cover the price of a single copy, and in one case, a copy was sold out for Rs 50. It was explained to the people that they were liable to be arrested and imprisoned for purchasing the proscribed literature, but for the moment, they had shed the fear of going to jail. The government, for its part, had conveniently taken the view that the proscribed books had not, in fact, been sold; what was sold was not held to qualify as proscribed literature. To sell the reprint did not constitute an offence under the law. This news caused general disappointment.[31]

Hazareesingh has made an insightful observation on the way Gandhi and Horniman came together during the protests against the Rowlatt Act. For Gandhi, the question was that whether the 'materialist' city people could adhere to the 'truth' of non-violence in their quest for justice; for Horniman, it was that whether satyagraha would enable the attainment of a new level of political pressure on the colonial state. In many ways, the twenty-four-hour hartal announced by the Satyagraha Sabha on 6 April represented a compromise between Gandhi's cautious and introspective orientation and Horniman's more activist approach. The 'National Humiliation Day' in Bombay city was marked by a negotiated amalgam of Gandhian techniques of 'self-purification' and urban forms of popular protest—demonstrations, processions, public speeches—which had been gathering momentum during the latter part of the war years.[32]

*Satyagrahi*, an unregistered newspaper, was issued by Gandhi on 7 April 1919 in defiance of the Indian Press Act. It was published from Mani Bhavan. The paper was the size of a half-sheet and priced at one pice. It declared that since the paper had not been registered under the law, there could be no annual subscription. And the paper would exist only until the withdrawal of the Rowlatt legislation.[33]

On 8 April, Gandhi left Bombay for Delhi. At Kosi station he was served with orders restricting his entry into Punjab and Delhi. But he refused to obey the orders. As he reached Punjab's Palwal station (now in Haryana), he was taken into police custody. He was prohibited from entering Punjab, for it was feared that his presence would disturb peace. He was brought back to Bombay on 11 April and released. He alighted at the Marine Lines station as advised by the accompanying police officer to avoid the demonstration at Colaba. A friend's carriage happened to pass by, and it left him at Revashankar Jhaveri's place. Umar Sobani and Anasuyaben took him to Pydhoni to pacify a huge, impatient crowd that had gathered there. The news of Gandhi's arrest had

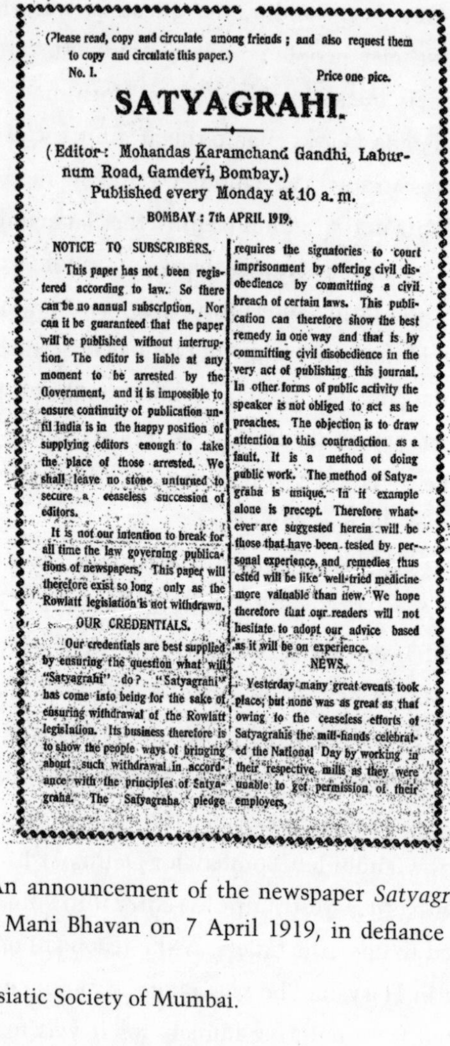

(Please read, copy and circulate among friends ; and also request them to copy and circulate this paper.)

No. I.                                    Price one pice.

# SATYAGRAHI.

( Editor : Mohandas Karamchand Gandhi, Laburnum Road, Gamdevi, Bombay.)
Published every Monday at 10 a. m.

BOMBAY : 7th APRIL, 1919.

**NOTICE TO SUBSCRIBERS.**

This paper has not been registered according to law. So there can be no annual subscription. Nor can it be guaranteed that the paper will be published without interruption. The editor is liable at any moment to be arrested by the Government, and it is impossible to ensure continuity of publication until India is in the happy position of supplying editors enough to take the place of those arrested. We shall leave no stone unturned to secure a ceaseless succession of editors.

It is not our intention to break for all time the law governing publications of newspapers. This paper will therefore exist so long only as the Rowlatt legislation is not withdrawn.

**OUR CREDENTIALS.**

Our credentials are best supplied by ensuring the question what will "Satyagrahi" do ? "Satyagrahi" has come into being for the sake of ensuring withdrawal of the Rowlatt legislation. Its business therefore is to show the people ways of bringing about such withdrawal in accordance with the principles of Satyagraha. The "Satyagraha" pledge

requires the signatories to court imprisonment by offering civil disobedience by committing a civil breach of certain laws. This publication can therefore show the best remedy in one way and that is by committing civil disobedience in the very act of publishing this journal. In other forms of public activity the speaker is not obliged to act as he preaches. The objection is to draw attention to this contradiction as a fault. It is a method of doing public work. The method of Satyagraha is unique. In it example alone is precept. Therefore whatever are suggested herein will be those that have been tested by personal experience, and remedies thus ested will be like well-tried medicine more valuable than new. We hope therefore that our readers will not hesitate to adopt our advice based as it will be on experience.

**NEWS.**

Yesterday many great events took place; but none was as great as that owing to the ceaseless efforts of Satyagrahis the mill-hands celebrated the National Day by working in their respective mills as they were unable to get permission of their employers.

**Figure 2.3** An announcement of the newspaper *Satyagrahi* issued by Gandhi from Mani Bhavan on 7 April 1919, in defiance of the Indian Press Act.

*Source*: The Asiatic Society of Mumbai.

roused anger among the people. As the procession emerged from Abdul Rehman Street into the Crawford Market square, it faced a wild charge by the mounted police, brandishing their lances to disperse the crowd. Some were trampled under feet; others were badly mauled and crushed. The crowd dispersed. Gandhi stopped at Bombay's police commissioner F.C. Griffith's office to complain

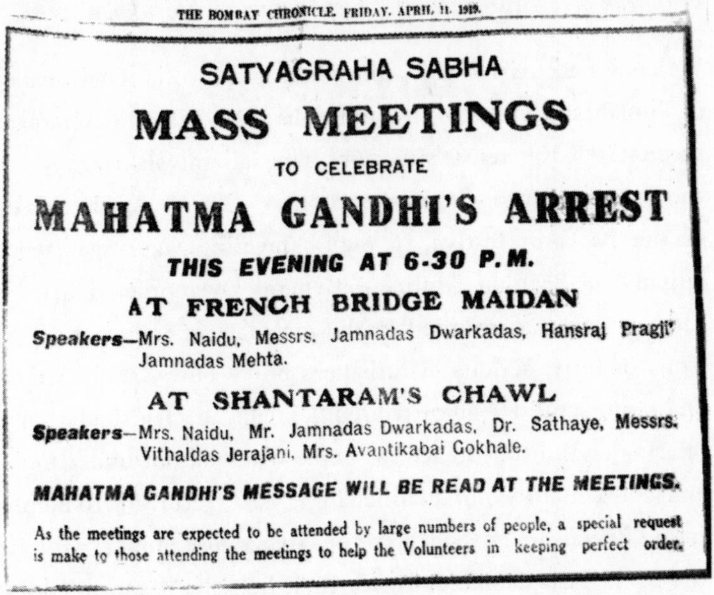

THE BOMBAY CHRONICLE. FRIDAY. APRIL 11. 1919.

SATYAGRAHA SABHA

**MASS MEETINGS**

TO CELEBRATE

**MAHATMA GANDHI'S ARREST**

***THIS EVENING AT 6-30 P. M.***

**AT FRENCH BRIDGE MAIDAN**

**Speakers**—Mrs. Naidu, Messrs. Jamnadas Dwarkadas, Hansraj Pragji, Jamnadas Mehta.

**AT SHANTARAM'S CHAWL**

**Speakers**—Mrs. Naidu, Mr. Jamnadas Dwarkadas, Dr. Sathaye, Messrs. Vithaldas Jerajani, Mrs. Avantikabai Gokhale.

***MAHATMA GANDHI'S MESSAGE WILL BE READ AT THE MEETINGS.***

As the meetings are expected to be attended by large numbers of people, a special request is make to those attending the meetings to help the Volunteers in keeping perfect order.

**Figure 2.4** An advertisement of mass meetings organized at French Bridge Maidan and Shantaram Chawl to 'celebrate' Gandhi's arrest.
*Source*: The Asiatic Society of Mumbai.

about the police's conduct. He was told about the disturbances that had occurred in various places. Thereafter, Gandhi held a meeting on the Chowpatty sands, where he spoke on the duty of non-violence and the limitations of satyagraha.[34] When he was arrested in April, there was a complete business hartal during which the cotton, cloth, and bullion markets were all closed, along with the Marwari bazar and the Mulji Jetha market.[35]

On 12 April 1919, Gandhi called a meeting of cloth merchants and vented his distress at the disturbances and violence. He appealed the people to remain peaceful in the spirit of satyagraha. He also attended a meeting at the Marwari chamber where he actually broke down hearing the news of disturbances in Ahmedabad and went without food the next day.[36]

Violence had marred the atmosphere of protests. Disturbances in Punjab and violence in Ahmedabad, Nadiad, and Viramgam precipitated the tense situation. The Jallianwala tragedy sent shock waves throughout the country. On 13 April, the day of the Baisakhi festival, a public meeting was organized at Jallianwala Bagh in Amritsar. General Dyer ordered firing at the meeting that resulted in the massacre of innocent people. Consequently, serious disturbances broke out. Gandhi felt sad and remorseful. He admitted his 'Himalayan miscalculation' in offering civil disobedience to people who had not understood it and, consequently, not qualified for it. After returning to Bombay from Gujarat, he raised a corps of satyagrahi volunteers through the Satyagraha Sabha, and with their help, he began to educate people about the meaning and significance of satyagraha. But it was a difficult task.[37] He fasted for three days and issued a statement on 18 April postponing satyagraha.[38] However, preaching and practising of truth and non-violence continued through the leaflets published in Bombay.

On 20 April 1919, he attended a meeting of the A.I.C.C. in Bombay. On 21 April 1919, the A.I.C.C. passed a resolution on the Punjab situation and Gandhi sent a telegram to the private secretary to the viceroy against the whipping of people arrested for disobeying orders under the martial law.[39] At a meeting in Bombay on 25 April, he advised people to do nothing contrary to the spirit of satyagraha.[40]

The government was obviously concerned about the growing political agitation and took some harsh steps. Horniman was served with an order to leave India and was deported. The *Bombay Chronicle* suspended publication. The deportation of Horniman on 26 April 1919 and the suspension of the *Bombay*

*Chronicle* generated a furore in the city. The news was published by the *Hindustan* and the *Sanj Vartaman*, the latter newspaper describing the action of the government as a gross blunder. Many were in favour of a strike the next morning, but Gandhi issued a manifesto strongly advocating that there should be no strike. He dissuaded many people, including the Hindus and Muslims who came to see him at his residence, from demonstrating and protesting against the action of the government. Because of this decision, he had to face criticism from many quarters[41] and he was flooded with complaints for his 'inactivity'. He was frequently visited by Jamnadas, Sathaye, Banker, Sobani, and a number of banias and Marwaris, and also by Anasuya Sarabhai, Pandit Malaviya, and Shantaram Dabholkar. On the evening of 29 April 1919, Gandhi discussed with Jinnah, Jamnadas, Sathaye, and others the future of the *Bombay Chronicle*.[42]

In *Satyagraha* leaflet no. 15, dated 5 May 1919, Gandhi declared that the Satyagraha Sabha had decided to observe 11 May as the day of observance of hartal, fasting for twenty-four hours, and private religious devotion in every home.[43] He elaborated the idea writing that 'it will be opportune also to explain to family gatherings Mr. Horniman's title to our affection'.[44] He wrote further: 'Where it is a question of determining the justice or otherwise of a particular act, there is no room for any other force but that of reason regulated by the voice of conscience.'[45]

Gandhi wrote to Commissioner Griffith on 6 May informing him about the proposed hartal.[46] And on the same day, he called a meeting at the Morarji Gokuldas Hall to explain to people how they should observe 11 May in honour of Horniman: they should stop their work that day, fast, and spend the day in devotion and peace.[47] On 8 May, he had discussions with the CID officers and also gave a lecture on swadeshi to a women's meeting at Vanita Vishram. Sarojini Naidu presided over this meeting.[48]

To ensure peace on the day of the hartal, Gandhi established his headquarters from 7.30 am at the Mulji Jetha market on Sheikh Memon Street. The satyagraha volunteers, considerably reinforced in numbers, were dispatched in small groups to move around the city. They were instructed to ensure that people were not, in any numbers, gathering in the usual open spaces—the Esplanade Maidan, Chowpatty beach, Shantaram Chawl, Madhav Baug, and Mastan Shah Tank.[49]

Gandhi was pleased that Bombay had set an example by observing a peaceful hartal on 11 May. He expressed his feelings: 'Bombay covered itself with glory by preserving perfect calm, and the citizens have shown by their peaceful hartal [that] they have understood a portion of satyagraha.... We shall learn the first chapter of swaraj and liberty when India adopts the example of Bombay as a permanent way of life.'[50]

Informal meetings of the satyagrahis continued in the city. A private meeting of the satyagrahis was held on the night of 29 May at the Morarji Gokuldas Hall. Gandhi said that he needed only intelligent, strong-willed, and well-educated people who were prepared to give an undertaking that they would adhere to the principles of satyagraha to the last.[51]

While on the one hand, people, by and large, were enthused with the spirit of nationalism, there were some who wanted to display their loyalty to the British empire. 24 August was celebrated as 'Empire Day' throughout India, including Bombay. A meeting, presided over by Sir Jugmohandas Vurjeevandas was held at Jhaverbaug, Kalbadevi Road, that day in the morning. The place was decorated with flags and bunting and a garlanded portrait of Queen Victoria was kept in the centre.[52]

The Satyagraha Sabha had organized a petition condemning the victimization of the *Bombay Chronicle* and the deportation of its editor, which was signed by over 50,000 citizens and presented to the governor George Llyod on the day preceding the hartal.[53]

Gandhi wrote to Crerar, the secretary to the Bombay government, on 29 May in unambiguous words that Horniman's deportation was 'totally unjustifiable' and the censorship orders on the *Bombay Chronicle* after his deportation were quite unnecessary.[54] He believed in the dissemination of the available information. On 30 April 1919, he published in *Satyagraha* leaflet no. 10 Horniman's letters to himself and Jamnadas from *S.S. Takada*.[55] From aboard *S.S. Takada*, Horniman had written to Jinnah, the president of the *Bombay Chronicle*'s board of directors, advising him to suspend the publication 'until the return of sanity'. This view, strongly backed by S.A. Brelvi and Gandhi, prevailed and the *Bombay Chronicle* was not published between 26 April and the end of May 1919. When the paper resumed publication on 31 May, its editorial columns were left conspicuously blank as a mark of protest against the pre-censorship imposed on it.[56]

Gandhi, a competent and consummate editor himself, appreciated Horniman and his work. He knew the power of vocal newspapers. He had favoured keeping the editorial columns of the *Bombay Chronicle* blank as a protest until the censorship was removed. Two of the directors of the newspaper, namely T.N. Malvi and S.N. Dabholkar, objected to the editorial columns being kept blank, but the other directors said that they were not inclined to disregard Gandhi's advice in this particular case. As a consequence, Malvi resigned. Gandhi had advised that copies of the *Bombay Chronicle* be sent to the editors of various papers in England and other foreign countries, particularly America, in order to show them the ruthless control the government exercised upon the Indian press. He had hoped that a copy would fall into the hands of President Wilson.[57]

When the *Bombay Chronicle* was put under censorship after Horniman's deportation, *Young India* was published from Bombay as a weekly in English. The management of *Young India* decided to make it a biweekly, so that it might serve, partly, the purpose the *Bombay Chronicle* had served and entrusted Gandhi with the supervision of its contents. *Young India* later became a powerful medium to express Gandhi's ideas. On 4 May 1919, he wrote about it to his friend C.F. Andrews from Bombay and asked, 'Can you find time to write for it? You may write on swadeshi, Hindu–Muslim unity, satyagraha, Rowlatt legislation.'[58] Around this time, on suggestions from friends, he also thought of starting a Gujarati paper. The founders of *Navajivan Ane Satyagraha* offered to place their weekly publication under his supervision. He took over the burden of running *Navajivan*.[59]

In his letter to T.L. Maffey on 5 May, Gandhi mentioned the 'restraining and sobering influence of Satyagraha' at the time of Horniman's deportation and enclosed the form of the swadeshi vow for the viceroy.[60] Earlier, on 30 April, he had sent letters with the form of the swadeshi pledge to Sir Stanley Reed and N.P. Cowie, the private secretary to the governor of Bombay, with a request to sign it.[61]

On the morning on 27 April 1919, he addressed a meeting of the Jains at Lalbaug on the anniversary of Muni Maharaj Mohanlalji and asked the monks to preach swadeshi. In the afternoon, he had a discussion with the police commissioner for two-and-a-half hours, and in the evening, he presided over a meeting of the Marwaris called by the Satyagraha Sabha at the Nar Narayan temple.[62] On 1 May 1919, he attended a meeting at the Jain Sabha Hall in Pydhoni, but a heavy rush of people upset this meeting.[63]

Gandhi spent a number of days in June 1919 in Bombay, and that summer he issued a number of satyagraha bulletins. He was restless and trying to take decisions that were not easy. In a letter dated 6 June to H.S.L. Polak, written from Laburnum Road, Gandhi wrote about the starting of civil disobedience on 1 July that would be 'intensive and not extensive' this time. According to him, the situation called for withdrawal of the Rowlatt Act, assurance of satisfaction to the Muslims, and an impartial committee with the power to revise sentences to look into the Punjab tragedy. He also stated that the present officials could not give an impartial version of affairs to Montagu and cited 'horrible misrepresentations' about Horniman. In addition, he expressed concern about the increase in the rate of exchange, resulting in a huge loss to India.[64]

In a letter dated 12 June, written from Laburnum Road, Gamdevi, Bombay, and addressed to the secretaries of the Satyagraha Sabha, he expressed his desire to renew the civil disobedience and to decide the time to start the movement, its manner, and the participating satyagrahis.[65] A private meeting of the members of the Satyagraha Sabha's executive committee was held at the organization's office at 6.30 pm on 15 June with Gandhi as the chair. The executive committee decided to give Gandhi absolute power.[66] He informed the viceroy on 18 June, in his letter to the latter's private secretary S.R. Hignell, that unless circumstances altered, civil disobedience would be resumed in July.[67] He also gave detailed instructions to the satyagrahis.[68]

In response to a grave warning given to Gandhi by the governor of Bombay that the resumption of civil disobedience was likely to have consequences for public security, and to the urgent desire publicly expressed by Dewan Bahadur Govinda Raghava Iyer and Sir Narayan Chandavarkar, Gandhi decided not to resume civil disobedience for the time being and wrote a letter from Laburnum Road to the press on the suspension of the movement. He advised the satyagrahis to use this as an opportunity for further discipline

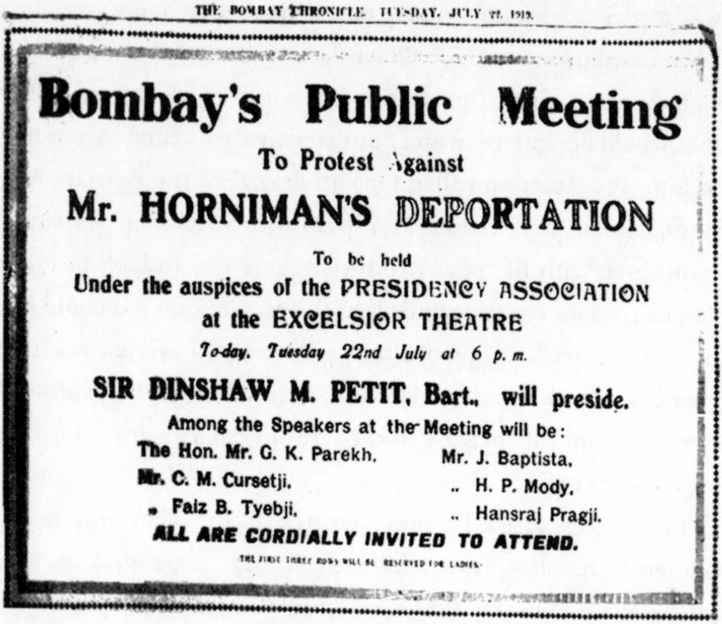

THE BOMBAY CHRONICLE TUESDAY, JULY 22, 1919.

# Bombay's Public Meeting

## To Protest Against

## Mr. HORNIMAN'S DEPORTATION

To be held

Under the auspices of the PRESIDENCY ASSOCIATION
at the EXCELSIOR THEATRE

*To-day,* *Tuesday* 22nd *July* at 6 p.m.

### SIR DINSHAW M. PETIT, Bart., will preside.

Among the Speakers at the Meeting will be:

The Hon. Mr. G. K. Parekh.          Mr. J. Baptista.

Mr. C. M. Cursetji.          „ H. P. Mody.

„ Faiz B. Tyebji.          „ Hansraj Pragji.

### ALL ARE CORDIALLY INVITED TO ATTEND.

THE FIRST THREE ROWS WILL BE RESERVED FOR LADIES.

**Figure 2.5**  An advertisement of the public meeting called on at Excelsior Theatre to protest against Horniman's deportation.
*Source*: The Asiatic Society of Mumbai.

and to promote Hindu–Muslim unity and propagate swadeshi.[69] The government had realized that any harsh step against Gandhi would precipitate the political situation, especially when the 1919 reforms were also being discussed.

G.S. Arundale wrote a letter to Gandhi on 26 July 1919, appealing him that since civil disobedience had been suspended, he should join the efforts to make the Montagu–Chelmsford constitutional reforms effective. Gandhi replied to it on 4 August 1919 from Laburnum Road. He maintained that he was incompetent for the task and that civil resistance had come to stay. It was an eternal doctrine of life. Further he wrote, 'My bent is not political but religious and I take part in politics because

I feel that there is no department of life which can be divorced from religion and because politics touch the vital being of India almost at every point.'[70]

On 19 August, a public meeting was held in the hall of Shri Cutchi Dassa Oswal Jain Pathshala, Bhat Bazar, Mandvi, under the joint auspices of the Jain Friendly Union and the Union Society, to protest against the deportation of Horniman, the passing of the Rowlatt Act, and the heavy sentences passed by the Punjab martial law commissioner. About 500 people were present. Gandhi presided over the meeting and the proceedings were conducted in Gujarati.[71]

Keen to have political discussions as required by the situation, Gandhi wrote a letter from his residence at Laburnum Road to the private secretary to the governor Sir George Lloyd on 19 August 1919, seeking an appointment with the latter for a discussion on swadeshi.[72]

## The Issue of Khilafat

During this time the issue of Khilafat acquired importance in the political scene of India. Turkey sided with Germany in the First World War and fought against Britain. The Muslims in India were dismayed to find that at the end of the First World War, the generous assurances given by the British government to Turkey were not honoured; the Khalifa, who was regarded as the religious head, was not given a fair treatment; the Turkish Empire was dismembered; and the holy places were not safeguarded. Soon mobilization started in India among the dismayed Muslim individuals and organizations on the issue of Khilafat.

On 19 March 1919, the Bombay Khilafat Committee was formed in a public meeting in the city with Mian Mohammed Haji Jan Mohammed Chhotani, a nationalist Muslim leader of

Bombay, elected as its president.[73] Six months later, the All India Muslim Conference convened at Lucknow by the Muslim League Council witnessed a clash between the moderates and extremist Pan-Islamists, the former led by the raja of Mahmudabad who opposed the pitting of the Muslim community against the government, but the extremists led by Maulana Abdul Bari won the day. The conference formulated the demands of the Indian Khilafatists and decided to observe 17 October as the 'All India Khilafat Day'. It also constituted an All India Khilafat Committee[74] headquartered in Bombay.

Gandhi viewed the Khilafat issue as one that could draw the Muslims in the nationalist movement and forge Hindu–Muslim unity. He had achieved success uniting Hindus and Muslims in South Africa against racialism and was now very hopeful to achieve Hindu–Muslim unity in India on this issue. He was concerned about the growing frustration among the Muslims over a religious issue and did not want it to erupt as a violent protest. Gandhi and some leaders among both the communities thought that the Hindus and Muslims together could exercise some pressure on the British government. According to him, his sense of moral responsibilities made him take up the Khilafat question.[75] The Ali brothers—Maulana Mohammed Ali and Maulana Shaukat Ali—Hakim Ajmal Khan, Dr Ansari, Maulana Abdul Bari, Maulana Azad, and Hasrat Mohani were among the main leaders of the Khilafat Movement. The Khilafat sentiment cut across the sectarian barriers of Muslims.

A special meeting of Anjuman Ziaul Islam under the presidentship of M.T. Kadarbhai, barrister-at-law, was convened at 9 pm on 9 May 1919 to consider the question of Khilafat, where a large number of Muslims were present. Gandhi, Jamnadas Dwarkadas, and Shankarlal Banker were among those who were specially invited. Gandhi delivered his speech in Gujarati and talked about his friendship with the Ali brothers, Dr Ansari, Maulana Abdul Bari, and the Muslims in South Africa. He said that he was devoting his life to two issues—the permanent unity between Hindus and Muslims and the satyagraha; satyagraha is an all-embracing movement and 'if we accept the law of Satyagraha, unity will come of itself'.[76] He expressed his sensitivity to the religious feelings of Muslims and supported their demand against any dismemberment of Turkey.[77]

Later in the year, on 18 September 1919, Gandhi spoke on the issue of Khilafat at a meeting of Muslims organized at Mastan Shah Tank in Nagpada. The meeting, presided over by Mian Mohammed Haji Jan Mohammed Chhotani, continued until 1.30 am.[78] The proceedings consisted of a procession and a meeting. The mass meeting at 8.30 pm was attended by around 10,000 people. Gandhi had come from Ahmedabad specially to attend this meeting.[79] He said that the Khilafat was 'a question among questions' and 'a great Empire question'. He also said that 'to die for a cause is the law of a man, to kill is that of the beast'.[80]

For the observance of 17 October as the 'Khilafat Day', Gandhi appealed the non-Muslims to join the Muslims in fasting, prayer, and hartal. In Bombay city, the hartal was partial, although the municipal markets, the share market, the cotton market, and two mills remained closed; practically no meat was available; and most victorias (horse carriages) stopped plying for hire. However, in the neighbourhoods such as the Jhaveri Bazar, where Gandhi's firm supporters lived, business went on as usual and there was nothing like the spirit that had been behind the hartals of April 1919.[81]

At the end of the war when the government started organizing peace celebrations, there was opposition to it from some quarters. An anti-peace celebration publicity board was established at Delhi to dissuade people from joining such celebrations. This board worked in conjunction with the members of the Khilafat Committee in Bombay in producing material for propaganda. On 5 December 1919, a poster published by the Delhi board was noticed in Bombay. Under the heading 'The Order of Mahatma Gandhi; the *fatwa* of Abdul Bari', it exhorted the Muslims and Hindus to refrain from joining the peace celebrations and to remember the martyrs of Punjab, Delhi, and Ahmedabad. There were such other leaflets also that were printed and distributed. Five thousand copies of such fatwas were printed in Bombay by Ahmed Siddick Khatri in addition to a thousand posters warning the Muslims not to take part in the peace celebrations. Around 6 December, Dhirajlal Ghelabhai Banker and K.M. Munshi gave orders at the Karnatak Press for 10,000 copies of a leaflet in Marathi and 5,000 copies of a leaflet in Gujarati. Moreover, Shankarlal Ghelabhai Banker also gave orders at the Gnana Sagar Litho Press for 250 wall posters in Marathi and 750 copies of the same in Gujarati. The members present at a meeting of the Muslims expressed indignation at the huge expense of nearly Rs 50,000 by the Municipal Corporation of Bombay for the peace celebrations.[82]

The protest over the Khilafat issue was to become more vociferous and strident in the following years.

## The Cause of Swadeshi

With his attention on political issues, Gandhi was also concerned about the welfare of the people and advocated the programme of swadeshi. In his leaflet on the swadeshi vow dated 16 June 1919, he elaborated his ideas on the mill-made and home-made cloth. In his opinion, a great objective of the propagation of swadeshi was to prevent the country's wealth from going out.[83] On 17 June, at a meeting chaired by him near the Carnac Bunder, he was more emphatic: 'So long as we do not bring ourselves to observe scrupulously the rule of *Swadeshi*, we shall not succeed in attaining Swaraj.'[84] In his speech on opening Shuddha Swadeshi Vastra Bhandar at the Morarji Goculdas Market on 18 June, he said that swadeshi was as much a necessity of daily life as air, water, and food, and only the direction of propagating swadeshi could rid people of their poverty.[85]

In his letter to the private secretary of the governor on 25 August written from Laburnum Road, he elaborated his idea and arguments on swadeshi to the governor and mentioned that 'although fraught with political consequences of a lofty, moral type in order that all may take part in it, the *swadeshi* propaganda is restricted to the religious and economic aspects only'.[86] He emphasized that at the moment he was concentrating on hand-spinning and hand-weaving. He even wrote,

If it is not a presumption, I would respectfully ask H.E. on my behalf to secure Lady George Lloyd's patronage for my spinning classes. Several titled ladies are, with a view to encouraging the industry among the poor classes, taking spinning lessons. I would consider it an honour to be allowed to present a spinning-wheel to Her Excellency and to send her a lady teacher or to give her the lessons myself.[87]

Gandhi had inspired many to spin and promote spinning. Revashankar Jagjivan announced in the *Navajivan* issue of 5 October 1919 that a prize money of Rs 5,000 would be offered to anyone inventing a portable spinning wheel of indigenous components, as far as possible, which could take on ten spindles at a time.[88] The merchants were supporters of Gandhi's swadeshi movement. Narandas Purshotam and Vithaldas Jerajani, both cloth merchants, were instrumental in starting a swadeshi concern in 1919, and when the National Swadeshi Stores Co. Ltd. was founded in 1920, a Jhaveri and other commodity dealers were behind it. The mill industry ridiculed the swadeshi movement through its journal—the *Indian Textile Journal*.[89]

Women were Gandhi's trusted workers and propagators of the message of swadeshi. Gandhi presided over a women's meeting on 13 June at the Jain Mangrol Sabha Hall and exhorted them to use swadeshi cloth and take the swadeshi vow regardless of the dictates of fashion. About 200 Gujarati women attended this meeting.[90] Gandhi was impressed with women's commitment and ability to make their work important and interesting. In his letter to Manubhai Nandshankar Mehta, the dewan of Baroda, written from Laburnum Road on 4 August 1919, he praised Gangabehn's work for spinning and weaving in Vijapur and the movement for swadeshi.[91] Women would not forget his birthday; the Bhagini Samaj organized a special function on 2 October at the Vanita Vishram Hall to celebrate the golden anniversary of his birth. He was presented with Rs 21,000. The day was filled up with work. He sent a telegram to Swami Shraddhanand and Andrews to collect evidence for the Hunter Commission, and another to the viceroy to decide on the early removal of the ban on his entry into Punjab. He also addressed the Muslim Students' Union at Chowpatty.[92] He said that he was grateful to the women for what they had done for him on his birthday, and that he would utilize the sum for the amelioration of the condition of Indian womanhood after careful consideration and would ask them for suggestions.[93] On 7 September 1929, he handed over the purse to the women's organization for constructing their building in Vile Parle.[94]

## Other Meetings

Gandhi was quick to defend the rights of journalists and citizens. When Babu Kalinath Roy, the editor of the now-defunct *Tribune*, was charged with sedition and imprisoned because of his writings, Gandhi protested against it.[95]

On 11 June 1919, a memorial was presented to the viceroy on behalf of the citizens of Bombay pleading him to release Babu Kalinath Roy. It was signed by Gandhi and others including Sir Narayan G. Chandavarkar, Sir Dinshaw Wacha, G.K. Parekh, and K. Natarajan. Another memorial on the same lines, presumably drafted by Gandhi, was sent to Chelmsford by the representatives of the journalists of the Bombay Presidency.[96] On 12 June 1919, he wrote from Mani Bhavan to S.T. Sheppard, the editor of the *Times of India*, Bombay, 'I enclose herewith a portion of *Young India* containing a reference to Babu Kalinath Roy's case. I hope you will find time to peruse the case and if you agree with my view that a gross injustice has been done to Mr. Roy, I trust you will join the movement for his release.'[97]

A public meeting was held in the evening on Saturday, 31 May 1919, at Shantaram Chawl to express appreciation of services rendered by Tilak to India and to appeal to people to contribute to the Tilak Purse Fund to defray the expenses incurred by him in his case against Sir Valentine Chirol taken in public interest. Gandhi admired Tilak and said that the latter 'has been in his life acting to the very letter up to what he has believed to be the essential teaching of the Gita. He devotes himself entirely to what he believes to be his karma, and leaves the result thereof to God. Who could withhold admiration from someone so great?'[98] Gandhi, as proposed by Dr Motiram Balkrishna Velkar, chaired the meeting. Prominent people including Yeshwantrao Vishnu Nene, Narandas Purushotamdas, Shivram Mahadev Paranjape, Raghunath Pandurang Karandikar, Vithaldas Vasanji Jairajani, Dr Moreshwar Gopal Deshmukh, and Dr Dinkar Dhondev Sathaye attended the meeting. Gandhi made a speech in Gujarati and had it read out in Marathi. Sarojini Naidu spoke in Urdu and read in English the resolution appreciating Tilak who had spent his entire life with selfless devotion for the betterment of his countrymen. It was carried unanimously.[99]

In the later part of the year, a meeting was organized at Excelsior Theatre, Bombay, to celebrate the 73rd birthday of Annie Besant on 1 October 1919. Gandhi presided over this meeting and paid her a rich tribute for toiling for the public cause, her ability to stand by her convictions, her working with zeal and earnestness, and the introduction of Home Rule by her in India.[100]

Amidst all the political work, he managed to find time to meet his well-wishers. On 5 April, he went to Narottam Morarji's house to compliment him, as the first Indian steamer *Loyalty* made by his company was sailing to Europe, and also to wish Morarji's son Shantikumar bon voyage. The voyage of the first Indian steamer must have been important to him. He also went to see the ailing Anandshankar Dhruv on 8 April.[101] He made it a point to attend the gathering for Hindi, the language he liked. On 19 April, at the Hindi Sahitya Sammelan he proposed the name of Pandit Madan Mohan Malaviya as its president, and the next day, he appealed Bombay to contribute money for its work of propagating Hindi.[102] On 21 April, he also attended a meeting at China Baug to meet John Scurr, a pacifist.[103]

———

The restrictions on Gandhi's entry into Punjab were removed on 15 October 1919. The Montagu–Chelmsford Reforms were discussed in the Congress session held at Amritsar from 27 December 1919 to 1 January 1920. Gandhi was not ready to call the reforms disappointing. In his opinion, the hand of friendship extended by Montagu should not be rejected.

Gandhi had made his presence felt in Bombay in 1919 and garnered many supporters. According to A.D.D. Gordon, there was a significant correlation between the leaders of various merchant groups and associations and the organizers of nationalist associations such as the All India Home Rule leagues and the Satyagraha Sabha. For instance, Gulabchand Devchand, H.V. Desai, and V.P. Shah, all nationalist organizers, were also prominent in the Bombay Shroffs' Association. Devchand was a close associate of Gandhi, and V.P. Shah was to be later known as the Bombay Congress 'Dictator'. Velji Lakhamsi Napoo, a close associate of V.J. Patel, and Lalji Vassanji were both prominent in the Grain Merchants Association, and Vithaldas and Mavji Govindji were well-known members of the Bombay Native Piece Goods Merchants' Association. The founder of the latter organization, Manmohandas Ramji, when still an active nationalist, was a leader in the Home Rule League, and another prominent piece-goods dealer Naranji Dayal was also an important activist. Jamnadas Dwarkadas was an importer of mill dyes. Jivraj G. Nensey, an active Home Ruler and Congressman, was also an important share broker. W.T. Halai had influence on both share and cotton brokers. Halai, like Nensey and the Govindjis, was a member of the original band of Home Rule League activists—Jamnadas, Banker, Tairsee, and Umar Sobani. Seth Narandas Purshotam, an important share and cotton broker, was another associate of these men in their early activities.[104]

The Rowlatt Satyagraha also attracted some criticism. According to Judith Brown, the power behind Gandhi's agitation was neither antagonism to the Rowlatt legislation nor loyalty to a new leader, but local discontent that found a focus and a means of expression in Gandhi's call for hartal.[105] Further, '[e]ven Gandhi needed a powerful organization of his own, and failing that a strong network of sub-contractors who would organize and control for him in places where his personal writ did not run: when he had neither he was as powerless as they had been.'[106] Disagreeing with this view, B.R. Nanda convincingly argues that even before people from Bombay went to Ahmedabad in February 1919 to seek Gandhi's guidance, the latter was thinking of launching civil disobedience if the Rowlatt bills were brought on the statute book. In fact, '[h]e was the script-writer, the producer, the director and the main actor of the drama of satyagraha'.[107]

Initially, the British government as well as the Indian intelligentsia had doubts about the efficacy of satyagraha against the Rowlatt Act, and it also could not achieve the immediate repeal of the act. However, what Gandhi achieved was remarkable. His satyagraha against the Rowlatt Act, his stand on the atrocities in Punjab, and his involvement in the Khilafat Movement strengthened his position in politics. His aura transcended local territories and spread throughout the country. As R. Kumar pointed out:

Given the structure of society and the web of social loyalties in India, the Rowlatt *Satyagraha*—a gesture of moral protest against a repressive law—was ideally suited to unleash a mass political movement in the country. By drawing different castes, communities, and religious groups into the penumbra of romantic politics, Gandhi sought to transform social groups which were loosely held together into a cohesive, articulate and creative political society.'[108]

The Rowlatt Satyagraha had propelled Gandhi into the national political scene. He was now entrusted with the role of guiding the nation. His unconventional approach to politics, innovative strategies, ability to bring together people of different ideological streams, and unusual capacity to mobilize people at all levels had put him in the position of an undisputed leader of India. Tagore, in his letter dated 12 April 1919, referred to him as

'Mahatmaji'—an endearing title that was already engraved in the hearts of people.[109]

## Notes and References

1. James Masselos, 'Some Aspects of Bombay City Politics in 1919', in R. Kumar (ed.), *Essays on Gandhian Politics: The Rowlatt Satyagraha of 1919* (Oxford: Clarendon Press, 1971), pp. 145–88.

2. Gandhi's letter to H.S.L. Polak, dated 14 October 1909 cited in Anthony J. Parel, *Hind Swaraj and Other Writings* (Cambridge: Cambridge University Press, 1997), p. 130.

3. *CWMG*, Vol. 15 (Delhi: Publications Division, Ministry of Information and Broadcasting, Government of India, 1965), p. 511. *Gandhijini Dinwari* mentions the date of Gandhi's surgery of piles as on 21 January 1919. See Dalal, *Gandhijini Dinwari*, p. 68.

4. Sandip Hazareesingh, *The Colonial City and the Challenge of Modernity: Urban Hegemonies and Civic Contestations in Bombay (1900–1925)* (Hyderabad: Orient Longman, 2007), p. 129.

5. *New India* dated 3 March 1919 cited in *CWMG*, Vol. 15, pp. 101–3.

6. B.R. Nanda, *Gandhi: Pan-Islamism, Imperialism and Nationalism in India* (Bombay: Oxford University Press, 1989), pp. 178–9.

7. H.F. Owen, 'Organizing for the Rowlatt Satyagraha of 1919', in *Essays on Gandhian Politics*, pp. 64–92.

8. 'Bombay Secret Abstract', 1919, p. 155, para 378 (g and l) cited in Phatak, *Source Material for a History of the Freedom Movement in India*, Vol. III, Part I, p. 104.

9. 'Bombay Secret Abstract', 1919, p. 203, 4, 5, para 500 (b and c) cited in Phatak, *Source Material for a History of the Freedom Movement in India*, Vol. III, Part I, pp. 108–9.

10. *Young India* dated 12 March 1919 and the *Bombay Chronicle* dated 28 March 1919 cited in *CWMG*, Vol. 15, pp. 132–3.

11. *The Bombay Chronicle* dated 1 March 1919 cited in *CWMG*, Vol. 15, pp. 120–2.

12. *The Bombay Chronicle* dated 1 March 1919 cited in *CWMG*, Vol. 15, pp. 120–2.

13. *The Bombay Chronicle* dated 12 March 1919 and *Young India* dated 12 March 1919 cited in *CWMG*, Vol. 15, pp. 118–20.

14. Dwarkadas, *India's Fight for Freedom*, pp. 98–9.

15. According to C.B. Dalal, Mrs Besant called in on 14 January. See Dalal, *Gandhi*, p. 21. The account of Kanji Dwarkadas, however, mentions this meeting in February.

16. 'Bombay Secret Abstract', 1919, pp. 187–8, para 476 (a and c) cited in Phatak, *Source Material for a History of the Freedom Movement in India*, Vol. III, Part I, p. 106.

17. *Mahatma Gandhi: His Life, Writings & Speeches* cited in *CWMG*, Vol. 15, pp. 135–6.

18. *The Bombay Chronicle* dated 4 April 1919 cited in *CWMG*, Vol. 15, pp. 174–6.

19. *CWMG*, Vol. 15, pp. 171–2.

20. Dalal, *Gandhijini Dinwari*, p. 72, footnote 1.

21. *The Bombay Chronicle* dated 5 April 1919 cited in *CWMG*, Vol. 15, pp. 177–8.

22. *The Bombay Chronicle* dated 7 April 1919 cited in *CWMG*, Vol. 15, pp. 183–8.

23. *The Bombay Chronicle* dated 7 April 1919 cited in *CWMG*, Vol. 15, pp. 183–8.

24. Hazareesingh, *The Colonial City*, p. 135.

25. *The Bombay Chronicle* dated 7 April 1919 cited in *CWMG*, Vol. 15, pp. 188–9.

26. *The Bombay Chronicle* dated 7 April 1919 cited in *CWMG*, Vol. 15, p. 189.

27. 'Bombay Secret Abstract', 1919, pp. 568–70, para 883 (j) cited in Phatak, *Source Material for a History of the Freedom Movement in India*, Vol. III, Part I, pp. 160–1.

28. *The Bombay Chronicle* dated 8 April 1919 cited in *CWMG*, Vol. 15, pp. 192–4.

29. *The Times of India*, 9 April 1919.

30. Hazareesingh, *The Colonial City*, p. 134.

31. Gandhi, *An Autobiography*, pp. 565–6.

32. Hazareesingh, *The Colonial City*, pp. 131–3.

33. *The Bombay Chronicle* dated 9 April 1919 cited in *CWMG*, Vol. 15, pp. 190–1; Gopalaswami, *Gandhi and Bombay*, p. 525.

34. Gandhi, *An Autobiography*, pp. 568–72.

35. *The Bombay Chronicle* dated 20 June 1919 quoted in A.D.D. Gordon, *Businessmen and Politics: Rising Nationalism and a Modernising Economy in Bombay, 1918–1933* (New Delhi: Manohar Publications, 1978), p. 167.

36. *The Bombay Chronicle* dated 15 April 1919 cited in *CWMG*, Vol. 15, pp. 214–15.

37. Gandhi, *An Autobiography*, pp. 575–7.

38. Dalal, *Gandhi*, p. 23.

39. *CWMG*, Vol. 15, p. 246.

40. *Gujarati* dated 4 May 1919 cited in *CWMG*, Vol. 15, p. 250.

41. 'Bombay Secret Abstract', p. 336, para 598 cited in Phatak, *Source Material for a History of the Freedom Movement in India*, Vol. III, Part I, p. 113.

42. Phatak, *Source Material for a History of the Freedom Movement in India*, Vol. III, Part I, p. 114.

43. *CWMG*, Vol. 15, pp. 273–4.

44. 'Satyagraha Leaflet No. 16' dated 6 May 1919 cited in *CWMG*, Vol. 15, p. 279.

45. 'Satyagraha Leaflet No. 17' dated 7 May 1919 cited in *CWMG*, Vol. 15, p. 286.

46. *CWMG*, Vol. 15, p. 280.

47. *Gujarati* dated 11 May 1919 cited in *CWMG*, Vol. 15, pp. 282–5.

48. Dalal, *Gandhi*, p. 23.

49. Hazareesingh, *The Colonial City*, p. 145.

50. 'Satyagraha Leaflet No. 21' dated 12 May 1919 cited in *CWMG*, Vol. 15, p. 303.

51. 'Bombay Secret Abstract', pp. 505–7, para 791 cited in Phatak, *Source Material for a History of the Freedom Movement in India*, Vol. III, Part I, p. 137.

52. *The Times of India*, 26 May 1919.

53. *Young India*, 10 May 1919.

54. *CWMG*, Vol. 15, pp. 259–60.

55. *CWMG*, Vol. 15, pp. 260–1.

56. Hazareesingh, *The Colonial City*, p. 146.

57. 'Bombay Secret Abstract', p. 527, para 827 cited in Phatak, *Source Material for a History of the Freedom Movement in India*, Vol. III, Part I, pp. 142–3.

58. *CWMG*, Vol. 15, pp. 271–2. *Young India* was a weekly founded by Jamnadas Dwarkadas in Bombay. Later on it passed on to a syndicate managed by Shankarlal Banker and Umar Sobani. When Horniman of the *Bombay Chronicle* was deported on 26 April 1919, *Young India* was placed in Gandhi's hands. It was made a biweekly first. Until October, it was published from Bombay. See Dalal, *Gandhi*, p. 27, footnote 2.

59. *Navjivan ane Satya* (Gujarati) dated July 1919 cited in *CWMG*, Vol. 15, pp. 419–21.

60. *CWMG*, Vol. 15, pp. 274–5.

61. *CWMG*, Vol. 15, pp. 261–2.

62. Dalal, *Gandhijini Dinwari*, p. 76.

63 Dalal, *Gandhi*, p. 23.

64. *CWMG*, Vol. 15, pp. 344–5.

65. *CWMG*, Vol. 15, pp. 364–5.

66. 'Bombay Secret Abstract', pp. 543–4, para 853(a) cited in Phatak, *Source Material for a History of the Freedom Movement in India*, Vol. III, Part I, pp. 146–7.

67. *CWMG*, Vol. 15, pp. 377–8.

68. *CWMG*, Vol. 15, pp. 412–6.

69. *Young India* dated 23 July 1919 cited in *CWMG*, Vol. 15, pp. 468–71.

70. *Young India* dated 6 August 1919 cited in *CWMG*, Vol. 16 (Delhi: Publications Division, Ministry of Information and Broadcasting, Government of India), pp. 5–7.

71. 'Bombay Secret Abstract', p. 769, para 1170 cited in Phatak, *Source Material for a History of the Freedom Movement in India*, Vol. III, Part I, pp. 198–9.

72. *CWMG*, Vol. 16, p. 44.

73. 'Fortnightly Report from Bombay', 1 October 1919, Home Political, Deposit, November 1919, no. 15 cited in K.K. Chaudhari, *Maharashtra State Gazetteers: History of Bombay—Modern Period* (Bombay: Gazetteers Department, Government of Maharashtra, 1987), p. 128.

74. Nanda, *Gandhi*, pp. 89–90.

75. *Young India* dated 28 April 1920 cited in *CWMG*, Vol. 17 (Delhi: Publications Division, Ministry of Information and Broadcasting, Government of India, 1965), pp. 349–51.

76. *Young India* dated 14 May 1919 cited in *CWMG*, Vol. 15, pp. 295–9.

77. *Young India* dated 14 May 1919 cited in *CWMG*, Vol. 15, pp. 295–9. The meeting was held at Jamal Hall, Tardeo. See Dalal, *Gandhi*, p. 23.

78. Dalal, *Gandhi*, p. 26.

79. 'Bombay Secret Abstract', 1919, pp. 823–5, para 1260 cited in Phatak, *Source Material for a History of the Freedom Movement in India*, Vol. III, Part I, p. 200.

80. *Young India* dated 20 September 1919 cited in *CWMG*, Vol. 16, pp. 151–2.

81. Judith M. Brown, *Gandhi's Rise to Power: Indian Politics, 1915–1922* (London: Cambridge University Press, 1972), p. 199.

82. K.K. Chaudhari (ed.), *Source Material for a History of the Freedom Movement in India: Khilafat Movement (1920–1921)*, Vol. X, e-Book edition (Bombay: Gazetteers Department, Government of Maharashtra, 2007), pp. 6–7.

83. *Young India* dated 18 June 1919 cited in *CWMG*, Vol. 15, pp. 372–4.

84. *Gujarati* dated 22 June 1919 cited in *CWMG*, Vol. 15, pp. 375–7.

85. *Young India* dated 21 June 1919 cited in *CWMG*, Vol. 15, pp. 378–81.

86. *CWMG*, Vol. 16, pp. 60–2.

87. *CWMG*, Vol. 16, pp. 60–2.

88. *CWMG*, Vol. 16, p. 217.

89. Gordon, *Businessmen and Politics*, p. 168.

90. 'Bombay Secret Abstract', 1919, p. 534, para 840 cited in Phatak, *Source Material for a History of the Freedom Movement in India*, Vol. III, Part I, p. 144.

91. *CWMG*, Vol. 16, pp. 8–9.

92. Dalal, *Gandhi*, p. 27.

93. *The Indian Review* dated October 1919 cited in *CWMG*, Vol. 16, p. 202.

94. Dalal, *Gandhi*, p. 27.

95. *Young India* dated 11 June 1919 cited in *CWMG*, Vol. 15, pp. 356–9.

96. 'Memorial to Viceroy', published in *Young India* dated 25 June 1919, and 'Memorial to Chelmsford' dated 11 June 1919 cited in *CWMG*, Vol. 15, pp. 360–1.

97. *CWMG*, Vol. 15, p. 365.

98. *Young India* dated 7 June 1919 cited in *CWMG*, Vol. 15, pp. 336–7.

99. 'Bombay Secret Abstract', pp. 536–9, para 849 cited in Phatak, *Source Material for a History of the Freedom Movement in India*, Vol. III, Part I, pp. 144–5.

100. *The Bombay Chronicle* dated 2 October 1919 cited in *CWMG*, Vol. 16, pp. 200–1.

101. Dalal, *Gandhijini Dinwari*, p. 73.

102. *CWMG*, Vol. 15, p. 245.

103. Dalal, *Gandhi*, p. 23.

104. Gordon, *Businessmen and Politics*, pp. 168–9.

105. Brown, *Gandhi's Rise to Power*, p. 185.

106. Brown, *Gandhi's Rise to Power*, p. 357.

107. Nanda, *Gandhi*, p. 187.

108. Kumar (ed.), *Essays on Gandhian Politics*, pp. 15–16.

109. R.K. Prabhu and Ravindra Kelekar (eds), *Truth Called Them Differently: Tagore–Gandhi Controversy* (Ahmedabad: Navajivan Publishing House, 1961), p. 14.

# 3

# CALL FOR NON-COOPERATION: 1920

GANDHI'S CALL FOR NON-COOPERATION BECAME THE CLARION CALL.
All protests against the British rule and the diverse unfulfilled
demands merged into this tidal wave that engulfed the country.
Indifference of the rulers, economic distress, and the shortage of
food and essential commodities had stirred discontent among
the people in the first two decades of the twentieth century. The
Congress, disillusioned with the apathetic attitude of the British
government that reflected in the report of the Hunter Committee
(the government or official committee looking into the
Jallianwala Bagh tragedy), was veering towards non-cooperation.
When Gandhi moved a resolution for non-cooperation at the
Congress session in Calcutta in September 1920, it was passed

by the majority despite opposition from some stalwarts such as C.R. Das. The non-cooperation programme was finally ratified at Nagpur in December 1920; the critics were won over, and Gandhi emerged as the undisputed leader. The non-cooperation programme included non-violent mass action such as the boycott of government-affiliated schools, colleges, courts, and foreign cloth; surrender of honours and titles; resignation from government service and positions; and non-payment of taxes. As the movement gathered momentum, programmes for constructive work were also developed, such as the promotion of swadeshi, establishment of national educational institutions, spinning and khadi work, eradication of untouchability, and fostering of Hindu–Muslim unity. People responded spontaneously and enthusiastically to the new programmes of the Congress and to Gandhi's charismatic leadership.

Despite his tours in various parts of the country in 1920, Gandhi remained closely connected with Bombay. The city was an important site for his Non-Cooperation Movement against the British rule. It was also at the forefront in supporting his work for the Khilafat and swadeshi movements.

The circumstances in the first quarter of 1920 were such that Gandhi had to come to the Bombay High Court. Gandhi was served with a notice of contempt of court. The matter was heard by justices Marten, Hayward, and Kajiji on 3 March. As the editor and publisher of *Young India*, Gandhi and Mahadev Desai were charged for publishing with their comments, in the issue dated 6 August 1919 of their paper, a letter addressed by Kennedy, the district judge of Ahmedabad, to the registrar of the high court complaining about the conduct of certain satyagrahi lawyers of Ahmedabad. These lawyers had signed the satyagraha pledge, also signed by Gandhi and others on 24 February 1919. Gandhi and Desai were asked to apologize, which they refused.

Gandhi argued that as a journalist he was entitled to do what he had done. Advocate General Sir Thomas Strangman, with Messrs Bahadurji and Pocock, appeared for the applicant; Gandhi and Desai appeared in person. The judgment delivered on 12 March was summed up by Justice Marten: 'The Court finds the charges proved. It severely reprimands the respondents and cautions them both as to future conduct.'[1]

## The Khilafat

The Khilafat issue had touched the sensitive chord of the Muslim community. Soon it became a powerful agitation, and Muslim organizations such as the All India Khilafat Conference and the Jamait-al-Ulema-e-Hind became prominent. Gandhi saw a way for the Hindu–Muslim unity in the Khilafat issue.

The tempo for the Khilafat Movement was rising in Bombay as in other places. When Shaukat Ali, Mohammed Ali, and Maulana Abdul Bari reached Mumbai's Victoria Terminus station on 29 January 1920, a huge crowd of thousands, mostly Muslims, was waiting to receive them. There was also a deputation from the Indian Home Rule League. In view of the rush at the Victoria Terminus station, the railway administration transferred them and their group at Kalyan into a special train, the engine of which flew Turkish flags. The procession to the Muzaffarabad Hall took more than three hours to traverse the distance of two miles. The crowds became enormous in the Muslim neighbourhood of Abdul Rehman Street and Pydhonie. A public meeting of around 35,000 people was held in the Chota Kabrastan on Grant Road where the three guests were presented addresses by the city's Muslims. The principal points made by these three were: the need for money, requirement of Rs 3 million for the deputation to England, the abandonment of cow sacrifice at Bakri-Id by Muslims, and the conversion of the Khilafat agitation into an all-India question. The next day, the Ali brothers had a consultation with Tilak possibly regarding the proposed Khilafat deputation to England. There was also a meeting at the Shantaram Chawl with Tilak as the chair and an audience of around 10,000 people who were mostly Hindus. It was organized by the Indian and All India Home Rule leagues, in conjunction with the Bombay National Union. The main point of the speeches was that the Khilafat had ceased to be a Muslim question alone; it was a matter of grave concern for India.[2]

A large meeting was organized on 31 January under the auspices of the Khilafat Committee to wish success to the deputation proceeding to Europe. About 10,000 people attended it, mainly Muslims. Although other sects were well represented, no notable Khojas were present. On the following day, 1 February, the first batch of the Khilafat deputation with Mohammed Ali, Sayed Hussain, and others left for England. The Khilafat had become 'the talk of the town'. The situation, however, had some inherent tensions. There were important factors such as the absence of Khojas from almost all these functions, general abstention of Hindus and Muslims from participation in each other's meetings, local opposition to any restriction on cow killing, and the insignificant headway made for the deputation fund. This showed that, in spite of much talk, Hindu–Muslim unity was still more formal than intimate.[3]

Soon thereafter, a meeting of the standing committee of the Central Khilafat Committee of India, Bombay, was held on 7 February with Chhotani as the chair. Shaukat Ali was elected as the secretary of the Central Khilafat Committee at this meeting. There were heated discussions and expressions of the religious sentiments.[4] There was, however, not much enthusiasm in all sections of society. The third session of the All India Khilafat Conference was held in Bombay on 15, 16, and 17 February 1920 with G.M. Bhurgri as its president. It was reported that the majority of delegates were Sunnis, with hardly five or ten Shias and three Hindus. Ajmal Khan, Dr Ansari, Hasan Imam, Gandhi, Tilak, Besant, and Madan Mohan Malaviya were some conspicuous absentees.[5]

Gandhi had linked the Khilafat issue to the programme of non-violent non-cooperation to protest against the government policy and had continued discussions with the Khilafat Committee. A huge meeting of about 5,000 Bombay Muslims with a few Hindus was called on 3 March to consider the Khilafat situation. It was attended by a strong contingent of Khojas, who were attracted by the presence of the Aga Khan and other Muslim leaders. Gandhi, in his address, exhorted his audience to direct their action to the Khilafat alone. Baptista and many Bombay Tilakites, as also Jinnah, Umar Sobani, M.K. Azad, Sheriff Devji Kanji, and a few other notable Muslims, however, were conspicuous by their absence.[6] The meeting was presided over by Chhotani.[7] On 7 March, Gandhi wrote a letter to the press about the Khilafat. In his opinion, non-cooperation became a duty when cooperation meant degradation or humiliation or an injury to one's cherished religious sentiment.[8]

When the Central Khilafat Committee met in Bombay from 11 to 14 March to discuss the future policy, Gandhi, apprehensive about the outbreak of violence, strongly suggested that the ground should be prepared thoroughly before non-cooperation was attempted.[9] Insisting on the importance of the Khilafat issue and the need to follow non-violence, he suggested that 19 March should be observed as the Khilafat Day, a day of national mourning betokened by fasting and hartal, and if the demands were not met, people should resort to non-cooperation.[10] The Central Khilafat Committee and Gandhi actively participated in the preparations for the hartal of 19 March in the city; efforts such as distribution of handbills in Gujarati and Urdu were made to make people aware of the issue.

The hartal on 19 March passed without any ugly incident. It was complete in the purely Muslim locality between Crawford Market and the Bhendi Bazaar, and fairly general throughout the centre of the Island. The advertised mass meeting commenced at about 10 pm. It was attended by 7,000 or 8,000 Muslims; about 200 or 300 Hindus; and a handful of Parsis, Khojas, Moghuls, and Arabs. Chhotani, who chaired the meeting, was supported by Shaukat Ali, Khatri, Kidwai, Zafar Ali Khan, Rafiuddin Ahmed, Gandhi, S.R. Bomonji, Neki Ram Sharma, S.G. Banker, and other local stalwarts.[11] At the meeting Gandhi expressed satisfaction that the hartal was spontaneous and voluntary; he congratulated the organizers and volunteers on the splendid success of the peaceful demonstration.[12] However, overall, a smaller number of citizens observed the second Khilafat Day as compared to the first, in spite of increased pressure from the satyagraha volunteers.[13]

Under the auspices of the Central Khilafat Committee and in connection with the National Week, a very well-attended public meeting of Muslims and Hindus was held on 9 April at about 10 pm in the open ground at French Bridge. Chhotani presided over the meeting.[14] Gandhi was impressed by Ali brothers' religiosity and ability to reach the Muslim masses. He remained involved with the meetings and discussions related to the Khilafat issue. He was present in the meeting of the Khilafat Committee on 12 April, when there was a discussion about sending a deputation with Gandhi and Azad to England, and also in the meeting on 21 April which was held to decide whether to send a delegation to England.[15] On 13 April, he wired to the private secretary to the viceroy seeking the latter's permission to go to England to acquaint ministers and the British public with the Khilafat issue.[16]

The All-India (Central) Khilafat Committee met in Bombay on 12 May 1920 to consider the programme of non-cooperation. All the groups in the three-way tug of war were present: Gandhi, the moderate merchants, and Shaukat Ali's enthusiasts. The moderates made a desperate effort to have the issue of tendering resignations from the police and military struck from the programme, but were defeated. Thus, they withdrew, resigning from their posts in the committee. Gandhi realized that the cooperation of Shaukat Ali's forces was very important for the mass movement. He spoke forcefully about the need for non-violence. He said that the Hindus would support the Muslims, but only if the Muslims took the lead and if they were careful not to indulge in needless scimitar-rattling.[17]

When the terms of the proposed peace treaty with Turkey were published in May, Gandhi described them in the press statement on Turkish peace terms as a staggering blow to the Indian Muslims and advocated non-cooperation as the only way to secure justice and avoid violence.[18] On 22 June, he wrote a letter to Viceroy Chelmsford and the governor general from Laburnum Road after the terms of the Turkish Peace Treaty and a message from the viceroy to the Indian Muslims were published in India on 14 May 1920. He found that these terms violated the ministerial pledges and utterly disregarded the Muslim sentiments. In this letter, he explained his connections with the movement and the causes that led to his taking up the Khilafat question. He reiterated that it was his duty to resist the injustice that had been done to the Muslim sentiment and pointed out the dire need of non-cooperation.[19] His advice to the Muslims and Khilafat leaders was to respect the creed of non-violence. When, on 29 July, he spoke at a Muslims' meeting at Muzaffarabad Hall, Grant Road, he advised them to be non-violent and talked about non-cooperation as a 'matchless and powerful weapon'.[20] Later, on 4 October, Gandhi also presided over a meeting to welcome Jinnah and the Khilafat deputation on their return from England.[21]

The propaganda about the Khilafat was carried enthusiastically by the Muslim leaders in the country; the ulema and Sufis were also active. There was also a move among some Muslim families for *hijrat* from India to Afghanistan. It is interesting that in May, a notice regarding hijrat had been pasted up at a mosque in Bhendi Bazaar recommending that men who wish to do it should go to Rawalpindi for hijrat to Afghanistan.[22]

There was much enthusiasm among the Muslims on the Khilafat issue but not among the Congress and Hindu leaders of that time, such as Motilal Nehru, Vallabhbhai Patel, C.P. Ramaswamy Aiyar, Madan Mohan Malaviya, and N.C. Kelkar. To Rabindranath Tagore, the Khilafat agitation seemed a manifestation of irrational and turbulent politics. C.F. Andrews also expressed his concern over the issue to Gandhi. But Gandhi saw the Khilafat issue primarily in moral terms. Some of his colleagues wondered why he had not chosen an issue with a wider and secular appeal. His hand, however, seems to have been forced by the intensity of the Muslim discontent and danger of its divergence into self-destructive channels. The Khilafat leadership was the victim of its own propaganda: it was under pressure from its own following, and Gandhi was under pressure from the Khilafat leaders. The non-cooperation programme was launched over the Khilafat issue in August 1920. And almost immediately, Gandhi embarked on a strategy to bring the Khilafat agitation into the mainstream of nationalist politics.[23]

## The First National Week

According to Gandhi, 6 April vitalized the whole of India; it saw the advent of satyagraha and inauguration of a definite plan of Hindu–Muslim unity and swadeshi. In the tragedy at Jallianwala Bagh on 13 April 1919, Hindu–Muslim blood flowed in a mingled stream and sealed the compact. Gandhi suggested that people fast on 6 April and hold public meetings for the repeal of the Rowlatt Act. Moreover, the week beginning from 6 April should be devoted to some work connected with the tragedy of 13 April and should be closed with meetings throughout India to urge the government to take effective steps to render a repetition of the tragedy impossible. This national week should be a week of purification, self-examination, sacrifice, exact discipline, and an expression of the cherished national sentiments. During the week, one must do their best to realize the principles of satyagraha, Hindu–Muslim unity, and swadeshi.[24]

People were enthused with this new idea. The entire week was devoted to the collection of funds for the Jallianwalla Bagh memorial, and Bombay responded generously. The week was celebrated in Bombay according to the programme laid down by Gandhi and published in the papers two or three weeks ago. Leaflets and posters were distributed and house-to-house collections for the Jallianwalla Bagh fund were made by volunteers, who, at times, marched in procession headed by a band and attended by Kitson lights. The normal life and appearance of the city, however, were undisturbed; there were no public prayers. An amount of about Rs 325,000 was subscribed to the Punjab funds. Gandhi addressed three meetings in Bombay. The resolutions passed at all these three meetings were substantially those drafted by Gandhi and published in the newspapers some time ago.[25]

A huge public meeting of the citizens of Bombay was held under the joint auspices of the Presidency Association, the provincial Congress committee, the Bombay branches of the Home Rule leagues, and the National Union, in an open space near the French Bridge on 6 April 1920. Dinshaw M. Petit chaired the meeting. Gandhi, Jinnah, Besant, and other leaders were present. V.J. Patel moved the resolution urging the repeal of the

Rowlatt Act. Gandhi seconded the resolution and emphasized the importance of truth and non-violence. According to him, theirs was a resolution not of despair but of confidence. He assured the meeting that so long as there were even a handful of satyagrahis left alive, there would be no peace in the land until the act was repealed before its statutory period.[26]

Another public meeting during the National Week was held under the auspices of the Central Khilafat Committee near the French Bridge on the night of 9 April. Chhotani presided over the meeting. According to Gandhi, two issues that stood out prominently in the last 12 months were the inauguration of the swadeshi and the laying of the foundation of genuine Hindu–Muslim unity.[27]

A public meeting under the auspices of the Home Rule League's Bombay branch and the National Union was held on 13 April in the open space near the French Bridge with Jinnah presiding over it. This was in connection with the National Week. C.F. Andrews read out a message from Rabindranath Tagore condemning the Jallianwala Bagh massacre. After that, Gandhi moved the resolution urging the government to take steps to render impossible acts of barbarity such as the Jallianwala Bagh incident and similar ones committed by responsible officers in Punjab during the administration of martial law. He was glad that the people of Bombay had contributed Rs 325,000 for the Jallianwala memorial, although he felt a little disappointed since it was not quite what he had expected from Bombay. He said that they could not forget, until life lasted, the memory of the Jallianwala Bagh victims. However, he entertained no thoughts of vengeance because it was the resort of the coward. All that they intended in erecting the memorial was to revere the memory of the innocent people who had died.[28] There was a very large attendance. Besides Gandhi and Jinnah, those present included Abdul Kassim, Chhotani, Rambhuj

Dutt Chaudhuri, C.F. Andrews, Jamnadas Dwarkadas, Ahmed Haji Siddick Khatri, C.V. Vaidya, Kanji Dwarkadas, Jamnadas K. Mehta, Moulvi Raffiuddin Ahmed, and others.[29]

## Launch of the Non-Cooperation Movement

In his letter dated 22 June 1920 to the viceroy, written from Mani Bhavan, Gandhi stated that Muslims and Hindus, as a whole, had lost 'faith in British justice and honour'. Under the circumstances, non-cooperation was the only dignified and constitutional way left, for 'it is the right recognized from time immemorial of the subject to refuse to assist a ruler who misrules'.[30] The movement was formally launched on 1 August 1920; it merged with the observance of fast, hartal, and processions on the day of Tilak's death.

Bombay was getting ready by the mid-1920 for the launch of the movement. The Non-Cooperation Committee issued a statement for public information and guidance before 7 July 1920. It stated that it wanted to enlist the passive sympathy, if not active cooperation, of the whole country in the method of non-cooperation. It had incorporated the following issues as part of the first stage: surrender of all titles of honour and honorary offices; non-participation in government loans; suspension by lawyers of practice and settlement of civil disputes by private arbitration; boycott of government schools by parents; boycott of the reformed councils; non-participation in government parties and such other functions; and refusal to accept any civil or military post in Mesopotamia, or to offer to work for the army, especially for serving in the Turkish territories (that were then administered in violation of pledges). It also focused on the task of propagating swadeshi. It was made clear that success depended entirely upon disciplined and concerted non-cooperation and the latter relied upon strict obedience to instructions, calmness, and absolute freedom from violence.[31] Before a crowded meeting of Muslims at Muzaffarabad, Bombay, on 29 July 1920, Gandhi declared confidently that the time for speeches on non-cooperation was past and the time for practice had arrived.[32]

The launch of the Non-Cooperation Movement opened a new chapter in the history of India. With his letter dated 1 August 1920 to the viceroy, Gandhi returned, 'not without a pang', the Kaiser-i-Hind gold medal granted to him by the British government for his humanitarian work in South Africa, the Zulu War medal granted in South Africa for his war services as the officer-in-charge of the Indian Volunteers Service Corps in 1906, and the medal for his services as the assistant superintendent of the Indian Volunteer Stretcher-Bearer Corps during the Boer War of 1899. He returned these medals 'in pursuance of the scheme of non-cooperation, inaugurated today in connection with the Khilafat Movement'. He wrote that in European countries the condonation of such grievous wrongs as the Khilafat and Punjab would have resulted in a bloody revolution by the people.

But one half of India is too weak to offer a violent resistance and the other half is unwilling to do so. I have therefore ventured to suggest a remedy of non-cooperation, which enables those who wish to disassociate themselves from the Government and which, if it is unattended by violence and undertaken in an ordered manner, will compel it to retrace its steps and undo the wrongs committed. But whilst I pursue the policy of non-cooperation in so far as I can carry the people with me, I shall not lose hope that you will yet see your way to do justice.[33]

The firm letter was politely signed as 'I remain, Sir, your faithful servant, M.K. Gandhi'.[34]

The Non-Cooperation Committee issued detailed instructions for the observance of full hartal on 1 August 1920. According to these, the day should be devoted to prayers and all those who can, should fast for the day. Meetings should be held all over the country, not excluding the smallest village at which the resolution—recording full sympathy with the Central Khilafat Committee to secure revision of the Turkish peace terms, approving non-cooperation adopted by the committee, and urging the imperial government for a just revision of the terms—should be adopted with or without speeches.[35]

The day of 1 August was also one when Tilak, a leader of great standing, passed away in Bombay. Two days before his death on 29 July, Gandhi had gone to see him. He went to Sardar Griha to join Tilak's funeral procession and paid him tribute in glowing terms. According to him, Tilak knew no religion but the love of

**Figure 3.1**   The funeral procession of B.G. Tilak on 1 August 1920.
*Source*: Pratap M.B. Velkar.

his country. He was a born democrat. 'The permanent essence of him abides with us forever. Let us erect for the only Lokmanya of India an imperishable monument by weaving into our lives his own bravery, his simplicity, his wonderful industry and his love for his country.'[36]

A meeting was convened on 1 August 1920 at Mastan Shah Tank, under the auspices of the Central Khilafat Committee and was presided over by Chhotani. The meeting recorded full sympathy with the movement of the Central Khilafat Committee to secure the revision of the Turkish peace terms consistent with the Muslim sentiments and Islamic law. It also approved that the non-cooperation adopted by the Central Khilafat Committee be continued until the peace terms were revised. Gandhi pointed out that the chief things essential for the success of the Non-Cooperation Movement were non-violence, renunciation of titles and honorary posts, and a vigorous propagation of swadeshi. He also stressed on the importance of withdrawing children from government schools, asking teachers to resign from their posts and legal professionals to give up their practice.[37]

There was a chain of meetings where people met and expressed their discontent with the foreign rule. Gandhi and his colleagues never got tired of organizing them. On 3 October, Gandhi presided over a public meeting convened by Sobani, Banker, and Pawar with the evident objective of introducing to the working classes the programme of non-cooperation. About 5,000 people, mostly mill hands and labourers, attended. The meeting was addressed by Gandhi, Shaukat Ali, N.D. Savarkar, Jinwala, Dattatraya R. Mayekar, and others, a combination of oratorical talent that was as significant as it was unusual. Gandhi stigmatized the government as bad and treacherous. After attending a few minor functions of welcome during the day, the returning delegates attended a meeting at the Mastan Shah Tank, where Gandhi presided over a crowd of 5,000 or more, almost exclusively Muslims. Pickthale, wearing a fez, was seated by Gandhi's side; Gandhi's wife, Anasuyaben, and Saraladevi Choudharani were well to the fore.[38]

## Students and the Movement

There were students in Bombay during this time who shared few of Gandhi's values, but were willing to join hands with him in the struggle for swaraj. S.A. Dange and a group of students—R.S. Nimbkar, R.V. Nadkarni, V.D. Sathaye, S.V. Ghate, and others— discussed politics and conducted study sessions in a library rich in Marxist literature. The 'socialists' around Dange were in close touch with another group of students consisting of V.H. Kulkarni, G.J. Madholkar, P.L. Purandkar, D.P. Navarne, K.N. Joglekar, and T.V. Parvate who were influenced by Gandhi's ideas but also read the literature of the Young Turk and the Irish Revolution avidly. These student groups contributed substantially to the strength of nationalism in Bombay. The young radicals around Dange, who were also students in Wilson College, had their brush with authority in the second week of August when they attempted to hold a meeting in the memory of their leader Tilak. The principal of Wilson College refused permission to hold such a meeting and it was subsequently held in the Marwari Vidyalaya Hall. However, the students who were in touch with Shankarlal Banker, V.J. Patel, and Jamnadas Mehta rushed to the offensive by installing a Ganapati idol in the college and celebrating a Ganapati festival. They also decided to take issue with the principal over a Bible class that was held daily in the college and at which attendance was compulsory. It soon turned into a public issue. The consequences of the agitation set afoot by Dange and his associates were apparent in the fourth annual convention of the Bombay Presidency Students Federation that met on 18 December 1920 at the Marwari Vidyalaya Hall, under the presidency of C.F. Andrews. Dange was the chief organizer. After much debate and discussion, the resolution committing the student community to the support of non-cooperation was passed with a majority of 48 against 19. The decision of the federation was the signal for around 500 students in Bombay, mostly Maharashtrians, some Gujaratis, with a sprinkling of Muslims, to quit schools and colleges. In these students who answered the call of swaraj in 1920, a generation was encountered which dominated politics in Bombay for the next two or three decades.[39]

Gandhi recognized the strength of the students and always found time to interact with them. He never missed an opportunity to say some words of advice to the students of Bombay. When some students of the Grant Medical College came to see him on 31 August, discussion with him helped clarify their views and they signed on the khadi pledge.[40] He said to a students' gathering at Shantaram Chawl on 14 November 1920 that until they realized the principles of non-violence and non-hatred, they would be able to do no service to their motherland which they genuinely loved. Gandhi called his non-cooperation 'non-violent non-cooperation'. He pointed out that his non-cooperation had no similarity with the non-cooperation movement of Ireland or Egypt, although the motive was nearly the same. Both Ireland and Egypt preached violence while he was against it. The use of the sword or force or abuse against an opponent was morally equally culpable, and they all amounted to violence. In addition, he said that the then British government was based on the worst principles. The rulers had cheated the Indians and issued false statements. He drew the audience's attention to the government's apathetic attitude towards the massacre in Punjab and to the pledge given to the Indian Muslims. According to Gandhi, the present universities and colleges had produced more slaves than scholars. Now they must destroy these slave-producing institutes and the only measure, in Gandhi's opinion, was non-cooperation with the government and the boycott of its institutions.[41]

## Swadeshi and Women

Mumbai was an important site for his advocacy of the idea of swadeshi and propagation of the khadi movement. Gandhi himself learnt the use of slivers from a carder who was passing by at Mani Bhavan. Women such as Avantikabai Gokhale, Ramiben (the widowed mother of Shankarlal Banker and Vasumatiben) were his trusted colleagues and followers in such activities. On 31 August 1920, he took a vow in Bombay: 'From today for life, I declare that I shall purchase for my [wear] only Khaddar cloth hand-made of hand-spun yarn, cap or head-dress and socks excepted.'[42]

Women from elite families took up the activities to advance the causes of swadeshi and khadi. They willingly gave their expensive foreign cloth and happily adopted the rough khadi cloth in their daily lives. Paying a tribute to Bombay's role, Gandhi wrote that in this city 'ladies of noted families have already taken up spinning. Their ranks have been joined by Dr. Mrs. Manekbai Bahadurji who has already learnt the art and who is now trying to introduce it in the Seva Sadan. Her Highness the Begum Saheba of Janjira and her sister Mrs. Atia Begum Rahman have also undertaken to learn the art.'[43]

Gandhi was accompanied by Saraladevi Choudharani when he declared open the khadi bhandar of Narandas Purushotamdas and Vithaldas Jerajani on 4 June. He referred to the work of the duchess of Sutherland who had popularized the use of home-woven and homespun Scotch tweed furnishing as the honourable and lucrative occupation of hundreds of Scottish women. He further said that he would not be satisfied until India recognized the true art in the homespun.[44]

Gandhi had developed a special way to draw women in the arena of political activities by erasing the dividing line between the personal and public/political spheres of their lives. In his speech on 7 July 1920 to a meeting of women organized by Gujarati Stree Mandal at Marwari Vidyalaya and presided over by Jaijee Petit, the wife of J.B. Petit, he asked women to read the Congress sub-committee's report on the Punjab atrocities carefully. He dwelt upon some of the happenings and pointed out their importance to women in Bombay and the need to protest against such injustice so that a repetition of the Punjab atrocities might be rendered impossible not only in that province but also in any other part of India. He urged women to show to the world that the soul power of India's womanhood was greater than the physical strength of those officials who had perpetrated the atrocities in Punjab and to stand by the side of their husbands, brothers, and sons and insist on their getting the Punjab wrongs redressed.[45]

The women of Bombay remembered Gandhi's birthday affectionately. Members of the Bhagini Samaj celebrated Gandhi's 52nd birthday at the hall of the Marwari Vidyalaya on Saturday evening. It was a large gathering of women presided over by Jaijee Petit. She gave them Gandhi's message in Gujarati. Gandhi felt that they recognized his affection. They knew that he had their self-respect at his heart and to preserve this, the easiest method he had shown them was swadeshi. Men could not help more than women in promoting it. He advised that all the women should always spend one hour spinning yarn.[46]

# Other Meetings

While the issues of the Khilafat, non-cooperation, and swadeshi took much of Gandhi's time and energy, other political issues and meetings were no less important for him. On 4 March 1920, he spoke at a public meeting presided over by G.K. Parekh at the Mathuradas Gokuldas Hall to welcome the formation of the Kathiawar Hitwardhak Sabha and pointed out the need to have truth, fearlessness, and straightforwardness in the working of the organization.[47]

Gandhi was a strong supporter of the freedom of the press. A meeting was held on 5 March 1920 under the auspices of the Indian Press Association, with Sir Narayan Chandavarkar as the chair. The meeting was one of the few occasions that found nationalists, liberals, and Home Rule leaguers on the same platform. A resolution demanding the repeal of the Press Act of 1910 was proposed by Gandhi and seconded by M.R. Jayakar. Advocating the repeal of the Press Act, Gandhi said that it was for the journalist to separate the grain from the chaff and it was his duty to throw light on every matter of public concern. His plea was not to gag newspapers because they were the representatives of public opinion. He also said that Horniman's issue could not be shelved. (Horniman was deported in April 1919 and he could return only in 1926.)[48]

A public meeting was held at Madhav Baug on 23 June, when Maharaja Scindia of Gwalior presided and Pandit Malaviya delivered a lecture on the Banaras Hindu University. Gandhi appreciated Malaviya's zealous efforts for the furtherance of the university and said that Bombay had always been famous for the ready manner in which it came to the help of a deserving cause and he had no doubt that Bombay would extend its support to the university with its wonted generosity.[49]

Under the joint auspices of the Imperial Indian Citizenship Association and the Bombay Presidency Association, the Indian Merchants' Chamber and Bureau, the Indian Home Rule League, the All India Home Rule League, the Bombay National Union, and the Bombay Provincial Congress Committee (BPCC), a public meeting of the citizens of Bombay was held at Excelsior Theatre on 13 July to consider the Indian situation in East Africa and Fiji and seek relief for the grievances of Indians living under the British empire. The meeting was presided over by Sir Chandavarkar. Attention was drawn to the grievances of the Indian residents there and deportation of Manilal Doctor by the Fijian government without any trial.[50]

Though running short of time, Gandhi had managed to go to open the Gujarati Rashtriya Shala (national school) started by Luhar-Suthar Dharma Jignasu Mandal at Malad on 17 November. He had received a complaint from some in the community of blacksmiths and carpenters that the proposed school was being started with the objective of minimizing their importance. He regretted to find class hatred manifest among the community. He advised them to stand on their own feet and to preach and practise non-cooperation in order to attain this. He emphasized that India required national education and not the education imparted in government schools.[51]

## The Home Rule League

Gandhi had close connections with the leaders of the Home Rule League; his own views and ways of working, however, were different. As time passed, he was urged by some to join the Home League. He wrote to friends seeking their views on the subject. He wrote to Mazharul Haque from Laburnum Road on 18 March 1920 that 'I can join an organization only if I can influence their viewpoint rather than get influenced myself. It does not mean that I do not have an open mind to accept new ideas. I only want to emphasize the fact that a fresh idea, with some extraordinary relevance alone can impress me now.'[52] He also wrote to V.S. Srinivasa Sastri on the same day saying:

[A]t my time of life and with views firmly formed on several matters I could only join an organization to affect its policy and not be affected by it. This does not mean that I would not keep or that I do not have an open mind to receive new light.... The League, according to my opinion, cannot become an anti-Congress organization but it should work as it is now doing to further the interests of the Congress.... Do you advise me, knowing me as you do with my qualifications and limitations, to join the League?[53]

After some deliberation, however, he agreed to be the president of the Home Rule League on 28 April 1920.[54]

On 26 June, the Bombay Home Rule League and the National Union organized a meeting with Jinnah presiding over it to protest against the Hunter Committee report. The meeting's main resolution moved by Gandhi protested against the majority report of the committee and its acceptance by the Indian government and the secretary of the state for India, and urged them to implement the recommendations of the Congress report on the Punjab disorder. Reasserting his faith in satyagraha, he said that there were three minimum demands: Lord Chelmsford's recall, return of the fines imposed on the people, and the burial of the Rowlatt Act.[55] This meeting was held at the Morarji Gokuldas Hall.[56] It was attended by 3,000 or 4,000 people of all creeds, and Malaviya, Shaukat Ali, Kitchlew, Jamnadas Dwarkadas, and Savarkar were among the speakers.[57]

Soon thereafter there were differences of opinion among the members about the way of functioning of the Home Rule League.

In September 1920, Gandhi assembled Home Rule leaguers at Calcutta and changed the league's creed into a form later adopted by the Congress at its Nagpur session.[58] A general meeting of the All India Home Rule League was held on 3 October 1920 in Morarji Gokuldas Hall. Gandhi chaired the meeting. It was decided to change the name of the league to Swaraj Sabha in Calcutta.[59] Jinnah and 19 others including M.R. Jayakar, Jamnadas M. Mehta, Hansraj Pragji Thackersey, K.M. Munshi, Jamnadas Dwarkadas, and Kanji Dwarkadas resigned through their letter dated 5 October 1920 because they were of the opinion that the constitution adopted by the league in its general meeting held on 3 October constituted a fundamental departure from the aims, objectives, and methods of work hitherto pursued by the league. Soon after this, the Swaraj Sabha began to identify itself fully with non-cooperation activities. The chief activity of this Swaraj Sabha was the establishment of national schools in Bombay.[60] In his reply to Jinnah dated 25 October 1920 from Laburnum Road, Gandhi gave his explanations and requested him to reconsider his decision.[61]

The tying up of the non-cooperation issue with that of the Khilafat had its own tensions. There was apprehension among many Congress as well as Muslim leaders about agitating over the Khilafat issue. Many moderate Muslims were also uneasy; they feared that the policy of non-cooperation and boycott would affect the opportunities of education and government jobs for the youth adversely. In addition, it was difficult to shake off the deep-rooted distrust of the Congress amongst the Muslim leaders. As pointed out by B.R. Nanda, the programme of Non-cooperation Movement, including the boycott of legislative councils, courts, schools, and foreign cloth; the building up of alternative educational and judicial structures; and the extension of hand-weaving and hand-spinning, was meant for all communities. Non-cooperation became a common platform for the restoration of the Khilafat and the achievement of Indian independence. The two campaigns were thus joined but never really merged into an integrated struggle. The INC and the All India Khilafat Conference had separate networks for their all-India committees, down to provincial, district, town, and village levels. They had two separate volunteer organizations and separate funds for financing their activities. Gandhi's primacy, despite the occasional criticism and doubts of his colleagues, was unquestioned within the Congress organization, but he had no such hold over the Central Khilafat Committee, the Muslim League, and the organization of the ulema which claimed to speak on behalf of the Muslim community. The Ali brothers were Gandhi's chief link with the Khilafat organization.[62]

Many mill owners also were not active participants in the agitation that took place between 1918 and 1922. Some were even active opponents. Under the presidency of D.E. Wacha, the liberals met in October 1920 and feared that non-cooperation would lead to violence. An anti-Non-Cooperation committee was also formed with Chimanlal Setalvad and Purshotamdas Thakurdas as secretaries. By November 1920, Besant and some of her theosophist followers were supporting the committee, and liberal sympathizers such as Sethna and C.V. Mehta were also involved. However, while the industrialists were fairly consistently pro-government during the 1918–22 period, the Marwari and Gujarati marketers remained pro-nationalist.[63]

In 1920, Bombay was in turmoil with workers' strikes, labour unrest, political agitation, and the Khilafat issue. Unfazed by the prevailing political unease and economic turmoil, Gandhi continued to tread his path of non-violent struggle.

His popularity was rising. By now, he had made inroads into the hearts of the people with his gentle manners, insistence on ethics in public life, and concern for all. He argued persuasively that non-cooperation, by reason of its non-violence, had become a religious and purifying movement. It was a movement of self-reliance; it was the mightiest force for revolutionizing opinion and stimulating thought. Since it was a movement of self-imposed suffering, it possessed automatic checks against extravagance or impatience.[64]

His immense faith in the efficacy of the Non-Cooperation Movement instilled new energy in the people. As Bhikhu Parekh has elucidated, the non-violent struggle empowered the people by activating their sense of agency and opening up new channels of collective action, and weakened the oppressive system by denying it moral and material support, thus undermining its self-confidence and demonstrating its fragility.[65]

## Notes and References

1. *Young India* dated 10 March 1920 cited in *CWMG*, Vol. 17, pp. 79–84.
2. Chaudhari, *Source Material for a History of the Freedom Movement in India*, Vol. X, pp. 50–2.
3. Chaudhari, *Source Material for a History of the Freedom Movement in India*, Vol. X, pp. 52–3.
4. Chaudhari, *Source Material for a History of the Freedom Movement in India*, Vol. X, p. 59.
5. Chaudhari, *Source Material for a History of the Freedom Movement in India*, Vol. X, pp. 101–6.
6. 'Bombay Secret Abstract', p. 331, para 453(f) cited in Phatak, *Source Material for a History of the Freedom Movement in India*, Vol. III, Part I, p. 257.
7. According to C.B. Dalal, the meeting was held on 4 March. See Dalal, *Gandhi*, p. 29.

8. *Young India* dated 10 March 1920 cited in *CWMG*, Vol. 17, pp. 73–6.

9. Brown, *Gandhi's Rise to Power*, p. 207.

10. *Young India* dated 10 March 1920 cited in *CWMG*, Vol. 17, pp. 73–6.

11. 'Bombay Secret Abstract', p. 401, para 524(1) cited in Phatak, *Source Material for a History of the Freedom Movement in India*, Vol. III, Part I, p. 259.

12. *Young India* dated 24 March 1920 cited in *CWMG*, Vol. 17, pp. 99–103.

13. Sabira Dossa, 1993, 'The Khilafat Movement in the Bombay City', PhD dissertation (history), SNDT Women's University, pp. 371–3.

14. Extract from the *Times of India* dated 10 April 1920 quoted in (o) C.I.D., Bombay Presidency, 12 April 1920 cited in Chaudhari, *Source Material for a History of the Freedom Movement in India*, Vol. X, p. 235.

15. Dalal, *Gandhi*, p. 30.

16. 'Bombay Secret Abstract', 1920, p. 574 cited in *CWMG*, Vol. 17, pp. 313–4.

17. Gail Minault, *The Khilafat Movement: Religious Symbolism and Political Mobilization in India* (New Delhi: Oxford University Press, 1982), p. 100.

18. *The Bombay Chronicle* dated 18 May 1920 cited in *CWMG*, Vol. 17, pp. 426–7.

19. N.A.I. Home, Political (A), November 1920, Nos 19–31 cited in *CWMG*, Vol. 17, pp. 502–4.

20. *Young India* dated 4 August 1920 cited in *CWMG*, Vol. 18 (Delhi: Publications Division, Ministry of Information and Broadcasting, Government of India, 1965), pp. 96–7.

21. Dalal, *Gandhi*, p. 33.

22. Chaudhari, *Source Material for a History of the Freedom Movement in India*, Vol. X, p. 364.

23. B.R. Nanda, 'Gandhi and Pan-Islamism', in *In Search of Gandhi: Essays and Reflections* (New Delhi: Oxford University Press, 2002), pp. 95–7.

24. *Young India* dated 10 March 1929 cited in *CWMG*, Vol. 17, pp. 77–9.

25. 'Bombay Secret Abstract', pp. 557–9, para 643(c) cited in Phatak, *Source Material for a History of the Freedom Movement in India*, Vol. III, Part I, p. 262.

26. *The Bombay Chronicle* dated 8 April 1920 and 7 April 1920 cited in *CWMG*, Vol. 17, pp. 305–6.

27. *The Bombay Chronicle* dated 10 April 1920 cited in *CWMG*, Vol. 17, pp. 309–10.

28. *The Bombay Chronicle* dated 14 April 1920 cited in *CWMG*, Vol. 17, pp. 314–15.

29. Extract from the *Bombay Chronicle* cited in Phatak, *Source Material for a History of the Freedom Movement in India*, Vol. III, Part I, p. 262,

30. N.A.I. Home, Political (A), November 1920, Nos 19–31 cited in *CWMG*, Vol. 17, pp. 502–4.

31. *Young India* dated 7 July 1920 cited in *CWMG*, Vol. 18, pp. 13–14.

32. *Young India* dated 4 August 1920 cited in *CWMG*, Vol. 18, pp. 96–7.

33. N.A.I.: Foreign: Political: File No. 100: 1921 cited in *CWMG*, Vol. 18, pp. 104–6.

34. N.A.I.: Foreign: Political: File No. 100: 1921 cited in *CWMG*, Vol. 18, pp. 104–6. According to C.B. Dalal, the government acknowledged it on 2 October 1920. See Dalal, *Gandhi*, p. 32, footnote 4.

35. B.G. Kunte (ed.), *Source Material for a History of the Freedom Movement in India, Non-cooperation Movement in Bombay City (1920–25)*, Vol. VI (Bombay: Gazetteers Department, Government of Maharashtra, 1978), pp. 6–7.

36. *Young India* dated 4 August 1920 cited in *CWMG*, Vol. 18, pp. 110–11.

37. *The Bombay Chronicle* dated 2 August 1920 cited in *CWMG*, Vol. 18, pp. 107–9.

38. Phatak, *Source Material for a History of the Freedom Movement in India*, Vol. III, Part I, pp. 333–4.

39. Ravinder Kumar, 'From Swaraj to Purna Swaraj: Nationalist Politics in the City of Bombay, 1920–32', in *Essays in the Social History of Modern India* (New Delhi: Oxford University Press, 1983), pp. 251–3.

40. Dalal, *Gandhi*, p. 32.

41. *The Bombay Chronicle* dated 15 November 1920 cited in *CWMG*, Vol. 18, pp. 461–3.

42. *CWMG*, Vol. 18, p. 215.

43. *Young India* dated 21 July 1920 cited in *CWMG*, Vol. 18, p. 71.

44. *Young India* dated 9 June 1920 cited in *CWMG*, Vol. 17, p. 479.

45. *The Bombay Chronicle* dated 8 July 1920 cited in *CWMG*, Vol. 18, p. 23; Dalal, *Gandhijini Dinwari*, p. 105.

46. *The Bombay Chronicle* dated 13 October 1920 cited in *CWMG*, Vol. 18, p. 338.

47. *The Bombay Chronicle* dated 5 March 1920 cited in *CWMG*, Vol. 17, p. 68.

48. *Navajivan* dated 14 March 1920 cited in *CWMG*, Vol. 17, pp. 69–70, 88–9.

49 *The Bombay Chronicle* dated 24 June 1920 cited in *CWMG*, Vol. 17, p. 511.

50. *The Bombay Chronicle* dated 14 July 1920 cited in *CWMG*, Vol. 18, pp. 38–41.

51. *The Bombay Chronicle* dated 22 November 1920 cited in *CWMG*, Vol. 18, p. 488; Dalal, *Gandhi*, p. 34.

52. *Ashiyana ki Awaz*, pp. 40–1 cited in *CWMG*, Vol. 97 (Supplementary Vol. VII) (New Delhi: Publications Division, Ministry of Information and Broadcasting, Government of India, 1994), pp. 32–3.

53. *CWMG*, Vol. 17, pp. 96–8.

54. *CWMG*, Vol. 17, p. 98.

55. *Navajivan* dated 4 July 1920 cited in *CWMG*, Vol. 17, pp. 513–14.

56. Dalal, *Gandhi*, p. 31.

57. 'Bombay Secret Abstract', 1920, p. 979, para 982 cited in Phatak, *Source Material for a History of the Freedom Movement in India*, Vol. III, Part I, pp. 287–8.

58. *CWMG*, Vol. 17, p. 348, footnote 2.

59. Dalal, *Gandhijini Dinwari*, p. 110.

60. Kunte, *Source Material for a History of the Freedom Movement in India*, Vol. VI, pp. 26–7.

61. *The Bombay Chronicle* dated 26 October 1920 cited in *CWMG*, Vol. 18, pp. 370–2.

62. Nanda, Gandhi, pp. 292–3.

63. Gordon, *Businessmen and Politics*, p. 159.

64. *Young India* dated 29 December 1920 cited in *CWMG*, Vol. 19 (Delhi: Publications Division, Ministry of Information and Broadcasting, Government of India, 1966), p. 171.

65. Bhikhu Parekh, *Debating India: Essays on Indian Political Discourse* (New Delhi: Oxford University Press, 2015), p. 253.

# 4

# BUILDING THE MASS BASE: 1921

---

BY THE BEGINNING OF 1921, GANDHI WAS FIRMLY ESTABLISHED IN THE
Congress. In September 1920, he had already declared at Calcutta
that India could attain swaraj within a year if its people followed
his plan of non-cooperation.[1] He expressed this belief again in
February 1921 and clarified that the essential preconditions
were the spirit of non-violence, Hindu–Muslim unity, abolition
of untouchability, establishment of the Congress organization in
every village, and a spinning wheel in every home.[2]

The year 1921 brought new vigour to the nationalist movement,
and Bombay remained one of its main centres. The Swaraj Sabha
made attempts to keep the people away from the attractions
of functions arranged in connection with the visit of the Duke

of Connaught in February. People, especially the youth, were touched by the spark of the movement. Efforts were made to mobilize them in the agitation and harness their energies for national education. The spirit of the Non-Cooperation Movement had caused considerable excitement among the students; the nationalist leaders were busy holding meetings for them and renowned colleges such as Wilson College and St. Xavier's College were seriously affected. Gandhi had instructed the local leaders to guarantee all non-cooperating students their maintenance. S.R. Bomanji was reported to be contributing Rs 10,000 towards the maintenance of non-cooperating students. It was reported that the new national college would start at the Marwari Vidyalaya with an attendance roll of about 60 and a staff consisting of Professor S.K. Puntambekar, the principal of the Surat Sarvajanik College; Professor Swami Narayan of the government college, Ahmedabad; Professor Muzumdar of the Fergusson College, Poona; J.B. Bhansali; and C.V. Vaidya of Kalyan. The subjects of instruction were to be spinning, Hindustani, and village organization. The opening of the new National Muslim School on 1 February by Haji Yusuf Sobani on the upper floor of Haji Abdus Satar Haji Umar's Madressah at Surti Mohalla was also announced.[3]

The fear of the state's repressive power could not dampen the public spirit and people's aversion to the foreign rule. There was an agitation to boycott the arrival of the new viceroy, Lord Reading, at two meetings in March 1921: on 6 March at Khadak, where about 2,000 residents of A and B wards attended the meeting presided over by V.J. Patel; and on 7 March 1921 at Jitekar's Wadi, where about 2,000 residents of C Ward attended the meeting over which Hirji Virji presided. The leaders expressed their determination not to welcome the new viceroy on his arrival and urged the municipal corporators not to vote on the address of welcome. Activities to propagate the message of swadeshi continued with vigour and detailed information about the place and timings of such activities was provided. The Swaraj Sabha had arranged public-spinning classes at the centres of the Gujarat National School, Princess Street (from 7.30 am to 9 am and from 8 pm to 9 pm daily); the Mandvi Swaraj Office (from 8 am to 10 am); Grant Road, Pannalal Terraces, Room 55-A, (from 8 am to 10 am); Nathuram's Wadi, Thakurdwar (morning and evening), and the Marwari Vidyalaya. Arrangements were also made to supply spinning wheels, yarn, ready rolls of cotton, and so forth, at Khadi Bhandar, Kalbadevi Road, or at Banker's place, Chowpatty Road.[4] The A.I.C.C. that met in Bombay from 28 to 30 July called for the boycott of foreign cloth and propagation of khadi. It also emphasized that people should not associate with functions connected with the visit of the Prince of Wales.

**Figure 4.1** The procession taken out by women in Bombay in 1921 to propagate swadeshi by spinning charkha and wearing khadi.
*Source*: Mani Bhavan Gandhi Sangrahalaya.

Enthused people, especially the merchants from the markets, responded effectively to Gandhi's call and organized many demonstrations and marches. As noted by Gordon, it was to become a pattern of the 1918–22 era that nationalist marches, described as going through the 'business' section of the city, always, upon closer examination, appeared to have wended their way through the bazaars and lanes of 'old' Bombay rather than down the wide boulevards of the 'westernized' section. Such was the Home Rule Day march of June 1918, and such was to be the case in almost all the subsequent marches, including those of the Civil Disobedience Movement.[5]

## Tilak Swaraj Fund

### Collection during the National Week

To the activities related to non-cooperation, a new element was added that gave a boost to people's determination and defiance. An announcement of Gandhi's resolve to collect a huge amount of Rs 10 million for the Tilak Swaraj Fund by the end of June 1921 stimulated people to get actively involved in the nationalist activities in the country. The people of Bombay were keen to contribute to this fund named after their favourite leader. (In March 1921, the Bezwada A.I.C.C. had decided to form the Tilak Swaraj Fund.) Gandhi made fervent appeals to people from all sections and sectors and made it known that his intention was to collect donations from as many people as possible and not from just a few donors. The purpose was very clear: 'There will be no statue. With that Fund, we are to win swaraj; it is to be utilized chiefly for providing education to children, for promoting the spinning-wheel movement and remunerating public workers, that is to say, the contributions we shall make to the Fund will be used entirely for us.'[6]

In response to Gandhi's appeal, the leaders and volunteers got busy collecting subscriptions for the fund from the National Week to the end of June 1921. Gandhi had great expectations from the people of Bombay, and they did not disappoint him. Various associations and groups such as merchants, carpenters and tailors, women, and artists donated generously. There were huge donations from some individuals such as Jainarayan Indumal Dani (Rs 500,000); Ardeshir Burjorji Godrej (Rs 300,000); Anandilal Podar (Rs 200,000); Haji Yusuf Sobani (Rs 100,000); Suraimal Harnandrai Ruia (Rs 60,000); Velji Lakhamsi Napoo (Rs 50,000); and Shankarlal Ghelabhai Banker, Revashankar Jagjivan, and M.R. Jayakar (Rs 25,000 each).[7] Industrialists and merchants, workers and activists, farmers and artists, young and old, men and women—all responded to Gandhi's call. No donation was too small for this fund being raised by the Mahatma.

The National or Satyagraha Week of 1921 (6 April to 13 April) was chiefly devoted to the collections of the Tilak Swaraj Fund and was observed with the spirit of service and sacrifice.

Gandhi's message for the observance of this week was published by Shankarlal Banker in the form of placards posted up in the city at various places. The message was as follows: 'Observe fast for 24 hours commencing from the evening previous to the 6th and 13th April. Observe *Hartal,* suspending business on the 6th and 13th April (1921). Pass the day in tranquility. Contribute to the Tilak Swaraj Fund according to your means and resolve to (i) gain *Swaraj* this year (ii) Solve the Khilafat Question and (iii) Obtain justice for the Punjab affairs.'

Some specific programmes were also arranged during this week. The audience was advised at all such programmes and meetings to contribute generously to the Tilak Swaraj Fund, to raise the membership of the Congress, and to introduce the spinning wheel

**Figure 4.2** The front page of the *Bombay Chronicle*, dated 1 July 1921. Bombay displayed generosity and upheld the country's honour.
*Source*: The Asiatic Society of Mumbai.

in every family. On the evening of 5 April, a public meeting under the auspices of the 'G' Ward District Congress Committee was held at Kirtikar's Wadi, Dadar. Narhar Shivram Paranjpe presided over this meeting attended by about 1,000 people. 'The People's

Duty during the National Week' was the theme of the speeches delivered by Sarojini Naidu and N.D. Savarkar.

On 6 April, the first day of the Satyagraha Week, a partial hartal was observed in the city. It was noticeable in localities such as Sheikh Memon Street, Mandvi Khadak, Chakla, and Share Bazaar. In the other parts of the city, only a few shops were closed. The day passed off without any untoward event except that around 20 volunteers asked the branches of cooperative stores at C.P. Tank and Princess Street to close down. At 6.30 in the evening, a public meeting was held at Shantaram Chawl under the auspices of the Swaraj Sabha, the Central Khilafat Committee, the Indian Home Rule League, and the Bombay National Union. Sarojini Naidu presided over the meeting, and Lala Lajpat Rai, Lala Gordhandas, V.J. Patel, and Marmaduke Pickthall addressed the audience of about 10,000. A resolution was passed at the meeting. Another meeting of a similar nature was held at Khadak, Mandvi, at 9.30 pm, which was presided over by Naranji Dayal. A resolution similar to the one passed at Shantaram Chawl was carried.

On 7 April, a public meeting of around 3,000 mill hands residing at Chinchpokli and neighbouring localities was held at 8.30 pm at Munji Shetts' Wadi, Chinchpokli. Achyut Balwant Kolhatkar, Lala Lajpat Rai, R.S. Nimbkar, D.R. Mayekar, and others explained the labourers why they needed to become members of the Congress and thus strengthen the prospects of India gaining swaraj in a few months. On 8 April, at 9.30 pm a public meeting of about 1,000 residents of Matunga was held in the open space near the Matunga railway station. V.J. Patel presided over this meeting. Prominent speakers such as Patel and Dr Savarkar exhorted the people to do their duty towards the country and the Congress by contributing to the Tilak Swaraj Fund, taking to spinning wheels, and enlisting as members of the Congress.

On 9 April, at 9 pm about 500 residents of Dadar held a meeting under the auspices of the 'G' Ward District Congress Committee at Kirtikar's Wadi, with V.J. Patel presiding over it. Patel, Jamnadas M. Mehta, and C.V.P. Shivam gave speeches. Gandhi returned from Madras (now Chennai) on 10 April in the morning. The Swaraj Sabha organized two public meetings on that day, one at 4.45 pm for the Mandvi merchants at Khadak and the other at 9 pm for the labourers at Elphinstone Road, Parel, a suburb of Central Bombay. At both these meetings, strong appeals were made by Gandhi and others to help the national cause by contributing to the Tilak Swaraj Fund and enlisting as members of the Congress committees. Gandhi emphasized the need for introducing spinning wheels and boycotting foreign cloth for the attainment of swaraj. At the Khadak meeting, an amount of about Rs 10,000 was collected and handed over to Gandhi. The sum included ornaments worth Rs 1,000 given on the spur of the moment by the women present and Rs 2,000 contributed by the merchants of Katha Bazar and the grocers of Mandvi.

On 13 April, the last day of the Satyagraha Week, the city observed only a partial hartal, similar to that of 6 April, and collections were made for the Tilak Swaraj Fund. The day ended with the holding of three public meetings at Shantaram Chawl, Mandvi, and the Marwari Vidyalaya.[8]

Gandhi was busy contacting individuals and associations to collect the contributions for the fund and keeping the tempo of the movement. He made a fervent appeal during the week on 10 April 1921 at a public meeting held under the auspices of the Swaraj Sabha and the Central Khilafat Committee that for the sake of swaraj within a year, for the sake of the Khilafat wrongs, and for the sake of the Punjab wrongs, the Indians must give up foreign-made goods. The A.I.C.C. had kept three tasks before the

country: enrol 10 million members (the fee for membership was
fixed at four annas), collect Rs 10 million for the Tilak Swaraj
Fund (Gandhi was sure that the rich mercantile community of
Bombay could easily collect that amount), and give up foreign
cloth and goods as well as cultivate the habit of spinning.
According to Gandhi, people must wear khadi and it was their
duty to use swadeshi only. It was an offence to wear clothes made
in foreign countries and discard those made in one's own country.
He wanted the cooperation of women and their blessings too,
and maintained that they must qualify for this by purifying
themselves, which could be done by discarding foreign clothes
and wearing Indian ones. In Bengal and Orissa (now Odisha),
women contributed to the Tilak Swaraj Fund liberally. He made
a special appeal to women to wear swadeshi clothes and discard
foreign ones, and put before them the ideal of Sita: suffer like Sita
and live like Sita—simply and plainly.[9]

His message on the last day of the Satyagraha Week was, 'Even
God will not grant us swaraj. It is for us to win it and there is only
one way of doing so. The moment we understand what it is and
follow it, swaraj will be ours.'[10]

## Reaching the Target

Gandhi's drive to collect the amount for the Tilak Swaraj Fund
was amazing. His words touched many hearts. He and his team
worked with vitality and intensity to make people aware of
the need of the day. Gandhi's messages were put on posters at
conspicuous places in the city and the word-of-mouth publicity
was very effective. Several meetings were held in different parts
of the city. After his tour of Bijapur District, Gandhi arrived in
Bombay on the morning of 29 May 1921. He was received at the
Victoria Terminus by the Ali brothers and put up in Revashankar

Jagjivandas's bungalow at Gamdevi. He addressed a mass meeting at Matunga in the evening where he was given a sum Rs 7,000 in aid of the Tilak Swaraj Fund by the people of Matunga.[11]

On 15 June, a meeting was held at Ghatkopar. Among those present were V.J. Patel, Hakim Ajmal Khan, Sarojini Naidu, Dr M.A. Ansari, Dr B.S. Munje, N.C. Kelkar, the Ali brothers, Maulana Abdul Bari, Maulana Abul Kalam Azad, Jamnalal Bajaj, and Shankarlal Banker. Accepting the amount of Rs 40,000 that was collected at Ghatkopar, Gandhi expressed his disappointment over the amount. He insisted, however, that the contribution should be made willingly, with *shraddha*, devotion, and faith. He also talked about other issues such as religion, cause of the Khilafat, the need for spinning, as well as the removal of untouchability and the Congress programme.[12]

Gandhi kept a tight watch over the collection drive, keeping the morale of his team high, and his team in turn supported him with all its energy and resources. There was an informal meeting in Gandhi's house on 17 June attended by Shankarlal Banker, Umar Sobani, Revashankar Jagjivan, Jamnalal Bajaj, and others. Gandhi discussed with them the subject of collection for the Swaraj Fund. He opined that Bombay must contribute at least Rs 600,000. Umar Sobani said that the people of Colaba had promised Rs 500,000, and that he was now canvassing to the mill owners of Bombay and had great hopes of collecting about Rs 200,000 in all. However, in case he failed, he would make good the difference from his own pocket. This drew a compliment from Gandhi. Revashankar Jagjivan said he had been promised Rs 75,000 by the merchants of the Jhaveri Bazaar and Rs 25,000 by the jewellers. Jamnalal Bajaj said that the Bombay Marwaris had promised him Rs 200,000, and if they failed him, he would go to Calcutta and collect the balance there. Gandhi expressed the desire that somebody should undertake the collection of

Rs 500,000 from the Mulji Jetha cloth markets and Rs 500,000 each from the Mangaldas, Narottam Morarji, and Lakhmidas markets.[13]

Gandhi tirelessly and enthusiastically attended various meetings and participated in deliberations. He was present at the meetings of the Congress Working Committee (CWC) and the A.I.C.C. on 14 and 15 June, and also at the meeting of the Central Khilafat Committee and a meeting in Ghatkopar on 15 June.[14] On 18 June, he spoke on non-cooperation at the Council of the Parsi Central Association. The meeting was presided over by Hormasji Adenwalla. Gandhi appealed the Parsis to join the movement.[15] On 19 June, he addressed a meeting at Vile Parle where he was presented with a purse for the Tilak Swaraj Fund.[16]

The merchants and residents of Mandvi Ward met in the afternoon of 26 June at New Chinch Bunder Road to present a purse to Gandhi for the Tilak Swaraj Fund. The meeting took place in a godown that could accommodate 10,000 or 12,000 people, but there must have been double that number present. The heat was oppressive, and due to the overcrowding, the audience endured much discomfort. Many of them, unable to bear it any longer, left the place before Gandhi arrived but dropped their contributions into the collecting boxes as they left. Gandhi, however, stuck it out to the end, intent only on the collection of as large a sum as possible. The women of the city had a tender corner in their hearts for Gandhi and his work. Khatri, a member of the Mandvi District Congress Committee, had collected Rs 500,000 in the ward and he presented the amount to Gandhi. On 21 June, he visited the spinning class conducted by the Hind Mahila Samaj in New Bhatwadi, at the invitation of Avantikabai Gokhale. She handed him over a sum of Rs 2,658 (on behalf of the Mahila Samaj); this amount included the sum (Rs 1,000) realized by the sale of her pearl bangles. At about 9.30 pm on the same day, Gandhi and

Kasturba were welcomed by the Surati Mahyavanshi community and other Parel residents at the hall of the Currimbhoy Kamgar Samaj at Delisle Road. A sum of Rs 106 was presented to him for the Tilak Swaraj Fund.[17]

The rising nationalism also manifested in the establishment of national schools. On 22 June, at about 9 am Gandhi formally opened the Lokmanya Rashtriya Kanya Shala, Bombay's first national girls' school, at Gandharva Mahavidyalaya Hall, Sandhurst Road. About Rs 2,000 and a few ornaments were collected on the spot. He was happy to find that they were able to secure the services of Krishnabai and Jasalakshmi Dalpatram Kavi as capable teachers. Both these women performed their duties towards the country.[18] There was another women's meeting where he could not go and had to be content by sending his message. That meeting was held under the auspices of Rashtriya Stree Samaj at Marwari Vidyalaya Hall with H.H. Nazli Begum Rafiya Sultana as the chairperson. Among the speakers were the Ali brothers and Sarojini Naidu. He conveyed that women should consider it a religious duty to use the charkha and khadi, although they might have to suffer inconvenience.[19]

On 25 June, he was presented with a purse of Rs 1,100 by the primary school teachers at Cutchi Dasa Oswal Jain Mahajanwadi, Khadak. He also attended a meeting of the Bhavsar community at Kanji Khetsey's Wadi, Modikhana. He was given a purse of Rs 1,600 by the Bhavsar community, and an amount of about Rs 1,000 was collected on the spot. On 26 June, he visited Santacruz, where a sum of Rs 40,000 was given to him. He was presented with a purse of about Rs 500,000 by the merchants and residents of Mandvi at New Chinch Bunder Road. A sum of about Rs 75,000 in addition was collected on the spot. He was welcomed by the shoemakers and cobblers of Bombay at Kazipura near Two Tanks, and a sum of Rs 2,000 was presented to him.[20]

As the deadline of 30 June approached, Gandhi and his team were charged with the drive and verve to reach the target of fund collection by midnight. Hence, the activities caught up the speed of a whirlwind. At such meetings they advised people to donate generously, use swadeshi clothes, give national education to their children, and take up national work. Gandhi's special advice to women was to give up luxurious habits, get engaged in picketing in front of shops selling liquor and foreign cloth, and propagate the idea of swadeshi.

It is interesting to have a look at his activities of 30 June. It has been reported that a sum of Rs 45,000 was presented at Borivali and of Rs 12,000 at Malad, and on 1 July at Bandra, he received Rs 15,000. To raise Rs 10 million by midnight, Gandhi visited the Mangaldas cloth market with the Ali brothers and Sarojini Naidu where he was given a purse of about Rs 35,000. Shaukat Ali put up a Khilafat note of Re 1 for auction that fetched Rs 1,001 from a Muslim merchant. Thereafter, Gandhi and his followers attended a meeting of the Lohanas at Daryasthan, Mandvi. About 3,000 people, including around 800 women, were present. The Lohana community presented a sum of Rs 110,000. A sum of about Rs 1,000 was collected on the spot. The Bombay jewellers met in a shamiana pitched in the compound of the Pannalal Terraces, Grant Road, to present a sum to Gandhi in aid of the fund. Almost 10,000 people, including about 500 women, attended. A sum of about Rs 232,000 was presented by Gulabchand Devchand together with an address that was written out on a khadi handkerchief and contained a prayer that God would help Gandhi in reaching the goal of swaraj to which they all aspired. Most of the jewellers of Bombay subscribed, although some prominent ones did not attend the meeting. Revashankar Jagjivan subscribed Rs 25,000 and exerted his influence to induce the others to subscribe. An amount of about Rs 60,000 collected from small associations and bodies, including that of grass merchants, plumbers, and so forth, was also handed over at the time. Collections were also made on the spot, which brought the total to about Rs 300,000.

After that, Gandhi attended the meeting of the cotton merchants and brokers held at the Colaba Cotton Green. About 7,000 people, mostly Marwaris and other cotton merchants, attended. Mathuradas Vasanji Khimji gave an amount of about Rs 154,000 on behalf of the Colaba cotton merchants. A motor car valued at about Rs 12,000 was presented by one Durgadutji and put up for auction, but the highest bidder offered only Rs 6,500. It was, therefore, not knocked down and remained a part of the assets of the Swaraj Fund. Two bales of cotton were also put up for auction; the one on which Gandhi was sitting went for Rs 6,100; the other, not so pleasantly favoured, only fetched Rs 2,500. A sum of about Rs 10,000 was collected on the spot. About 2,000 residents of the Fort presented him with a sum of approximately Rs 150,000 at Kanji Khetsi's Wadi, Mint Road. The Parsis—numbering about 1,000 and headed by K.K. Suntoke, Barjori Framji Bharucha, and K.F. Nariman—met at Excelsior Theatre and presented a sum of Rs 30,000 as the contribution of the Parsi friends and admirers of Gandhi.

The members of the Swaraj Sabha Volunteer Corps and the other public workers presented a sum of Rs 5,000 through Shaukat Ali as Gandhi, hard-pressed for time, could not attend the meeting held at Chikhalwadi, Grant Road. A public meeting under the auspices of the Mandvi District Congress Committee was held in a godown at Chinch Bunder Road, Mandvi, attended by about 10,000 people. Admission to this meeting was through tickets worth Rs 2 and Re 1 each. Speeches advising the use of swadeshi instead of foreign cloth and the adoption of the charkha were made by Gandhi, the Ali brothers, and Sarojini Naidu.

A sum of about Rs 100,000 was given to Gandhi along with some collections on the spot and a few ornaments. On 1 July, he visited Bandra in the morning with Sarojini Naidu. A sum of about Rs 15,000 was presented to him. In the evening, he was presented with another sum of about Rs 400 by the Dalits of Walpakhadi, Mazagaon. About 3,000 people attended.[21]

Gandhi was overwhelmed with the generosity of the people. He took a special note of the contribution by the Parsis. He stated: 'I wish also to testify that, during the collection week in Bombay, not a day has passed without Parsi donations. Parsi ladies and gentlemen are also making door to door collections. Parsis are also working as pickets. Among the news-papers, too, not all the Parsi papers are hostile to the movement.'[22] He further said, 'If Bombay was beautiful, if Bombay was noted for its generosity, if Bombay was noted for its public spirit, it was due to the Parsi community. If it were not for the Parsis, Bombay would be like any other city in India.'[23]

It is interesting to note that the figures given by the *Bombay Chronicle* of 1 July 1921 differed slightly from those in the official account. According to it, the rich merchants at the Cotton Green gave about Rs 400,000 to Gandhi. The piece-goods dealers comprised another group of business that contributed to the fund, and Gandhi told them it was they who had made possible the Bezwada promise regarding the Tilak Swaraj Fund. The *jhaveris* (jewellers) alone contributed Rs 300,000, presumably under the prompting of the pearl merchant and shroff Seth Gulabchand Devchand, who also contributed his house, Shanti Bhavan, to the movement.[24]

The administration of the fund was as important as its collection. A private meeting of the council of the BPCC was held at 5.15 pm (for about one-and-a-half hours) on 3 July at the hall of the Presidency Association to meet Gandhi and consider his proposals for the administration of the Tilak Swaraj Fund. Among those present, besides Gandhi, were S. Banker, M.B. Velkar, N.D. Savarkar, D.D. Sathaye, V.A. Desai, L.R. Tairsee, Sarojini Naidu, Jivraj G. Nensey, Umar Sobani, B.N. Meisheri, P.G. Sahasrabudhe, Revashankar Jagjivan, K.G. Sanzgiri, Govindji Vasanji, and Moazamali. Two resolutions proposed by Gandhi were discussed and passed unanimously. First, Jamnalal Bajaj, Umar Sobani, L.R. Tairsee, Velji Lakhamsi Napoo, A. Godrej, Raghavji Purshotam, and Revashankar Jagjivan were appointed as trustees of the Tilak Swaraj Fund collections made in the city of Bombay. Second, the amount collected for the fund in Bombay was to be spent only for national education, home industries, famine, elevation of the suppressed classes, and temperance. It was decided that the money collected in Bombay City would not be utilized for any purpose outside the Presidency of Bombay unless the A.I.C.C. made a recommendation to that effect and such recommendation received the approval of the Bombay Provincial Committee.[25]

The outcome of the large-heartedness and kindness of the people of Bombay was outstanding: a sum of about 375,000 was collected for the Tilak Swaraj Fund from the city.[26] Bombay's generosity earned the city the sobriquet 'the beautiful' by Gandhi. Writing in *Young India* on 6 July 1921 under the heading 'Bombay the Beautiful', he said: 'Bombay is beautiful, not for its big buildings for most of them hide squalid poverty and dirt, not for its wealth for most of it is derived from the blood of the masses, but for its world-renowned generosity. The Parsis set the tone, and Bombay has ever lived up to her reputation.'[27] He further said, 'Bombay's charity has covered a multitude of her sins. In respect of the Tilak Swaraj Fund, Bombay has beaten her past records. Between the sixteenth and the thirtieth June, she subscribed at the rate of two lakhs and a half per day. She enabled

India to keep her promise.'[28] He drew attention to the fact that
'[t]he subscription is but a milestone on the journey. The crore
cannot give us swaraj, not the riches of the whole world can
give it. Before we can be wholly free, we must be economically
independent.' He then said that the burden of boycott had to be
principally borne by Bombay, just the way the city had borne
the largest part of the financial obligation. A complete boycott
of foreign cloth was required to achieve swaraj, and Bombay's
responsibility in this context was heavy. 'Bombay the Beautiful
has a golden opportunity. She must add to her beauty, or be
prepared to lose what she has.'[29]

## Boycott of Foreign Cloth and Bonfire

After the successful completion of the Tilak Swaraj Fund
project, Gandhi concentrated his attention on the issue of
boycott of foreign cloth. There was no vindictive motive behind
such boycott; it was an essential component of the movement
along with spinning that was a tool for the nation's economic
regeneration. Gandhi suggested a complete boycott of foreign
cloth before 1 August, the death anniversary of Tilak. He cancelled
his plan to go to Madras, as he considered it necessary to be in
Bombay to manage the boycott campaign. He also suggested that
the meeting of the A.I.C.C., which was to be held in Lucknow
on 22 July, should be held in Bombay, as he did not want to leave
Bombay during the month, not even for that short period. He
called the important piece-goods merchants to his house and
tried to persuade them to sign a declaration that they would not
import foreign piece goods henceforth, and that whatever stocks
they might have on hand would be disposed of outside India.
Some merchants such as Narandas Purshotam, Narotam Bhanji,
Raghavji Purshotam, Naranji Dayal, Dwarkadas Govardhandas,

and Mansukhlal Oghadbhai signed the undertaking not to import foreign piece goods.[30]

A committee with the Bombay merchant L.R. Tairsee as its convener and some prominent leaders such as Lala Lajpat Rai, N.C. Kelkar, Hasrat Mohani, and Shankarlal Banker met in Bombay in July 1921 and recommended the boycott of all foreign cloth not only to free India from foreign exploitation but also as one of the means to get swaraj. After considering its report, the A.I.C.C. decided to concentrate on the boycott of foreign cloth and its substitution by indigenous and preferably handspun and hand-woven khadi.[31]

Two meetings in support of the movement were held in Bombay on 16 and 17 July in which Gandhi and Mohammed Ali spoke. Gandhi also addressed the Jains on 15 July at the Jain temple, Lalbag, and the handloom weavers on 17 July at Madanpura at Yusuff Bagh, Ripon Road. Under the auspices of the Parsi Rajkiya Sabha, a meeting of liquor contractors—both Parsis and Hindu Bhandaris—was also held on 19 July at the Marwari Vidyalaya Hall.[32]

On 19 July, he gave a speech in Hindustani at the meeting held at Mrs Haji Yusuf Sobani's bungalow at Nepean Sea Road in the afternoon; the meeting was attended by more than 500 Muslim women. He advised women to give up luxury, wear khadi, and spin for swaraj and the Khilafat.[33] On 23 July, he gave a lecture at Madanpura on the life work of Tilak and paid tribute to his fearlessness, self-sacrifice, and simplicity, the qualities necessary to gain swaraj.[34]

The movement to induce merchants to boycott foreign cloth had caught momentum in July. Leaflets were distributed in the city, advising people to discard foreign cloth and wear khadi. Gandhi addressed a meeting of volunteers at Morarji Gokuldas Hall and spoke on swadeshi at another meeting at

Hirjee Govindji's godown, Mandvi, on 21 July.[35] Umar Sobani was reported to have given clothes worth Rs 30,000. Two of the several meetings organized in connection with the boycott of foreign cloth were held at Chowpatty on 27 and 29 July 1921 in which most of the leaders who had been in Bombay to attend the A.I.C.C. meeting addressed the people, numbering about 3,000 to 4,000, on the boycott of foreign cloth.[36]

A historic meeting inaugurating the swadeshi campaign with a bonfire of foreign clothes was held near the Elphinstone Mill at Parel on 31 July 1921. Printed copies of Gandhi's speech were distributed in advance at the meeting and the translation was published in the newspapers. He said:

I regard this day as sacred for Bombay. We are removing today a pollution from our bodies. We are purifying ourselves by discarding foreign cloth which is the badge of our slavery. We attain today fitness to enter the Temple of Freedom (swaraj). Some say that destruction of discarded clothing is a token of anger and ill-will. Whether it is or not depends upon the point of view from which we burn such clothes. Why should we bear ill-will towards the English, the Americans, the Japanese or the French? They will continue to dump down their cloth in our midst as long as we choose to buy it. Therefore, if we are angry, we should vent our anger against ourselves. We shall cease to think ill of foreign nations when we have ceased to be tempted by foreign fineries.... I am sure that the best method of perpetuating Lokamanya's memory is the attainment of swaraj. And swaraj is impossible without swadeshi. And the inauguration of swadeshi can only be signalized by a complete and permanent boycott of foreign cloth. Hence I look upon the ceremony of burning as a sacrament. And I consider myself fortunate that the sacred ceremony is to be performed by me.[37]

A large crowd witnessed this first bonfire of foreign cloth that was lit in the compound of Elphinstone Mill that belonged to Umar Sobani. A vivid description of the scene is recorded in a report. It states that the clothing was arranged circularly in a pile about 20 feet high from which were draped saris of different colours. A good number of the A.I.C.C. members attended. There were roughly about 10,000 to 12,000 people present. According to the government report, the pile was not a very imposing one and consisted mainly of old clothes. Volunteers guarded the entrance to the mill compounds and everybody who entered had his headgear removed if it was not made of khadi. The crowd quietly dispersed after the bonfire and there was no disturbance of any kind. The Gandhi cap was very noticeable on this occasion.[38]

The actions of the people expressed their earnestness and enthusiasm. According to a report, clothes meant for the bonfire on 31 July at the Elphinstone Mills were displayed at the Ashoka building. They included new and expensive clothes given by Umar Sobani, a very expensive sari by M.R. Jayakar's family, and newly bought clothes worth Rs 1,200 from Asquith & Lords by Mansukhlal Oghadbhai.[39]

The day of 31 July was an assiduous and active one for Gandhi. He was present in the meeting of the working committee. He inaugurated the khadi exhibition organized by the Rashtriya Stree Sabha at Rambaug on C.P. Tank. He also visited the spinning classes at Madanpura. He gave a speech on swadeshi to Kutchi Dasha Oswal community at Mandvi Mahajan Wadi. He also spoke on swadeshi at a meeting held in the compound of Motisha's Jain temple at Byculla. In the course of his speech, Gandhi said that the charkha was their sword with which they must fight the battle of swaraj and win it for their country. He exhorted people to wear khadi, spin charkha, and propagate swadeshi. He told them that their salvation depended only on swadeshi.[40]

It is interesting that Gandhi also found time to attend the CWC meeting at Mani Bhavan on 31 July at 8.30 am to consider

the resolution related to the recent A.I.C.C. elections held in
Bengal and Madras.[41]

There was a huge meeting on 1 August at Chowpatty on
the spot where Tilak was cremated a year before. In his speech,
Gandhi recorded the presence of 200,000 men and women at
Sobani's mill compound on 31 July and called it 'a soul-stirring
sight'. He further said: 'Bombay the Beautiful lit yesterday a
fire which must remain ever alive even as in a Parsi temple and
which must continually burn all our pollutions as yesterday
we burnt our greatest outward pollution, namely, our foreign
clothing. Let it be a token of our determination never to touch
foreign cloth.'[42] Bombay's example in swadeshi, symbolized by
the bonfire, created waves throughout India. Perhaps this was the
first bonfire of foreign cloth.[43]

Under the auspices of the Parsi Rajkiya Sabha, a public
meeting presided over by Gandhi was held in Excelsior Theatre
on 2 August in aid of the Smyrna Relief Fund. Entry was by
ticket. About 3,000 people—Muslims, Parsis, and Hindus—were
present. Gandhi, Lala Lajpat Rai, Sarojini Naidu, Hales, Yakub
Hasan, K.F. Nariman, K.K. Suntoke, Marmaduke Pickthall, and
the Ali brothers addressed the meeting.[44]

The visit of the prince was being arranged by the government
despite severe opposition from the people and the Congress and
at a time when India was 'seething with discontent'. The CWC,
which met in Bombay on 5 October 1921, opined that every
government employee, military or civilian, should withdraw
from government service. As the day of the landing of the prince
drew nearer, Gandhi provided guidelines to the people:

What are we to do in the circumstances? We must organize a complete
boycott of all functions held in the Prince's honour. We must religiously
refrain from attending charities, fetes or fireworks organized for the

purpose. We must refuse to illuminate or to send our children to see the organized illuminations. To this end we must publish leaflets by the million and distribute them amongst the people telling them what their duty in the matter is and it would be true honour done to the Prince if Bombay on the day of his landing wears the appearances of a deserted city. But we must isolate the Prince from the person. We have no ill-will against the Prince as man. He probably knows nothing of the feeling in India, he probably knows nothing about repression.... Any injury or insult to the Prince by us will be a greater wrong done by us to Islam and India than any the English have done.[45]

The next instance of bonfire of foreign clothes took place on the evening of 9 October in the compound of the Elphinstone Mill. The enthusiasm of the people was matched by their overwhelming numbers. From early afternoon, people were moving towards the Elphinstone Road, clothed in khadi, and later in the evening, it was impossible to pass along the Elphinstone Bridge and its precincts. But the meeting, despite such a large crowd, was extremely orderly, perhaps the most orderly of all the meetings of this kind in Bombay. The entire crowd was quiet all throughout, and for this, a great deal of credit was due to the large number of volunteers. In the middle of the area, a large platform was erected for the leaders, and near it, the foreign clothes that had been collected during the past few days were arranged in the shape of a pyramid. All sorts of clothes of foreign make were there— expensive silk saris, brocades, costly coats, shirts, hats, and in fact everything that was considered necessary up until this time was there thrown in a heap. The heap was well-arranged, soaked in kerosene, and mixed with crackers. Sarojini Naidu presided over the meeting, and before the meeting, Gandhi moved the principle, and the only, resolution supported by various leaders such as Lala Lajpat Rai, Maulana Azad, Sobani, Babu Rajendra, and so forth. Gandhi's speech was full of pathos and it moved all who were present. He had tears in his eyes—so moved was he by sorrow at the failure on people's part in doing their duty towards the country. The Mahatma lighted the heap of foreign clothing, and it burned on merrily amidst the loud noise of crackers and bursting flames. The sight was extremely impressive: the vast audiences, the burning clothes, and the passionate speakers under God's sky in the growing night.[46]

The city's spirited atmosphere helped maintain the tempo of the activities. For instance, it was reported on 31 October that Shankarlal Banker had published about 2,000 copies of a poster in Marathi and Gujarati, which contained Gandhi's message to the people of Bombay. These posters were displayed at conspicuous places in the city. About 50 students of the

**Figure 4.3** A poster in the *Bombay Chronicle* announcing the second bonfire of foreign cloth that took place on 9 October 1921 at the Elphinstone Mill compound in Bombay.
*Source*: The Asiatic Society of Mumbai.

Gazi Mustafa Kemal Pasha Muslim High School went around several mohallas in the city on 26 and 27 October, collecting foreign clothes and distributing handbills titled 'Khilafat and Mahatma Gandhi's Message'. They collected a large number of old clothes.[47]

The third bonfire of foreign cloth was arranged on 17 November, yet again in the Elphinstone Mill compound; Gandhi presided over it. The Prince of Wales landed in Bombay the same day. Gandhi, in his speech, emphasized that it was important for the people to believe in non-violence, swadeshi, and Hindu–Muslim unity.[48] More than 25,000 people attended the event. Speeches were made by Gandhi, Maulana Abdul Kadir, Azad, Sobani, and Pandit Nekiram Sharma. In spite of appeals by the non-cooperators to observe a hartal on that day, there was no general hartal. After the prince's procession had passed, a local train with large crowds wearing Gandhi caps was seen coming from the north of the city. This train presumably carried back crowds who had been at the Elphinstone Mill. They alighted at Charni Road and Marine Lines and insulted those who were returning home after attending the prince's state procession. At around 12.30 pm, disorder spread in the city, which synchronized with the arrival of the crowds from the Elphinstone Mill.[49] South Bombay was the focus of the events, where trainloads of Congress and Khilafat volunteers returning from the bonfire disembarked at Marine Lines and Charni Road railway stations and found themselves face-to-face with Parsis and Europeans leaving the route of the prince's procession. Full-scale rioting broke out across the city from Tardeo and Girgaum in the west to the lower reaches of Parel Road. Stones were thrown at cars and trams and decorations were dragged down and burnt. The situation deteriorated rapidly the next day.[50] Violent disturbances broke out and crowds went out of control.

**Figure 4.4**  Volunteers going for a meeting in Parel.
*Source*: Mani Bhavan Gandhi Sangrahalaya.

Gandhi, after a round in the city, was shocked and anguished
to find that peaceful passengers in the tramcars were molested,
two tramcars and a motor car were burnt, liquor shops were
smashed, and two badly wounded policemen were lying
unconscious on cots without anybody caring for them. He went
around the troubled areas with other leaders to quench the thirst
for bloodshed. He went to Bhendi Bazaar with Maulana Azad and
Sobani, reasoned with the crowd, and told them that they were
insulting their religion by hurting innocent men. The inmates of
the shop were able to come out because of the efforts of Pandit
Nekiram Sharma and others. Six Hindu and Muslim volunteers
had come back to Gandhi with their heads smashed and bleeding
heavily. They had gone to Parel led by Maulana Azad, Sobani,
and Mouzam Ali to pacify the agitated crowd. They, however,

were unable to proceed to their destination. Gandhi was greatly perturbed after witnessing the unfortunate disturbances in the city and harassment of the Parsis and others who had gone to welcome the prince. Giving the details of the happenings and disturbances in the city, he wrote:

The reputation of Bombay, the hope of my dreams, was being stained yesterday even whilst in my simplicity I was congratulating the citizens upon their non-violence in the face of grave provocation.... I confess my inability to conduct a campaign of civil disobedience to a successful issue unless a completely non-violent spirit is generated among the people. I am sorry for the conclusion.... If I can have nothing to do with the organized violence of the Government, I can have less to do with the unorganized violence of the people. I would prefer to be crushed between the two.[51]

Gandhi called back his son Devdas to Bombay on 19 November and said that the latter had been brought on purpose. He was to be sent out as a 'sacrifice' for slaughter by the rioters, should a fresh outbreak occur in the neighbouring areas.[52]

Gandhi, in penance, announced a fast from 19 November onwards until peace was restored in the city. On 21 November 1921, Gandhi broke his fast in the midst of a gathering of cooperators, non-cooperators, Hindus, Muslims, Christians, and Parsis. He stressed that permanent friendship among all communities can be established only if all concerned would incessantly strive to build it up.[53]

A meeting of the CWC was called on 22 and 23 November 1921. It was held at Mani Bhavan on 23 November. The members agreed that the disturbances in Bombay were a setback to the activities of the non-cooperators. The working committee also warned all the provincial Congress committees against embarking upon mass civil disobedience without ensuring a peaceful atmosphere.[54]

Gandhi appealed to the citizens of Bombay for peace and called
for amity among the Hindus, Muslims, Parsis, and Christians. He
and his colleagues such as Azad, Sobani, M.P. Jayakar, Jamnadas
Mehta, Sathe, Mouzam Ali, Sarojini Naidu, and Pandit Nekiram
Sharma worked hard to restore peace. He believed that violence
undermined the causes of the Khilafat, Punjab, and swaraj. He
also commented:

The khadi cap came in for much attention during the late disturbance
in Bombay. Dr. Sathe was severely assaulted because he would not
surrender his khadi cap. Now I hear that sailors in the Fort forcibly
dispossessed many innocent wearers of their khadi caps. I can only hope
that this senseless persecution will stiffen the resolve of the nation and
that thousands will be prepared to die for the khadi cap which is fast
becoming a visible mark of swadeshi and swaraj.[55]

During the year 1921, the unrest among the people in Bombay
was on the rise due to awakening nationalism, escalating labour
unrest, strikes, and incarceration of the Ali brothers. The Moplah
outbreak in Malabar in 1921 was a blow to the Non-Cooperation
Movement and Hindu–Muslim unity. It disturbed the atmosphere
as nothing else had since the inauguration of non-cooperation.[56] It
is interesting, in this context, to refer to an open letter criticizing
Gandhi's policy. It was written by 'Non-violent Spirit' to the editor
of the *Times of India*. According to the writer, Gandhi could not
succeed in India as he did in South Africa because India was a
land of leaders while in South Africa he was the solitary leader.
Union there was possible among a few thousands bound by the
tie of common interest, but it was impossible in India among
millions separated by varying interests.[57] However, undaunted by
criticism, Gandhi continued his work. His call for swadeshi and

the boycott of foreign cloth attracted people from all strata. As S. Bhattacharya comments, the swadeshi and boycott programme of 1921 was a dramatic effort, however limited in scope (being confined primarily to cottons) and achievement, to sever the colonial–metropolitan nexus. As such, it had the support of the Indian bourgeoisie as well as the masses. However, the boycott programme did not mean the same thing to all men—the merchant, the petty trader, the cotton mill owner, and the Indian consumer. But overriding the short-term advantages and disadvantages was the long-term perspective of an anti-imperialist struggle.[58]

The outbreak of violence in Bombay, however, had disturbed Gandhi immensely. He wanted the guilty to come forward and confess their guilt. His appeal to the citizens of Bombay was, 'The easiest method of achieving peace is to give up the idea of complaining against one another in a court of law and to concentrate our attention upon preventive measures, so that there is no recurrence of such madness. And I hope that Bombay will retrieve her lost reputation by adopting these measures.'[59] Gandhi's immediate concern was peace in the city and his ultimate vision was that of freedom based on non-violence, tolerance, and love for all. In his opinion, 'The complete victory of non-violent non-cooperation will be possible only if we conquer the enemy inside us.'[60] He respected the rights of minorities and maintained that '[w]hat we want in a free India is not a dead level but a variety of opinion and conduct in which the sanest will prevail by the weight not of might but of right.'[61]

Gandhi wanted to identify completely with the deprived. He had given up material comforts long back. In 1921, he reduced his needs even further. On 22 September, he took a momentous decision in Madura to dress only in a loincloth and a chaddar whenever necessary, and on 31 October, he took a vow to spin half an hour every day before the second meal and forgo the meal

in case he failed to do so. His urge to identify with the poor was
intense. Sucheta Kriplani had observed, 'Gandhi knew India
better than most people, the real India, India of the poor and
the villages.'[62] He had before him the ideal of a just and humane
society rooted in the principles of truth and non-violence. The
ideal was magnificent, but the road was full of impediments with
the clouds of violence gathering over.

## Notes and References

1. *Young India* dated 22 September 1920 cited in *CWMG*, Vol. 18,
   pp. 270–3.
2. *Young India* dated 23 February 1921 cited in *CWMG*, Vol. 19, pp.
   383–5.
3. Kunte, *Source Material for a History of the Freedom Movement in
   India*, Vol. VI, pp. 51–2.
4. Kunte, *Source Material for a History of the Freedom Movement in
   India*, Vol. VI, p. 52–3.
5. Gordon, *Businessmen and Politics*, p. 167.
6. *Navajivan* dated 20 March 1921 cited in *CWMG*, Vol. 19, p. 460.
7. Kunte, *Source Material for a History of the Freedom Movement in
   India*, Vol. VI, p. 59.
8. The above details regarding the National Week are from Kunte,
   *Source Material for a History of the Freedom Movement in India*,
   Vol. VI, pp. 54–7.
9. *The Bombay Chronicle* dated 11 April 1921 cited in *CWMG*, Vol. 19,
   pp. 552–4.
10. *Navajivan* dated 14 April 1921 cited in *CWMG*, Vol. 19, p. 554.
11. 'Bombay Secret Abstract', 1921, p. 737, para 461(24) cited in Phatak,
    *Source Material for a History of the Freedom Movement in India*,
    Vol. III, Part I, p. 401.
12. *The Bombay Chronicle* dated 16 June 1921 cited in *CWMG*, Vol.
    20 (Delhi: Publications Division, Ministry of Information and
    Broadcasting, Government of India, 1966), pp. 233–6.

13. 'Bombay Secret Abstract', 1921, p. 866, para 511 (52) cited in B.G Kunte (ed.), *Source Material for a History of the Freedom Movement in India, Mahatma Gandhi in Maharashtra (1915–1946)*, Vol. IX (Bombay: Gazetteers Department, Government of Maharashtra, 1980), p. 99.

14. Dalal, *Gandhi*, p. 39.

15. *The Bombay Chronicle* dated 19 June 1921 cited in *CWMG*, Vol. 20, pp. 238–44.

16. *The Bombay Chronicle* dated 20 June 1921 cited in *CWMG*, Vol. 20, pp. 245–6.

17. 'Bombay Secret Abstract', 27 June 1921, p. 928, para 523 (38), Bombay City cited in Phatak, *Source Material for a History of the Freedom Movement in India*, Vol. III, Part I, pp. 412–14.

18. *CWMG*, Vol. 20, pp. 262–4; 'Bombay Secret Abstract', 27 June 1921, p. 928, para 523 (38), Bombay City cited in Phatak, *Source Material for a History of the Freedom Movement in India*, Vol. III, Part I, p. 414.

19. *The Bombay Chronicle* dated 23 June 1921 cited in *CWMG*, Vol. 20, pp. 264–5.

20. 'Bombay Secret Abstract', 27 June 1921, p. 928, para 523 (38), Bombay City cited in Phatak, *Source Material for a History of the Freedom Movement in India*, Vol. III, Part I, p. 414.

21. Details of the collection on 30 June and 1 July are taken from 'Bombay Secret Abstract', 4 July 1921, pp. 964–7, para 548 (14), Bombay City cited in Phatak, *Source Material for a History of the Freedom Movement in India*, Vol. III, Part I, pp. 415–17.

22. *CWMG*, Vol. 20, p. 286.

23. *CWMG*, Vol. 20, p. 307.

24. Gordon, *Businessmen and Politics*, pp. 166–7.

25. 'Bombay Secret Abstract', 4 July 1921, pp. 964–7, para 548 (14), Bombay City cited in Phatak, *Source Material for a History of the Freedom Movement in India*, Vol. III, Part I, pp. 417–18.

26. Kunte, *Source Material for a History of the Freedom Movement in India*, Vol. VI, p. 57.

27. *Young India* dated 6 July 1921 cited in *CWMG*, Vol. 20, p. 329.

28. *Young India* dated 6 July 1921 cited in *CWMG*, Vol. 20, p. 329.

29. *Young India* dated 6 July 1921 cited in *CWMG*, Vol. 20, pp. 330–1.

30. 'Bombay Secret Abstract', 7 July 1921, pp. 969–72, para 552 (A, B, C), Bombay City cited in Phatak, *Source Material for a History of the Freedom Movement in India*, Vol. III, Part I, pp. 418–19.

31. Nanda, *Gandhi*, pp. 263–4.

32. 'Bombay Secret Abstract', p. 1056, para 605 (3) and pp. 1065–7, para 608 (16) cited in Phatak, *Source Material for a History of the Freedom Movement in India*, Vol. III, Part I, p. 429.

33. *The Bombay Chronicle* dated 20 July 1921 cited in *CWMG*, Vol. 20, pp. 396–8; Dalal, *Gandhi*, p. 40.

34. 'Bombay Secret Abstract', 25 July 1921, p. 1117, para 652 (1), (4), (4) Bombay cited in Phatak, *Source Material for a History of the Freedom Movement in India*, Vol. III, Part I, p. 434.

35. Dalal, *Gandhi*, p. 40.

36. Kunte, *Source Material for a History of the Freedom Movement in India*, Vol. VI, p. 78.

37. *The Bombay Chronicle* dated 1 August 1921 cited in *CWMG*, Vol. 20, pp. 454–5.

38. Kunte, *Source Material for a History of the Freedom Movement in India*, Vol. VI, p. 78.

39. *Mahasabha Suvarna Mahotsava*, p. 7.

40. *The Bombay Chronicle* dated 1 August 1921 cited in *CWMG*, Vol. 20, p. 456; Dalal, *Gandhijini Dinwari*, p. 132.

41. 'Bombay Secret Abstracts', 1921 cited in *CWMG*, Vol. 20, p. 452.

42. *Young India* dated 4 August 1921 cited in *CWMG*, Vol. 20, p. 458.

43. Dalal, *Gandhijini Dinwari*, p. 132. It further mentions that the first bonfire of foreign cloth was on 28 February 1896 at Ahmednagar. There was another of foreign goods at Poona on 8 October 1905. At that time, only the 'British' was considered foreign.

44. 'Bombay Secret Abstract', 8 August 1921, p. 1183, para 706 (5), Bombay cited in Phatak, *Source Material for a History of the Freedom Movement in India*, Vol. III, Part I, p. 435. In its resolutions, the meeting expressed its horror over the atrocities committed by the Greek troops and their adherents in the homelands of the

Turkish race. In view of the prevailing boycott of the foreign cloth in India, it was resolved that, as much as possible, such discarded cloth should be sent to Turkey for the sufferers of the Greek aggression. It further expressed no-confidence in Great Britain's declaration of neutrality.

45. *Young India* dated 27 October 1921 cited in *CWMG*, Vol. 21 (Delhi: Publications Division, Ministry of Information and Broadcasting, Government of India, 1966), pp. 351–2.

46. Kunte, *Source Material for a History of the Freedom Movement in India*, Vol. VI, p. 79.

47. 'Bombay Secret Abstract', 31 October 1921, p. 1688, para 1147 (12), Bombay City cited in Kunte, *Source Material for a History of the Freedom Movement, Mahatma Gandhi in Maharashtra*, Vol. IX, p. 145.

48. *The Bombay Chronicle* dated 18 November 1921 cited in *CWMG*, Vol. 21, pp. 459–61.

49. Kunte, *Source Material for a History of the Freedom Movement in India*, Vol. VI, p. 85.

50. Richard Newman, *Workers and Unions in Bombay, 1918–1929: A Study of Organisation in the Cotton Mills*, Australian National University Monographs on South Asia 6 (Canberra: Australian National University, 1981), p. 98.

51. *Young India* dated 24 November 1921 cited in *CWMG*, Vol. 21, pp. 462–5.

52. D.G. Tendulkar, *Mahatma: Life of Mohandas Karamchand Gandhi (1920–1929)*, Vol. II (Bombay: Vithalbhai K. Jhaveri and D.G. Tendulkar, 1951), p. 93. Illustrations collected and arranged by Vithalbhai K. Jhaveri and D.G. Tendulkar.

53. *Navajivan* dated 24 November 1921 cited in *CWMG*, Vol. 21, pp. 475–7. According to Dalal, Gandhi ended his fast on 22 November. See Dalal, *Gandhi*, p. 43.

54. Kunte, *Source Material for a History of the Freedom Movement in India*, Vol. VI, pp. 92–3; *Gandhiji and Mani Bhavan* (New Delhi: Gandhi Smarak Nidhi, 1959), p. 20.

55. *Young India* dated 1 December 1921 cited in *CWMG*, Vol. 21, p. 507.

56. *CWMG*, Vol. 21, p. 70.

57. *The Times of India*, 24 November 1921.

58. S. Bhattacharya, 1976, 'Cotton Mills and Spinning Wheels: Swadeshi and the Indian Capitalist Class, 1920–22', *Economic & Political Weekly*, 11(47), p. 1833.

59. *Young India* dated 1 December 1921 cited in *CWMG*, Vol. 21, p. 486.

60. *Navajivan* dated 4 September 1921 cited in *CWMG*, Vol. 21, p. 49.

61. *Young India* dated 1 December 1921 cited in *CWMG*, Vol. 21, p. 501.

62. Usha Thakkar and Jayshree Mehta (eds), *Understanding Gandhi: Gandhians in Conversation with Fred J. Blum* (New Delhi: SAGE Publications, 2011), p. 428.

## 5

# INTERVENING YEARS: 1922–9

THE VIOLENCE THAT BROKE OUT IN CHAURI CHAURA IN THE UNITED
Province was a major setback to the movement. On 5 February
1922, a large group of protesters at Chauri Chaura turned violent
after police firing and retaliated by burning the police station,
killing more than 20 policemen. Saddened beyond words, Gandhi
suspended the movement. The dampening of people's zest and
enthusiasm was apparent in Bombay as in the whole nation.
However, the activities related to khadi continued throughout
the year and there was no important agitation in the city. Gandhi
had discussions with the leaders after his arrival in Bombay on
13 January. He presided over the working committee of the A.I.C.C.
that met at Mani Bhavan in the afternoon of 17 January 1922.[1]

A resolution of the working committee, presumably drafted by Gandhi, wanted the withdrawal of all notifications and notices prohibiting the formation of volunteer corps and declaring illegal public meetings, picketing, and other general activities of the Congress and the Khilafat committees. It also demanded the release of prisoners undergoing prosecution or conviction in respect of such notices. It also stated that the offensive civil disobedience contemplated at the Ahmedabad Congress will not be started until 31 January 1922 or pending the result of the negotiations undertaken by the committee appointed by the Malaviya Conference for a round table conference, whichever might be earlier.[2]

There was an apprehension of disturbance when Gandhi and Banker were arrested at Ahmedabad on 10 March 1922 for spreading disaffection by articles published in the *Young India* issues of 29 September 1921, 15 December 1921, and 23 February 1922.[3] The leaders and volunteers in Bombay were prompt in their response. Placards put up by the Congress and Khilafat committees advised the people to remain calm, and there was no sign of restlessness in the city. A public meeting was held on the night of 11 March 1922 in the Cutchi Dasa Oswal Jain Mahajanwadi with V.J. Patel presiding over it. About 600 people were present. K.P. Khadilkar, V.J. Patel, Jamnadas Mehta, and N.D. Upadhya advised people to keep quiet and not disturb the peace, and extolled the virtues of non-violence.[4]

# 1923

The rise of the Swaraj Party in early 1923 under the leadership of C.R. Das and Motilal Nehru created waves for a short time. The party was formed with the aims of contesting elections for the central and provincial assemblies and opposing the government measures from within the system. Its leaders, however, did not cut off their links with the Congress. The 'no-changers' or the orthodox members of the Congress wanted the original programme of non-cooperation to be strictly followed and opposed the entry to the councils. But the members of the Swaraj Party wanted to get elected and follow obstruction within the councils. Gandhi did not agree with the idea of entering the councils since it was inconsistent with non-cooperation. But he clarified that he would be 'no party to putting any obstacle in their way'.[5] He kept emphasizing the importance of constructive work. The Bombay branch of the Swaraj Party was formed, and by May, it had leaders such as V.J. Patel, Jamnadas Mehta, M.R. Jayakar, Purshottamdas Tricumdas, A.G. Mulgaonkar, and K. Natarajan. However, soon differences amongst the members began to surface.[6]

The political scene of the BMC was also changing. The new franchise contributed to the emergence of party politics. The 1923 elections largely crystallized into a contest between the Nationalist Municipal Party (NMP, led by Vithalbhai Patel) and the Progressive Party (led by H.P. Mody); they had different views on municipal matters and reforms. The NMP was closer to Gandhi's Congress. Some of the NMP's leading members such as Patel and K.F. Nariman were also members of the Bombay Swaraj Party.[7] Some leaders and some of Gandhi's supporters in the NMP, such as Patel, Jamnadas Mehta, Sarojini Naidu, D.D. Sathaye, Bachuben R. Lotwalla, and Chhotani were elected to the municipal corporation in January 1923. Prominent persons such as Avantikabai Gokhale and Umar Sobani were co-opted.[8]

In the last quarter of 1923, the NMP boycotted the functions to bid farewell to the outgoing governor Sir George Lloyd and to welcome the incoming governor Sir Leslie Wilson. It held protest meetings on the Chowpatty sands and other places the day before the outgoing governor's departure.[9]

Bombay responded enthusiastically to Nagpur flag satyagraha (May–August 1923). This satyagraha was launched under the leadership of Jamnalal Bajaj to exercise the right to hoist the national flag against the restrictions imposed by the British rule. Many volunteers went to Nagpur from Bombay. The Bombay Grain Merchants' Association, the Gold and Silver Satta Bazar, and Marwadi Bazar marked their protest by closing for a day. In the beginning of July, miniatures of the national flag for wearing on Gandhi caps and shirt buttons were sold to the public by the Bhuleshwar District Congress Committee at one pice each. Flag processions were organized in the city. Two peaceful processions were organized on 18 July—which was also observed as the Gandhi Day—one in the morning (1,500 people marched with flags from the Congress office to Madhav Baug) and the other in the evening (5,000 people, including 500 women, with flags marched from Chowpatty to Madhav Baug). Before joining the procession in the evening, women had a meeting at the Marwari Vidyalaya Hall; Kasturba presided over it. Among those convicted in connection with the Nagpur satyagraha were many volunteers from Bombay.[10]

## 1924

Gandhi was charged with promoting disaffection against the government through his writings in *Young India*. He was sentenced to a six-year imprisonment and taken to the Yerwada prison in March 1922. He suffered acute pain in the stomach there and was operated for appendicitis by Dr Maddock. The day of 18 January was observed throughout the presidency and Sind as a day of prayer for the recovery and release of Gandhi. Five meetings were held in Bombay city alone for this purpose—the meeting of the Chowpatty sands attended by around 5,000 people.

Thereafter, he was released unconditionally on 5 February 1924. The news of his release brought joy to the people. The rejoicing Share Bazar was closed. The sharebrokers collected Rs 500 on the spot to feed the cows. Sweets were also distributed. The Bullion Bazar and a few cotton associations at Sheikh Memon Street also stopped business.[11]

Gandhi stayed for a few days in Sassoon Hospital at Poona and arrived in Bombay on 11 March 1924. He stayed at Narottam Morarji's bungalow 'Palm Van' in Juhu for convalescence until 28 May following his disciplined routine of getting up very early, offering prayers, reading, walking, attending to correspondence and visitors, and seeing political and other friends as well as a large number of visitors. Walks along the seashore found a special place in his routine. Shantikumar Morarji recorded a delightful incident of this period: 'Sir Ness Wadia, Sir Cowasji Jehangir and other mill owners called on Gandhiji. In the course of the talk Sir Cowasji referred to him as "Gandhi Seth" which aroused amusement. Correcting his mistake, Sir Cowasji said, "I mean Mahatma Seth." There was a roar of laughter.'[12]

It was during his stay at Juhu that Gandhi wrote, on 2 April 1924, the preface of his book *Satyagraha in South Africa*. He elaborated the importance and meaning of satyagraha by giving the context of the abolition of Viramgam customs, ending of indentured labour, the Champaran Satyagraha, struggles of the mill hands in Ahmedabad, struggle in Kheda, satyagraha against the Rowlatt Act, and the struggle to set right the Khilafat and Punjab wrongs and to win swaraj. According to Gandhi, satyagraha came up to oneself, one need not go out searching for it.[13]

Gandhi decided to resume the editorship of *Young India* and *Navajivan* from the first week of April 1924. For the convenience of the readers of these papers, an arrangement was made to open a branch office at Princess Street opposite Ashoka stores, where the copies of these papers were made available for sale.[14]

Gandhi's visit to Mumbai from the end of August to the first week of September in 1924 was hectic. He arrived from Ahmedabad at the Grant Road railway station in Bombay on the morning of 29 August 1924. It was raining, and there were about 50 people headed by Sarojini Naidu and Jivraj G. Nensey, the secretary of the BPCC, to receive him. They went to Mani Bhavan from the station. The same evening the BMC's address to Gandhi was presented at Sir Cowasji Jehangir Hall. The hall, with a capacity of 1,200, was packed to the fullest despite the rainy season. About 2,000 people had to wait outside. After the reading of the corporation's address, Gandhi made a short speech, first in Gujarati and then in English. The proceeding lasted for only half an hour, both the address and the reply being brief.[15] V.J. Patel was, at that time, the mayor of the corporation and K.F. Nariman the leader of the NMP. The corporation had presented such address earlier to Dadabhai Naoroji. It expressed joy at Gandhi's recovery from illness and appreciated his invaluable services. In his reply, Gandhi elaborated the importance of the spinning wheel and the need to have unity among Hindus, Muslims, Parsis, Christians, Jews, and others and to remove untouchability among the Hindus. He reiterated that '[f]or me the humanitarian service, or rather service of all that lives, is religion. And I draw no distinction between such religion and politics. Indeed I cannot conceive a life full of service without its touching politics.' He invited all those present to join him in his work. It is interesting to note what he said at the outset: 'I need offer no apology for my having addressed you first in my mother tongue. But as Bombay is an essentially cosmopolitan city, it is but meet that I should give you the substance of my reply in English also.'[16]

On 30 August, Gandhi visited the National School at Princess Street and spoke on khadi and the spinning wheel. From there he went to a women's meeting at 4 pm in the Marwari Vidyalaya Hall under the auspices of the Rashtriya Stree Sabha. Sarojini Naidu presided over this meeting attended by about 500 women. On this occasion two purses were handed over to Gandhi, one amounting to Rs 1,000 from the Bhuleshwar District Congress Committee and the other amounting to Rs 4,536 from the Rashtriya Stree Sabha. A collection of about Rs 500 was taken for the Malabar flood victims.[17]

On 31 August, Gandhi presided over a prize distribution ceremony of the Girls' National School (Lokmanya Kanyashala) at the Muzaffarabad Hall where about 150 scholars and 150 parents and guardians were present. Naidu gave away the prizes. The principal, Tulaskar, described their difficulties that had resulted in the reduction in their numbers from 370 to 150. Gandhi expressed his satisfaction at seeing four Dalit boys being educated in the school. He appealed to the people to show their faith in the removal of untouchability by continuing to send their children to the school.[18]

A large public meeting was organized by the Parsi Rajkiya Sabha at Excelsior Theatre on the morning of Sunday, 31 August. The meeting had two objects: the first was to honour Gandhi and the second to raise money for Malabar relief. Admission to the meeting was by way of tickets, from the sale of which an amount of nearly Rs 4,000 was collected. In addition, M.R. Jayakar contributed Rs 1000 and other contributions amounting to Rs. 1,000 were also received. There were about 1,500 people present at the meeting. Jayakar, Vimadalal, Pickthall, Jamnadas Dwarkadas, B.F. Bharucha, Sarojini Naidu, and others praised Gandhi. The audience expressed their displeasure at Jamnadas Dwarkadas since he referred to the guest of honour as 'Gandhiji'

instead of 'Mahatma', and when it was Gandhi's turn to speak, he
vigorously upbraided the audience for their conduct.[19]

Gandhi addressed public meetings at Vile Parle and
Mandvi on 2 September 1924.[20] On the same day he visited the
khadi bhandar at Princess Street. In the evening, he paid a brief
visit to the National Medical College where he appealed for khadi
and for contributions to the institution. Later that evening he
attended a meeting organized in his honour by the BPCC, which
was held in the godown of Ramchandra Ramvallabh in Dhana
Bunder. Sarojini Naidu presided over this meeting of about 5,000
people. Gandhi left Bombay by the night train on 3 September for
Poona and arrived back at Dadar on the morning of 5 September
where he visited the Ganpati Mandap and addressed an audience
of 500.[21]

Gandhi undertook a 21-day fast starting from 17 September
1924 at Delhi for self-purification against communal disharmony.
The city of Bombay felt concerned about it. On the day preceding
the breaking of his fast, the Mandvi District Congress Committee
had organized a procession to celebrate the termination of the
week of special prayers observed by the Jains of the locality in
their temple at Kharak Bazar. These prayers were offered from
1 to 7 October to ask for more strength to Gandhi to enable him
to face the ordeal. The procession consisted of about 500 people,
some of whom carried posters bearing the words such as 'Hindu–
Muslim Unity' and 'Wear Khaddar'.[22]

Gandhi returned to Bombay from Delhi on 20 November.
He held discussions at his residence at Gamdevi with various
leaders. The main point underlying the discussion was the
alteration of the Congress programme in such a way as to bring
on the Congress platform all the parties that had seceded from it.
The issues regarding the differences between the liberals and the
swarajists and non-cooperation were important. The Congress

president Mohammed Ali opened the All Parties Conference on 21 November at the Muzaffarabad Hall. Sir Dinshaw Petit, who did not belong to any party, chaired the meeting. Nearly 275 members of the A.I.C.C., about 200 people from different political parties, and about 50 people who did not belong to any party, such as solicitors, doctors, and merchants, attended the conference. Prominent amongst those present were Gandhi, Mohammed Ali, Shaukat Ali, Annie Besant, Sarojini Naidu, Lady Emmily Lutyens, Sastri, Dinshaw Petit, Motilal Nehru, C.Y. Chintamani, B.S. Kamat, V.J. Patel, Vallabhbhai J. Patel, M.A. Jinnah, M.R. Jayakar, C.R. Das, G.B. Deshpande, A.N. Surve, B.C. Pal, J.B. Petit, Jamnadas Dwarkadas, Kanji Dwarkadas, Sir Purshottam Thakordas, C.R. Reddy, S. Satyamurthy, K.P. Khadilkar, K.F. Nariman, B.N. Motiwala, K. Natarajan, Pickthall, B. Chakravarti, Sethna, Dr Sukhia, Dr Ansari, Abdul Kalam Azad, Hakim Ajmal Khan, S.A. Brelvi, M.K. Patel, and N.D. Savarkar.[23] Leaflets in Gujarati protesting against the aforementioned conference and condemning the attitude of Gandhi and Mohammed Ali towards the Sanatan Hindus were distributed in the vicinity of the conference hall. Gandhi was criticized for favouring the abolition of untouchability and for his support to khadi, charkha, and the Khilafat.[24]

The A.I.C.C. met on 23 November at the Muzaffarabad Hall to consider the Gandhi–Das–Nehru pact (that was arrived at earlier at Calcutta). Mohammed Ali presided over the meeting and about 200 members attended. Gandhi made it clear that there should not be any amendment; it should be accepted or rejected in toto. Eventually, it was accepted. It paved the way for political unification of the members of the Congress and the Swaraj Party.[25]

Gandhi continued with his efforts to keep all the communities and various sections of society together.

On 23 November, a mammoth meeting of 4,000 people of Bombay was presided over by Sarojini Naidu. It was held on the Chowpatty sands under the joint auspices of the BPCC, the Central Khilafat Committee, the Rashtriya Stree Sabha, the Parsi Rajkiya Sabha, the national Home Rule League, and the Bombay Swaraj Party. Gandhi, C.R. Das, Hakim Ajmal Khan, Shaukat Ali, Avantikabai Gokhale, and Sarojini Naidu addressed the audience, and eulogized the services of Bi Amma (the mother of the Ali brothers) for India. They exhorted the people to follow in her footsteps and to win swaraj for their country.[26] On 31 December 1924, Gandhi also attended the meeting of the All-India Muslim League at Globe Theatre, Sandhurst Road.[27]

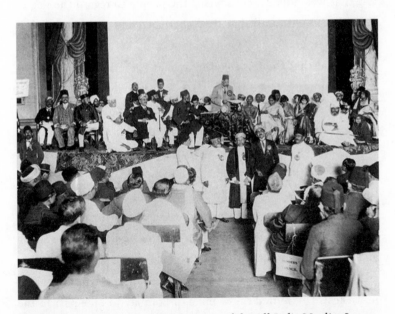

**Figure 5.1** Gandhi at the annual session of the All-India Muslim League at Globe Theatre, Bombay, on 31 December 1924.
*Source*: Vithalbhai Jhaveri Collection/Dinodia Photos.

# 1925

Gandhi visited Bombay in 1925 for the opening of the Congress House and other meetings. He arrived from Madras on the morning of 26 March. He was presented an address of welcome at a meeting of the depressed classes. S.V. Puntambekar translated the Hindi speech in Marathi. Gandhi said that the Vycom Satyagraha was offered to open the eyes of caste Hindus.[28] He then formally opened the Congress House before a gathering of about 400 people by hoisting the national flag. Prayers showering blessing on the Congress House were offered by a Parsi priest, a maulvi, an Indian Christian minister, a Sikh, and a Sanatanist. Gandhi made a short speech in Gujarati, explaining the unique occasion of opening the Congress House and the significance of maintaining, at the cost of one's life, the prestige of the national flag that was hoisted. He advised the people to regard the flag as an embodiment of all that they cherished and honoured just as Englishmen did.[29]

He said that the flag hoisting meant something more than a mere ceremony. Once the flag was hoisted, it should never be lowered no matter what happened, even if they all had to die for it. He drew the attention of the audience to the important fact that the house was purchased out of the Tilak Swaraj Fund, to which Bombay was the largest contributor. The house was consecrated to the Congress work and he asked them all to take advantage of the building.[30] He had also addressed a meeting of about 200 women that met under the auspices of the Rashtriya Stree Sabha and was presided over by Sarojini Naidu at the Congress House and had appealed to them to take to khadi and the spinning wheel in earnest. He invited the women of Bombay to take part in the national functions that were to be held in the Congress House, which would be the centre of all national activities in this city.

The women of Bombay had given him much, but he asked them to give him something more for the country and that was: to devote half-an-hour daily.[31]

During the National Week, about half-a-dozen volunteers hawked khadi in the morning, and in the evening, a public meeting was organized on 13 April 1925, held under the auspices of the BPCC at the Congress House, Girgaum, to observe the Jallianwala Bagh Day. Sarojini Naidu presided over the meeting. About 1,000 people attended and Sarojini Naidu, V.J. Patel, K.P. Khadilkar, Shaukat Ali, and Gandhi gave speeches. V.J. Patel deplored the prevailing state of political lethargy and wrangling between the parties. Gandhi replied to V.J. Patel's criticism of the spinning franchise and once again emphasized that without the threefold programme (of Hindu–Muslim unity, removal of untouchability, and adoption of khadi), it was impossible to achieve swaraj. He was ready to resort to satyagraha at any time if he believed that the people were prepared for it, but he knew well that the country was not ready at that time. Real satyagraha required insistence on truth, peace, and non-violence and these were essentials in the fight for freedom.[32] He asked the satyagrahis to unite with each other. He realized that the people were ready for *duragraha* and to break each other's heads, and after doing it, they wanted to run away. Those, to him, were not the ways of winning swaraj. He knew that if not even a few men were ready to make sacrifice for the country, they could never hope to win in the end. He declared confidently that he knew something about satyagraha, for he was its author. He further said that for him there was no swaraj without Hindu–Muslim unity, the charkha, and the removal of untouchability.[33]

Gandhi's involvement in political issues did not diminish his interest in social matters. He realized the importance of cows for Hindus and took interest in their protection. The draft

**Figure 5.2**  Gandhi attending a meeting at the Congress House, Bombay, on 13 April 1925 to observe the Jallianwala Bagh Day. Seen with him are Sarojini Naidu and Shaukat Ali.
*Source*: Vithalbhai Jhaveri Collection/Dinodia Photos.

constitution of the All-India Cow-Protection Association was presented for approval to the public meeting held at Madhav Baug, Bombay (the meeting should have been held in Delhi, but the venue was changed to Bombay particularly for Gandhi's convenience), on 28 April 1925. Gandhi stopped by in Bombay that morning—he was on his way to Calcutta. He presided over the meeting and spoke in Gujarati. He said that he was always interested in cow protection and drew attention to the establishment of tanneries and dairies. His opined that people should take control of the milk supply and the disposal of the dead cattle; religion must take into account practical affairs and help to solve them.[34] About 4,000 people attended the meeting. Prominent persons present in the meeting included Shaukat Ali, Sir Purshottamdas Thakurdas, Dr B.S. Munje, Sarojini Naidu,

Jamnadas Dwarkadas, Mahadeo H. Desai, Radhakant Malaviya,
and Ramanujacharya, the preceptor of the Vaishnawas.[35]

At the Cow Protection Conference held at Belgaum in December 1924, a committee was appointed to frame a constitution for the founding of a permanent all-India cow-protection organization. This committee met at Delhi on 24 January 1925 and accepted a draft constitution for the All-India Cow-Protection Mandal prepared by Gandhi for submission to a meeting of the general public.[36]

Gandhi arrived in Bombay on the morning of 3 September 1925 at the Victoria Terminus station. He was received by Sarojini Naidu and several other friends. He stayed in Revashankar Jagjivan's house at Laburnum Road—'his usual Bombay residence'. A representative of the *Bombay Chronicle* had an interview with him on the same day. He asked: 'What remedy would you suggest against the prevailing stagnation in the country?' Gandhi fixed a fond look on the twirl gig, drew out a fine long thread, and said with a beaming smile: 'Well, I have already prescribed my remedy. Spin, spin, spin, till stagnation vanishes. That is my remedy and it holds the field till another or an alternative remedy is suggested and a case made out for it.'[37] When it was pointed out that the establishment of village panchayats was being suggested in several places, especially in Maharashtra, and also cooperative societies for khaddar work as adjuncts for village organizations, Gandhi said:

They are all right where they can properly be worked out in a spirit of absolute self-reliance. Where this spirit prevails, I would welcome almost any organization as better than none, but I fear that in many cases these institutions might turn out to be additional instruments to accustom people to lean on officials or their agents. What we want to unite and vitalize the whole nation is a common industry which all can carry on entirely by themselves. Universal spinning is the thing.[38]

In the evening of 4 September, he presided over a public meeting held at Sir Cowasji Jehangir Hall to celebrate the birth centenary of Dadabhai Naoroji. The hall was packed with about 2,500 people from all castes. The meeting was representative of around 43 political and social associations of Bombay. Speeches were made by J.E. Needham, D.G. Padhye, K.M. Munshi, H.P. Mody, Mirza Ali Mohamed Khan, M.R. Jayakar, M.D. Altekar, M.C. Chagla, J.J. Vimadalal, Sarojini Naidu, and Shaukat Ali. The speakers paid tributes to the memory of Dadabhai Naoroji and appealed to the people to emulate his example. Gandhi made a short speech in Gujarati, narrating his personal recollection of Dadabhai Naoroji and appealed to the audience to act on the principles laid down by Dadabhai for the general uplift of the country.[39]

On 3 September 1925, Gandhi attended a performance entitled 'Shoor Abala' (Brave Woman) organized by the girls of the Tilak Girls School under the guidance of the principal Krishnabai Tulaskar. A sum of about Rs 500 was realized by the sale of tickets. Gandhi appealed to the audience to support the institution.[40]

Gandhi was back in Bombay while on his way to Kutch by steamer on 21 October 1925. He addressed a large number of people who had gathered at Ferry Wharf, Carnac Bunder, to see him off. He thanked the Kutchi residents of Bombay and the people of Kutch for extending him an invitation to visit their province. He said that he was nearing death, but all the same his ideals and ambitions remained unlimited. He only requested them that they should all shower their blessings on him and pray to God to give him the strength and courage to stick to his ideals and work. He reminded them that in everything he did, he was prompted by his love for *truth* and *dharma*. He also said that he was in urgent need of rest and he looked forward to getting that in Kutch. He was then taken to *S.S. Rupavati* of the Bombay Steam Navigation Company, which was specially chartered for

**Figure 5.3** Gandhi attending a garden party in honour of the delegation of the South African government in Bombay on 19 September 1926.
*Source*: Vithalbhai Jhaveri Collection/Dinodia Photos.

the trip by Sheth Kanji Jadhavji, and was escorted to his cabin. His party included Mahadev Desai, Vallabhbhai Patel, Manilal Kothari, and Jivraj G. Nensey.[41]

Gandhi was in Bombay again on 19 September 1926. He had a discussion with the delegation of the South African government and attended the reception in their honour by the Indian Merchants' Chamber.[42]

## 1927–8

Gandhi continued to travel to different parts of the country. He visited Bombay only for two days in 1927. He visited Ghatkopar Sarvajanik Jivdaya Sanstha on 24 March 1927.[43]

By the end of the 1920s, new leaders such as Nariman, Yusuf Meherally, S.K. Patil, and Abidali Jafferbhai had emerged on the political scene of Bombay. The appointment of the all-British Simon Commission in late 1927 and its arrival on 3 February 1928 had evoked many protest meetings and angry reactions in Bombay as in other places of the country. There was not a single Indian member on the commission that was sent to play an important role in deciding the next political course. Demonstrations against it with slogans and placards of 'Simon Commission, go back', raising of black flags, processions, and meetings were organized in Bombay. It was observed that in the European business quarters, many of the shops stayed open. But in the Indian business quarters, everything was practically at a standstill. No business was carried out in the share, bullion, cotton-seeds, and piece-goods markets. Excepting a mill here and there, all cotton millworkers came out in a procession through the northern parts of the town led by Spratt and other labour leaders. They were joined by the workers of the G.I.P. Matunga workshop. The B.B. and C.I. workshops were partly working. At Foras Road, a labour meeting was held in which the effigies of Stanley Baldwin, Lord Birkenhead, John Simon, and Ramsay MacDonald were burnt.[44]

In his appeal to the people of Bombay, Gandhi hoped that the boycott would 'pass peacefully and show the nation's strength of purpose'.[45] He had refrained from writing anything about the boycott of the commission 'with great deliberation and not without the exercise of great self-restraint', as he recognized that his interference would bring the masses prominently into the movement and 'possibly embarrass the promoters'. He drew attention to the fact that the hartal had to be 'followed by sufficient and persistent action... I suggest that there is nothing before the nation other than boycott of foreign cloth which can be brought about effectively and quickly.'[46] He wrote this 'by way of a humble appeal to the different parties who are jointly acting in order to vindicate the national honour'.[47]

There were protest meetings in Bombay too, before the arrival of the Simon Commission. A mass meeting of the citizens of Bombay was held on 19 November 1927 at the Cowasji Jehangir Hall. The meeting passed a resolution that the commission was not acceptable to the people of India. On 3 December 1927, another public meeting was held on the requisition signed by the leading citizens of Bombay including Jayakar, Jinnah, Bhulabhai Desai, and Purshottamdas Thakurdas. Authorities, on the contrary, were making efforts to divide the Muslims from the Hindus as regards their opposition to the commission. On 3 February 1928, a crowded meeting of the citizens of Bombay was held on the Chowpatty sands and the commission's appointment was condemned. The Bombay Youth League had organized a demonstration against the commission. A procession of 700 students assembled at the gate of Alexandra Docks. Yusuf Meherally was in charge of the procession. The procession was subjected to lathi charges which caused considerable injury to the people. Subsequently, prosecution was launched against Sergeant Carter who was responsible for the lathi charge. Although the magistrate found Carter guilty and fined him Rs 50, the conviction was set aside by the high court. Soon afterwards, Meherally, who had passed his LLB examination, applied to the high court for *sanad* to practise on the appellate side, but his application was turned down by the court without citing any reasons. Meherally applied again, and his application was supported by the bar council. Even then, the high court did not grant his request, and Pandit, the magistrate who convicted Sergeant Carter, was not confirmed in his post.[48]

While the Simon Commission was carrying on its work, an all-parties conference was held in Bombay on 19 May 1928;

Dr M.A. Ansari presided over it. The conference appointed a committee under the chairmanship of Motilal Nehru to draft a constitution for India that would be acceptable to all political parties. This report that came to be known as the 'Nehru Report' was a milestone in the constitutional history of India. It was considered favourably by the Congress. But it was not approved by the Khilafat leaders such as Shaukat Ali, as it did not have special provisions for Muslims. Young and energetic leaders in the country, such as Jawaharlal Nehru, Subhas Chandra Bose, Nariman, and Yusuf Meherally, also did not like it, as it did not demand complete independence. The British government remained adamant and did not accept the Congress demands, ultimately leading the Congress to its resolution of complete independence for India at the Lahore session.

In Bombay, the year 1928 was marked by the spontaneous and patriotic expression of the students of the Victoria Jubilee Technical Institute (VJTI) at Matunga in August. At the institute, the students were banned from weaving Gandhi's portrait on a loom.[49] When the chairman of the VJTI's board refused to allow the students to make a portrait of Gandhi, about 40 students held a meeting at Matunga protesting against his decision.[50] About 75 students of the institute assembled again on 13 August outside the premises of the college to protest against the attitude of the chairman in disallowing the weaving of M.K. Gandhi's portrait on the loom. Bhagwanji Bhimbhai Desai, an ex-student and a weaving master in the Kaiser-i-Hind Mills, presided. He congratulated the students on their decision to not weave any portrait unless that of Gandhi was allowed to be woven.[51] A meeting of the VJTI's textile students was held on the maidan opposite the institute at Matunga on 25 September. K.N. Gokli presided over the meeting. He said that the decision of the board's chairman was regrettable and a great insult to the patriot and leader. He further said that

the decision should have been displayed on the institute's notice
board, but apparently the authorities were afraid of the criticism
in the press. He asked the students to unite as they had done at
the time of the arrival of the Simon Commission and continue
to protest against the decision until they were successful. A
resolution protesting against the board's decision was passed.[52]

A public meeting under the auspices of the Bombay Youth
League to protest against the ban on Gandhi's portrait was
held at the People's Jinnah Hall on 4 December. Horniman,
who presided over the meeting, criticized the tendency of the
education department to belittle the greatness of India and her
national heroes and asked how the VJTI could consider Gandhi
as an undesirable man whose portrait could not be woven. A
resolution protesting against the attitude of the VJTI authorities
for imposing a ban on the weaving of Gandhi's portrait and
requesting the members of the municipal corporation to support
K.F. Nariman's motion on the subject was moved by M.C. Chagla
and seconded by Meherally. It was passed unanimously. About
200 people, mostly students, attended the meeting. Jamnadas M.
Mehta suggested that the students should wear fine miniature
photos of Gandhi and should not submit to any unjustifiable
order given by the principal in respect thereof. He said that he was
assured by a Bombay merchant that the students who suffered on
that account would be amply compensated for.[53] Finally, it was
in 1934 that Babubhai M. Chinai, a Congressman of Bombay who
was then a student of the VJTI, obtained the permission of the
institute authorities to weave a portrait of Gandhi. Ten thousand
smaller portraits were later woven and distributed as calendars.[54]

Gandhi's non-violence was a dynamic concept and not
just a ritual. Some of his decisions such as killing a suffering
calf had come under severe criticism. Under the auspices of
the Humanitarian League, Bombay, a public meeting of the

city's Hindus was held on 18 October in the Godiji Maharaj Temple, Pydhonie, to protest against Gandhi's action of killing a sick calf by a poisonous injection and also against his alleged intention of killing the monkeys infesting the Gandhi Ashram at Ahmedabad. Jain Acharaya Maharaj Shri Ladha Vijaysurji presided over the meeting. About 300 people attended it and passed a resolution expressing their views. Jayantilal Mankar, Rao Saheb Harjivan Velji, W.T. Halai, and the president spoke, protesting against Gandhi's views that were offensive to the religious susceptibilities of many Hindus. A large number of people objected to the word 'Mahatma' used with reference to Gandhi and pressed for its deletion from the resolution. The word was accordingly deleted.[55]

## 1929

Gandhi arrived in Bombay from Ahmedabad on 5 April 1929. He was received at the Grant Road railway station by Nariman, Meherally, and about 10 other people. Under the auspices of the BPCC, he addressed an audience of about 500 people at the Congress House on the importance of khadi and the boycott of foreign cloth. He appealed to the audience to discard their foreign clothes as a token of their sincerity. About 50 foreign caps and a few other clothes were thrown on the platform. At the close of the meeting, the foreign-made clothes were burnt inside the Congress House compound. A gold ring was presented to Gandhi in the meeting, and it was thrice auctioned, ultimately fetching Rs 446 in all. He then opened the Umar Sobani Library in the newly erected building in the Congress House compound. (Umar Sobani had passed away in July 1926.) He also inaugurated the khadi bazaar organized by the Bombay Youth League in the People's Jinnah Hall. The bazaar contained about 18 stalls of khadi and other India-made articles. He thereafter opened the Khadi Printing and Dyeing at 113, Girgaum Back Road. Gandhi addressed another public meeting at Ranchhoddas Kanji's Wadi in the same area. In his brief speech, he advocated the use of khadi and boycott of foreign cloth. Several women threw off their necklaces and other ornaments that were auctioned after the meeting and a sum of about Rs. 760 was realized. This amount, along with Rs 446 realized by the auction of the ring at the Congress House, was given to the Boycott Propaganda Committee.[56]

On 24 and 25 May 1929, a meeting of the A.I.C.C., presided over by Motilal Nehru, was held in Bombay at the People's Jinnah Hall. About 300 people attended each day including about 100 members of the A.I.C.C. Prominent among those who attended included Dr M.A. Ansari, Pandit Madan Mohan Malaviya, C.V. Vaidya, Dr N.S. Hardikar, Horniman,

**Figure 5.4**   Gandhi at the opening of the khadi bhandar in Bombay in 1929.
*Source*: Vithalbhai Jhaveri Collection/Dinodia Photos.

Suhashini Nambiar, A. Rangaswami Iyengar, S. Srinivas Iyengar, S. Sattyamurti, Meherally, Jawaharlal Nehru, Jamnadas Mehta, Jamnalal Bajaj, N.C. Kelkar, Nariman, C.Y. Chintamani, Pattabhi Sitaramayya, D.D. Sathye, B.S. Munje, Vallabhbhai Patel, Babu Rajendra Prasad, and Jairamdas Dawalatram. Gandhi attended the meeting only on 25 May.[57] He also attended the All-India Native States Peoples' Conference, presided over by C.Y. Chintamani, on 25 May at the Royal Opera House.[58]

———

The situation after 1921, however, was getting uneasy. In addition to the differences in opinions among leaders in the political arena, disregard for the concept of non-violence and movements of *shuddhi* (purification), *sangathan* (consolidation), *tabligh* (conversion), and *tanzim* (unification) were aggravating religious tensions. Communal disharmony started erupting in violence. The Moplah rebellion in Malabar in 1921 was a blow to the Non-Cooperation Movement and the Hindu–Muslim unity. Gandhi's painful decision to withdraw the movement after the Chauri Chaura incident was a huge setback. There were communal riots in various places in the country in 1923 and 1924. The prestige of the Khilafat cause had suffered further damage by allegations of misuse of its funds against the Central Khilafat Committee. Communal riots in Gulbarga, followed soon by riots in Kohat in 1924, caused deep anguish and concern in Gandhi. When the riots in Kohat started, he was in Delhi at Mohammed Ali's home. He decided to undertake a fast there, although Mohammed Ali tried to dissuade him from doing so. According to Rajmohan Gandhi, after Kohat the Ali brothers gradually drifted away from Gandhi.[59]

The severest blow to the Khilafat Movement came from an unexpected place. In 1922, the Turkish Grand National Assembly

abolished the sultanate and declared Turkey a republic in 1923.
Mustafa Kemal became the president of the republic, and in
1924, the institution of Khilafat itself was abolished. By 1924,
Gandhi had realized that the Khilafat, as the glue between the Ali
brothers and himself, had gone dry and, therefore, the time had
come to place the idea of unadulterated swaraj before everyone,
including the Ali brothers.[60]

When Gandhi came out of jail in 1924, he was disappointed
to see that his success in bringing the Muslims in the national
political stream was short-lived. Many Khilafat leaders had
broken their ties with the allies in the Non-cooperation
Movement. Maulana Abdul Bari blamed Gandhi and became a
supporter of the raj. S.D. Kitchlew plunged into the movements
of conversion and unification of the Muslims as a counterblast
to the Hindu movement of purification. Hasrat Mohani became
critical of Gandhi and the Congress and joined the Muslim
League. The Ali brothers found it difficult to accept the abolition
of the Khilafat. They became increasingly isolated. Mohammed
Ali tried to work with the Congress leaders for some time.
Gandhi observed his 21-day fast for Hindu–Muslim unity at
Mohammed Ali's home in October 1924. But the Ali brothers
were under great strain and broke with Gandhi. Mohammed
Ali criticized Gandhi's launching of civil disobedience in
1930. After his death, Shaukat Ali lost his anchor and toed the
government line. Some Khilafat leaders such as Hakim Ajmal
Khan and M.A. Ansari stayed with Gandhi and steered away of
sectarian politics. Maulana Azad later bloomed as an outstanding
nationalist Muslim leader of India.[61]

The Indian politics changed its complexion after the Khilafat
brought the issue of religion in politics. Relations between
the Hindus and Muslims started getting torn due to tension
and strife. Jinnah had opposed the Khilafat, as he did not want

religion to determine politics and did not favour pan-Islamism for the Muslims in India. It was, however, a twist of history that he later achieved power and position through the use of religion in political arena. Gandhi must have felt dissipated and frustrated when he admitted later that 'I dare not touch the problem of Hindu–Muslim unity. It has passed out of human hands, and has been transferred to God's hands alone.'[62]

The semblance of communal harmony that had appeared during the Khilafat and Non-cooperation movements of 1920 had slowly disintegrated. After his release from jail in 1924, Gandhi had focused his attention and energy on constructive work for some time. Political developments such as the recommendations and later the report of the Simon Commission displayed the apathy and impassivity of the British government. The Backbay scandal furnished the nationalists with their greatest triumph in city politics of the decade from 1920 to 1930. Nariman accused the government of mismanagement and malpractice. He pursued the Bombay government over the issue from 1924 onwards both in the municipal corporation as well as the legislative council. As a result of the scandal, the government was put under a cloud—a cloud that was all the blacker because the scandal was exposed by a nationalist.[63]

The nationalist leaders had been emphasizing the issue of the boycott. The response of the business was complex. According to Sabyasachi Bhattacharya, in the early 1920s, the attitude to the Congress in Bombay business groups was sharply divided. Some sections, small merchants in particular, showed a marked sympathy for the non-cooperation and boycott movements. On the contrary, many industrialists were wary of the disruptive potentials of the movement. In the mid-1920s, the tone towards the Congress began to change. The boycott of foreign goods had gained for Indian mills a larger share of the home market.

Moreover, the Congress in its periods of quiescence was not as much a threat as it was in periods of political turmoil. Above all, the Congress and particularly its more moderate leaders were useful allies in the Indian business groups' struggle to gain concessions.[64]

A.D.D. Gordon has noted that the Foreign Cloth Boycott Committee was set up in 1929 in Bombay, with Jairamdas Daulatram, a businessman, as the secretary and chief organizer and Swami Anand as president; Jamnalal Bajaj was also deeply involved. By August 1930, the CWC had established a list of 56 mills to be boycotted, 24 of them in Bombay.[65]

Disappointed with the unresponsive attitude of the British government, the Congress passed a resolution demanding complete independence at its Lahore session on 31 December 1929. The resolution was proposed by Gandhi at midnight. People were now enthused to march forward under Gandhi's leadership. The CWC met at the Sabarmati Ashram in February 1930 and entrusted Gandhi with all the powers to launch the Civil Disobedience Movement. Gandhi had a brilliant plan, meticulously worked out; he had decided to launch the Dandi March. In his letter dated 2 March 1930, he wrote to the viceroy that the British rule 'has impoverished the dumb millions by a system of progressive exploitation' and 'has reduced us politically to serfdom. It has sapped the foundation of our culture.'[66] He further wrote that 'on the 11th day of the month, I shall proceed with such co-workers of the Ashram as I can take, to disregard the provisions of the Salt Law'.[67] The nation, filled with new energy, watched with admiration and prepared to follow its unsurpassed hero leading the march to Dandi on 12 March 1930. Bombay was hit by recession, economic depression, and volatility of the labour due to retrenchment and unemployment. The textile strikes of 1928 and 1929 had accentuated the crisis. However, despite all this, the city of Bombay was not to be left behind.

## Notes and References

1. 'Bombay Secret Abstract', 1922, pp. 131–2, para 104 cited in Kunte, *Source Material for a History of the Freedom Movement*, Vol. IX, p. 145.

2. *Young India* dated 19 January 1922 cited in *CWMG*, Vol. 22 (Delhi: Publications Division, Ministry of Information and Broadcasting, Government of India, 1966), pp. 210–11.

3. Kunte, *Source Material for a History of the Freedom Movement in India*, Vol. VI, p. 96.

4. 'Bombay Secret Abstract', 1922, p. 400, para 364 cited in Phatak, *Source Material for a History of the Freedom Movement in India*, Vol. III, Part I, p. 467.

5. *CWMG*, Vol. 23 (Delhi: Publications Division, Ministry of Information and Broadcasting, Government of India, 1967), pp. 413–18.

6. Kunte, *Source Material for a History of the Freedom Movement in India*, Vol. VI, pp. 151–60.

7. For details on municipal reforms and local politics, see Hazareesingh, *The Colonial City*, pp. 186–98; Gordon, *Businessmen and Politics*, pp. 131–40.

8. Kunte, *Source Material for a History of the Freedom Movement in India*, Vol. VI, pp. 148–50.

9. Kunte, *Source Material for a History of the Freedom Movement in India*, Vol. VI, pp. 124–5.

10. Kunte, *Source Material for a History of the Freedom Movement in India*, Vol. VI, pp. 172–6.

11. 'Bombay Secret Abstract', 1924, p. 68, para 156 and p. 103, para 221, section (12) cited in N.R. Phatak (ed.), *Source Material for a History of the Freedom Movement in India, Mahatma Gandhi*, Vol. III, Part II: 1922–1929 (Bombay: Directorate of Printing and Stationery, Maharashtra State, 1968), pp. 287–8.

12. Gopalaswami, *Gandhi and Bombay*, pp. 183–5.

13. M.K. Gandhi, 'Preface', in *Satyagraha in South Africa*, Valji Govindji Desai (tr.) (Madras: S. Ganesan, 1928), pp. 1–7.

14. 'Bombay Secret Abstract', 1924, p. 252, para 515, Bombay City, S.B., March 19 cited in Kunte, *Source Material for a History of the Freedom Movement in India*, Vol. IX, p. 151.

15. 'Bombay Secret Abstract', 1924, p. 565, para 1260(8), Bombay City, S.B., August 30 cited in Kunte, *Source Material for a History of the Freedom Movement in India*, Vol. IX, p. 153.

16. *The Bombay Chronicle* dated 30 August 1924 cited in *CWMG*, Vol. 25 (Delhi: Publications Division, Ministry of Information and Broadcasting, Government of India, 1967), pp. 52–3.

17. 'Bombay Secret Abstract', 1924, p. 565, para 1260(8), Bombay City, S.B., August 30 cited in Kunte, *Source Material for a History of the Freedom Movement in India*, Vol. IX, pp. 153–4.

18. 'Bombay Secret Abstract', 1924, p. 578, para 1294(12), Bombay City, S.B., 5 September cited in Phatak, *Source Material for a History of the Freedom Movement in India*, Vol. III, Part II, p. 317.

19. 'Bombay Secret Abstract', 1924, p. 578, para 1294(12), Bombay City, S.B., 5 September cited in Phatak, *Source Material for a History of the Freedom Movement in India*, Vol. III, Part II, p. 316.

20. Dalal, *Gandhi*, p. 51.

21. 'Bombay Secret Abstract', 1924, p. 578, para 1294(12) cited in Kunte, *Source Material for a History of the Freedom Movement in India*, Vol. IX, p. 157.

22. 'Bombay Secret Abstract', 1924, p. 658, para 1491(14), Bombay City, S.B., 13 October cited in Phatak, *Source Material for a History of the Freedom Movement in India*, Vol. III, Part II, p. 333.

23. 'Bombay Secret Abstract', 3 December 1924, p. 753, para 1703(6), S. B. Bombay Presidency, Poona, pp. 754–5 cited in Phatak, *Source Material for a History of the Freedom Movement in India*, Vol. III, Part II, pp. 334–8.

24. 'Bombay Secret Abstract', 1924, pp. 754–5 cited in Phatak, *Source Material for a History of the Freedom Movement in India*, Vol. III, Part II, p. 341.

25. Kunte, *Source Material for a History of the Freedom Movement in India*, Vol. VI, p. 200.

26. 'Bombay Secret Abstract', 25 November 1924, p. 776, para 1738(8), Bombay City, S.B. cited in Phatak, *Source Material for a History of the Freedom Movement in India*, Vol. III, Part II, p. 342.

27. 'Bombay Secret Abstract', 1925, p. 33, para 66 cited in Phatak, *Source Material for a History of the Freedom Movement in India*, Vol. III, Part II, p. 350.

28. *The Bombay Chronicle* dated 27 March 1925 cited in *CWMG*, Vol. 26 (Delhi: Publications Division, Ministry of Information and Broadcasting, Government of India, 1967), pp. 420–1.

29. 'Bombay Secret Abstract', 1925, p. 196, para 509 cited in Kunte, *Source Material for a History of the Freedom Movement in India*, Vol. IX, pp. 174–5.

30. *The Bombay Chronicle* dated 27 March 1925 cited in *CWMG*, Vol. 26, pp. 421–2.

31. *The Bombay Chronicle* dated 27 March 1925 cited in *CWMG*, Vol. 26, pp. 419–20.

32. 'Bombay Secret Abstract', 14 April 1925, p. 232, para 612 (6), Bombay City, S.B. cited in Phatak, *Source Material for a History of the Freedom Movement in India*, Vol. III, Part II, pp. 359–60.

33. *The Bombay Chronicle* dated 14 April 1925 cited in *CWMG*, Vol. 26, pp. 505–7.

34. *Young India* dated 7 May 1925 cited in *CWMG*, Vol. 26, pp. 555–8.

35. 'Bombay Secret Abstract', 1925, p. 270, para 694 cited in Phatak, *Source Material for a History of the Freedom Movement in India*, Vol. III, Part II, pp. 362–4.

36. 'Bombay Secret Abstract', 1925, p. 270, para 694 cited in Phatak, *Source Material for a History of the Freedom Movement in India*, Vol. III, Part II, p. 362.

37. *The Bombay Chronicle* dated 4 September 1925 cited in *CWMG*, Vol. 28 (Delhi: Publications Division, Ministry of Information and Broadcasting, Government of India, 1968), p. 153.

38. *The Bombay Chronicle* dated 4 September 1925 cited in *CWMG*, Vol. 28, pp. 153–4.

39. 'Bombay Secret Abstract', p. 562, para 1403(2) cited in Kunte, *Source Material for a History of the Freedom Movement in India*, Vol. IX, pp. 182–3. See also *The Bombay Chronicle* dated 7 September 1925 cited in *CWMG*, Vol. 28, pp. 156–7.

40. 'Bombay Secret Abstract', p. 562, para 1403(2) cited in Kunte, *Source Material for a History of the Freedom Movement in India*, Vol. IX, p. 182.

41. *The Bombay Chronicle* dated 22 October 1925 cited in *CWMG*, Vol. 28, pp. 357–8.

42. Dalal, *Gandhi*, p. 63.

43. Dalal, *Gandhijini Dinwari*, p. 215.

44. S.R. Bakshi, *Simon Commission and Indian Nationalism* (New Delhi: Munshiram Manoharlal Publishers, 1977), pp. 65–6.

45. *The Bombay Chronicle* dated 3 February 1928 cited in *CWMG*, Vol. 36 (New Delhi: Publications Division, Ministry of Information and Broadcasting, Government of India, 1970), p. 8.

46. *Young India* dated 9 February 1928 cited in *CWMG*, Vol. 36, pp. 14–5.

47. *Young India* dated 9 February 1928 cited in *CWMG*, Vol. 36, pp. 14–5.

48. T.K. Tope, *Bombay and Congress Movement* (Bombay: Maharashtra State Board for Literature and Culture, 1986), pp. 66–7.

49. Dalal, *Gandhi*, p. 72, footnote 5 (b).

50. 'Bombay Secret Abstract', 1928, p. 528, para 1296 cited in Phatak, *Source Material for a History of the Freedom Movement in India*, Vol. III, Part II, pp. 402–3.

51. 'Bombay Secret Abstract', 14 August 1928, p. 546, para 1336, Bombay City, S.B. cited in Phatak, *Source Material for a History of the Freedom Movement in India*, Vol. III, Part II, p. 404.

52. 'Bombay Secret Abstract', 25 September 1928, p. 642, para 1561, Bombay City, S.B. cited in Phatak, *Source Material for a History of the Freedom Movement in India*, Vol. III, Part II, p. 407.

53. 'Bombay Secret Abstract', 5 December 1928, p. 840, para 1957, Bombay City, S.B. cited in Phatak, *Source Material for a History of the Freedom Movement in India*, Vol. III, Part II, p. 409.

54. Gopalaswami, *Gandhi and Bombay*, p. 235.

55. 'Bombay Secret Abstract', 19 October 1928, p. 698, para 1654 (2), Bombay City, S.B. cited in Phatak, *Source Material for a History of the Freedom Movement in India*, Vol. III, Part II, p. 408.

56. 'Bombay Secret Abstract', 6 April 1929, p. 273, para 710 (2), Bombay City, S.B. cited in Phatak, *Source Material for a History of the Freedom Movement in India*, Vol. III, Part II, p. 429.

57. 'Bombay Secret Abstract', 26 May 1928, p. 411, para 1014, Bombay City, S.B. cited in Kunte, *Source Material for a History of the Freedom Movement in India*, Vol. IX, p. 193.

58. Dalal, *Gandhi*, p. 77.

59. Rajmohan Gandhi, *Mohandas: The Story of a Man, His People, and an Empire* (New Delhi: Penguin, 2006), p. 297.

60. Rakhahari Chatterji, *Gandhi and the Ali Brothers: Biography of a Friendship* (New Delhi: SAGE Publications, 2013), p. 183.

61. Nanda, 'Gandhi and Pan-Islamism', pp. 102–4.

62. *Young India*, 13 January 1927.

63. Gordon, *Businessmen and Politics*, pp. 152–4.

64. Sabyasachi Bhattacharya, 'The Colonial State, Capital and Labour: Bombay, 1919–1931', in S. Gopal, Sabyasachi Bhattacharya, and Romila Thapar (eds.), *Situating Indian History* (New Delhi: Oxford University Press, 1986), p. 188.

65. Gordon, *Businessmen and Politics*, p. 208.

66. *Young India* dated 12 March 1930 cited in *CWMG*, Vol. 43 (New Delhi: Publications Division, Ministry of Information and Broadcasting, Government of India, 1971), p. 3.

67. *CWMG*, Vol. 43, p. 7.

$6\partial$

# 6

# MAKING BOMBAY 'THE CITADEL OF NATIONAL MOVEMENT': 1930–1

AS GANDHI STARTED HIS EPIC JOURNEY FROM SABARMATI ASHRAM TO
Dandi on 12 March 1930, Bombay was agog with excitement. The
city was humming with activities after Gandhi picked up salt
at Dandi.

## Protests in Bombay

Activities in Bombay gathered momentum by the beginning of
April. Three centres of opposition to the British rule sprang up in the
city. At the prosperous suburb of Vile Parle with many residences of
Gujarati and Marwari families, Gandhi's close confidant Jamnalal

Bajaj set up a camp that housed satyagrahis such as Kishorlal Mashruwala, Rishabdas Ranka, Gokulbhai Bhat, Swami Anand, and M.R. Mehta. At the Congress House in Girgaum, the middle-class Maharashtrian area, K.F. Nariman, Yusuf Meherally, Abid Ali, S.K. Patil, and other leaders of the BPCC were involved in the work. Kandalkar and Ruiker were persuading the railway workers at Parel and Matunga to associate their strike with the broader struggle about to be launched in the city.[1]

The suburb of Vile Parle became a lively hub of non-violent action. Gandhi had nominated Jamnalal Bajaj as the first 'dictator'. A grand camp was established and elaborate arrangements were made. Besides Bajaj, eminent leaders of Bombay and Maharashtra participated in this satyagraha at Vile Parle. They included Shankarrao Dattatraya Deo, S.D. Javadekar, G.V. Ketkar, Vasudeo Vithal Dastane, V.V. Athalye, and Anant Vasudeo Sahastrabuddhe. Kasturba Gandhi and Janakidevi Bajaj were also busy camping in the Vile Parle camp.[2] On 6 April, Jamnalal Bajaj unfurled the national flag at a gathering in Vile Parle. Thereafter, the satyagrahis went to a saltwater pool in the nearby area, where Kishorlal Mashruwala and four volunteers prepared salt. The GIP Railwaymen's Union also launched a big strike that day.[3]

The National Week's celebrations started from that day. Under the auspices of the BPCC, a huge procession of around 2,000 people started from the Congress House in the morning and went along Lamington Road, Sandhurst Road, Girgaum Back Road, Bhuleshwar, Kalbadevi Road, Mumbadevi, Princess Street, Girgaum Road, and back to the Congress House. In the evening a meeting of around 5,000 people, presided over by D.R. Gharpure, was held in Chowpatty. In the early morning of 7 April, a large crowd of people assembled at the Congress House to accompany the 10 satyagrahis in their march to Hornby Vellard to breach the Salt Act. At 6.30 am these satyagrahis, headed by K.F. Nariman,

marched out of the Congress House and were joined by thousands
on their way. They made their way to Mahalaxmi in procession
through Lamington Road and Tardeo. On arrival at Mahalaxmi,
Pandit Sunderlal and Nariman informed the people that a batch
of four volunteers would fetch sea water from which salt would
be prepared by boiling it. The four volunteers went to the sea
with buckets in their hands and brought sea water to the public
park near Race Course. Avantikabai Gokhale and Kamaladevi
Chattopadhyaya lighted *segrees* to boil the water. Nariman and
Ali Bahadur Khan took prominent part in the making of the salt.
The salt, which looked like a fine white powder, was exhibited
to the public and photographed. In the evening a public meeting
of about 10,000 people was held at Chowpatty to celebrate the
breach of the Salt Act. K.F. Nariman presided over the meeting.[4]

Nariman, Bajaj, Mashruwala, and Gokulbhai Bhat were
arrested, and in response to these arrests, the shops in Mulji
Jetha Market, Crawford Market, Jhaveri Bazar, and the nearby
areas were closed. These arrests, however, did not dampen the
spirit of the satyagrahis and the BPCC. On 8 April, some of them,
including D.R. Gharpure, Yusuf Meherally, and Kamaladevi,
marched from the Congress House to Chowpatty, where they
participated in the ritual of preparing salt, watched all the
while by a huge crowd. The BPCC showed remarkable power
of endurance in its non-violent confrontation. Fresh batches of
satyagrahis, escorted by tens of thousands of people, continued to
go from the Congress House to Chowpatty or Worli.[5]

Bombay's response to the Salt Satyagraha created history. A
programme of making salt from sea water on the terrace of the
Congress House was launched from 8 April. This was done by
boiling water and making salt in cement salt pans on the terrace.
A meeting of about 30,000 people, including around 200 women,
was held in Chowpatty to congratulate K.F. Nariman, Jamnalal

Bajaj, and the other satyagrahis on their arrest. Contraband salt was enthusiastically sold. On 10 April, the police searched the Congress House and made their way with considerable difficulty to the terrace of the BPCC's office where they found 30 salt pans made of cement. Women such as Perin Captain and Kamaladevi were in the forefront. Three prominent members of the war council—Meherally (the vice-president of the Bombay Youth League), Abid Ali Jafferbhai (the secretary of the BPCC), and M. Sadik (the editor of a nationalist weekly)—were arrested.[6]

The last day of the National Week—13 April—witnessed large processions to Chowpatty where they turned into a mass rally of about 50,000 including around 1,000 women. The cloth markets observed a hartal. In response to Jawaharlal Nehru's arrest, various markets in the city were closed. The BMC also adjourned its meeting on the motion of Jamnadas Mehta. Eminent lawyers and solicitors, such as Bhulabhai J. Desai, M.C. Setalvad, K.M. Munshi, and Mangaldas M. Pakvasa, pledged to support the swadeshi movement. On 20 April, there was a massive rally (of 8,000 as reported by the government authorities and a 100,000 according to the Bombay Chronicle) in Chowpatty. Speakers included Sarojini Naidu, Avantikabai Gokhale, Kamaladevi, K.M. Munshi, Lilavati Munshi, V.V. Jerajani, Ganapatishankar N. Desai, and others. The police repression failed to suppress the spirit of the satyagrahis.[7]

The Salt Satyagraha had touched the lives of many in different parts of the country from Malabar to the North West Frontier Province. Not anticipating such a massive resistance, the government was 'puzzled and perplexed'.[8] Gandhi and his followers were undeterred and determined to continue with the satyagraha. Finally, the government arrested him on 4 May 1930. People protested against it vociferously: the streets and roads in Bombay were oozing with protesting crowds drawing various sections of society including merchants and textile and railway workers. The repressive steps of the government no longer frightened the people in Bombay. Merchants, shopkeepers, women, and students became engrossed in Gandhi's political activities. Going to jail was no longer a stigma but an honour; observing hartal was no longer a solitary protest but a part of the mainstream connected with the national movement. Nonviolent demonstrations and meetings in the city became familiar sights. The satyagrahis kept on courting arrest, and import of cloth from Britain fell down drastically.

A succession of raids on the Wadala salt depot was an important phase in the Salt Satyagraha in Bombay. Kamaladevi and many others were arrested. Hundreds of volunteers dashed to the salt pans and, despite police resistance, removed salt. They got arrested almost every day. From 22 May 1930, this drama was enacted every day and the government responded with increasingly repressive measures. The most demonstrative raid was on 1 June for which the War Council had been diligently preparing. Nearly 15,000 volunteers and other citizens participated in the great mass action in Wadala salt areas. Successive batches marched up to the Port Trust level crossing and the police cordon there held up the swelling crowds. Soon the raiders, including women and children, broke through the cordon, splashed through slime and mud, and ran over the pans. Some raiders were injured. The way in which the police dealt with the raiders caused considerable public indignation and protest.[9] The fullest preparations of the police to deal with the situation could not succeed in dampening the spirit of the volunteers. A large number of women took part, adding to the difficulties of the police. Lilavati Munshi insisted on her arrest.[10] Women's participation in the movement was impressive. Sarojini Naidu had attracted the nation's attention by her leadership at the Dharasana Salt Satyagraha in Gujarat.

The Parsis, though a small community, were visible because of their contribution to the cause of freedom. They participated actively in the constructive programme outlined by the Congress. Under the auspices of the Parsi Rajkiya Sabha, a public meeting of Parsis was held at Blavatsky Lodge, French Bridge, on 21 May 1930 to congratulate the Parsi satyagrahis who were arrested in Bombay and elsewhere. The president of the meeting K.K. Suntoke, B.F. Bharucha, K.K. Dadachandji, and Perin Captain made speeches congratulating Nariman, Dr Choksey, Sidwa, and Pestonji of Peshawar. Resolutions were passed advising the boycott of foreign cloth and participation in the satyagraha movement by the Parsis.[11]

The *Bombay Chronicle* dated 13 June 1930 reported about the enthusiastic scenes at the meeting of Parsis held at Sir C.J. Hall on 12 June when the whole hall and the galleries were overflowing and, amidst the crowd, there were many women as well. More than half-a-dozen speakers made speeches, exhorting the audience to join the national movement. It is interesting that the admission to the meeting was by tickets, with the understanding that the amount collected (over Rs 900) would go to the Parsi Satyagrahis Fund. The chair was kept vacant, as Perin Captain, who was to preside, was prevented from coming by the police blockade at the Congress House. In her message to the audience, she conveyed that 'the minority communities have the power to become the majority communities by their sacrifice and service to the cause of our country's freedom'[12] B.F. Bharucha condemned the excesses committed on the Dharasana satyagrahis as inhuman. Professor Shroff earnestly appealed to the Parsis to take to swadeshi, which was the most powerful weapon to compel the government to give up their economic and political domination. Dinshaw Gagrat spoke about the great self-sacrifice of several Parsis. Erward Kutar, a Parsi *mobad* (priest), pointed out that the Parsis must join in the struggle to demonstrate that soul force was more powerful than bayonets and machine guns. Chollu, one of the Parsi satyagrahis who were arrested at Wadala, compared Mahatma Gandhi to their Prophet Zoroaster who had refused to give up his religion despite persecution. Rustom H. Wadia, Homi Kapadia, Nosheerwan Jhabvalaand, and Kaikhosru Dadachanji delivered spirited speeches.[13]

The prabhat pheris were very visible in the city around this time. They were small bands of people who paraded in the city in the morning, sang patriotic songs, and urged people to do their duties towards the motherland. Not only Hindus but also Parsis and Muslims joined the groups as did men and women. The great bulk of the groups was in parts of the town that covered the Marathi and Gujarati middle class and the service areas such as Girgaum, Bhuleshwar, Kalbadevi, and Thakurdwar. In time, the pheris produced their own heroes and martyrs. The most prominent, early in the campaign, was Hargovind Lalji who led the group of the Pavagad Vijay Prabhat Pheri. He lived in Dhobitalao and owned a washing company. On 2 August 1930, he was at the head of the group marching and proudly waving the national flag when a European policeman rushed at him, hit him on the head, and knocked him to the ground. Lalji defended the flag at the risk of his life; he was seriously injured. He was taken to the K.E.M. Hospital where he died on 4 August.[14] Singing was an important facet of the prabhat pheris. In this context, it is interesting to know that Balkrishna Kapileshwari, a disciple of Abdul Karim Khan and the principal of Shri Saraswati Sangeet Vidyalaya at Kalbadevi Road, offered to give free lessons in music to the members of the prabhat pheris.[15]

People's spirit of nationalism was reflected in their daily life and festivals. It is reported that a noticeable feature of the Ganapati festival was that the parties carrying the Ganapati

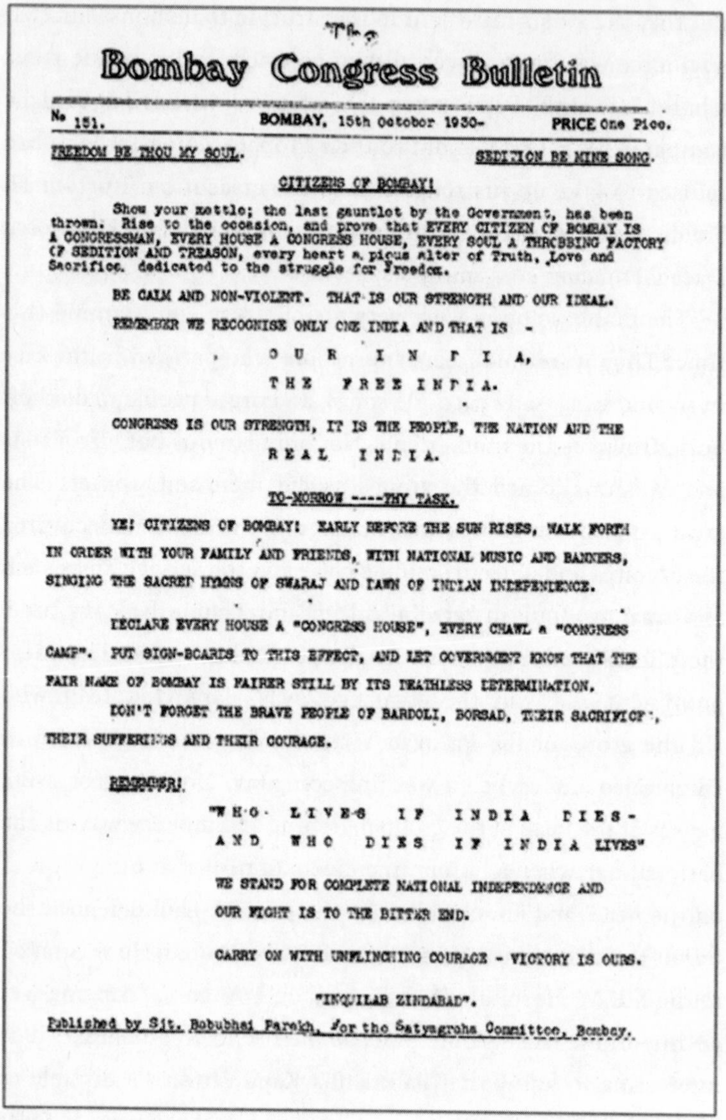

The
# Bombay Congress Bulletin

No. 151.          BOMBAY, 15th October 1930-          PRICE One Pice.

FREEDOM BE THOU MY SOUL.                    SEDITION BE MINE SONG.

### CITIZENS OF BOMBAY!

Show your mettle; the last gauntlet by the Government, has been thrown. Rise to the occasion, and prove that EVERY CITIZEN OF BOMBAY IS A CONGRESSMAN, EVERY HOUSE A CONGRESS HOUSE, EVERY SOUL A THROBBING FACTORY OF SEDITION AND TREASON, every heart a pious alter of Truth, Love and Sacrifice, dedicated to the struggle for Freedom.

BE CALM AND NON-VIOLENT. THAT IS OUR STRENGTH AND OUR IDEAL.

REMEMBER WE RECOGNISE ONLY ONE INDIA AND THAT IS -

> OUR INDIA,
> THE FREE INDIA.

CONGRESS IS OUR STRENGTH, IT IS THE PEOPLE, THE NATION AND THE
> REAL INDIA.

### TO-MORROW ----THY TASK.

YE! CITIZENS OF BOMBAY! EARLY BEFORE THE SUN RISES, WALK FORTH IN ORDER WITH YOUR FAMILY AND FRIENDS, WITH NATIONAL MUSIC AND BANNERS, SINGING THE SACRED HYMNS OF SWARAJ AND DAWN OF INDIAN INDEPENDENCE.

DECLARE EVERY HOUSE A "CONGRESS HOUSE", EVERY CHAWL A "CONGRESS CAMP". PUT SIGN-BOARDS TO THIS EFFECT, AND LET GOVERNMENT KNOW THAT THE FAIR NAME OF BOMBAY IS FAIRER STILL BY ITS DEATHLESS DETERMINATION.

DON'T FORGET THE BRAVE PEOPLE OF BARDOLI, BORSAD, THEIR SACRIFICE, THEIR SUFFERINGS AND THEIR COURAGE.

REMEMBER!

> "WHO LIVES IF INDIA DIES - AND WHO DIES IF INDIA LIVES"

> WE STAND FOR COMPLETE NATIONAL INDEPENDENCE AND OUR FIGHT IS TO THE BITTER END.

> CARRY ON WITH UNFLINCHING COURAGE - VICTORY IS OURS.

> "INQUILAB ZINDABAD".

Published by Sjt. Robubhai Parekh, for the Satyagraha Committee, Bombay.

**Figure 6.1**   The Bombay Congress Bulletin dated 15 October 1930.
*Source*: Mani Bhavan Gandhi Sangrahalaya.

generally had a Congress flag in front of them. Some images of Ganapati were decked with Gandhi caps.[16] Gandhi was imprisoned on 5 May 1930. To mark the end of his first month of imprisonment, 5 June was observed as 'Gandhi Day' in Bombay. Thousands of white-capped adherents of the passive-resistance movement passed through the streets of Bombay in a procession with banners exhorting people to boycott British goods.[17]

Leaders and other people from different walks of life courted arrest for being active in the struggle, and people lauded their courage and grit. Hansa Mehta, the president, and four other members of the BPCC's War Council were arrested for disobeying the order of the chief magistrate prohibiting the publication of the Congress Bulletin.[18] Ramibai Kamdar, Dilshed Sayid, and other members of the War Council were also sent to jail for the same offence. A large public meeting presided over by Morarji Kamdar, Ramibai's husband, was convened at the Esplanade Maidan to congratulate them.[19]

There was notable picketing against liquor and foreign cloth. On 12 December 1930, Babu Genu, a mill worker, offered courageous satyagraha by trying to prevent a truck carrying foreign cloth and sacrificed his life as the truck crushed him.

## Women's Participation

The martyrdom of Babu Genu moved the people, especially women, who participated in the demonstration with the spirit of nationalism and admiration for the martyr. A rare report of the Desh Sevika Sangh (established in 1930 as the voluntary group of the Rashtriya Stree Sabha of Bombay) notes an unprecedented move of women:

The courage of our Sevikas was proved when they faced the bayonets of the military surrounding the mortal remains of Babu Genu. That procession was headed by Shrimati Vijayabehn Parekh and Vimlabehn Jhaveri and Smt. Snehlata Hajrat, the then president of the war council, who were throughout the year some of our most resolute and prominent workers. Perhaps for the first time in the history of recorded Hinduism high caste Hindu women led [a] funeral procession and did the last loving service to the mortal remains by setting the torch to the pyre.[20]

The women of Bombay were actively participating in this struggle in a determined way. They manufactured and sold contraband salt, organized prabhat pheris and flag salutations, distributed leaflets, and mobilized the various sections of society. Women like Kamaladevi Chattopadhyaya, Avantikabai Gokhale, Perin Captain, Lilavati Munshi, Hansa Mehta, and Ratanben Mehta were in the forefront. The leaders of the Desh Sevika Sangh encouraged women to join the non-violent struggle led by Gandhi. Women picketed effectively against the shops of foreign cloth and liquor in various areas of the city. They picketed the auction of toddy licences at the Town Hall and ensured that it was a complete failure. They organized a number of impressive demonstrations and processions. About 5,000 women dressed in orange saris marched from Chowpatty to the Azad Maidan to defy the government's decision to declare the Desh Sevika Sangh an illegal organization. On Gandhi's birthday, too, their huge procession was notable. The fearless Desh Sevikas showed tremendous discipline, efficiency, boldness, energy, and courage throughout the Civil Disobedience Movement of 1930–1.[21]

The Congress had asked the people to abstain from voting in the elections for the legislatures under the British rule. The Congress volunteers and the Desh Sevikas in Bombay enthusiastically took up the task of persuading the people to boycott the elections. In this context, women's effective picketing at the polling booths at the Town Hall on 18 September 1930 is noteworthy. A government report gives a vivid description of the scene of the election to the Bombay Council that took place at the Town Hall. Although the polling was to commence at 8 am, people started reaching the Town Hall much earlier. A batch of

**Figure 6.2** The defiance procession by Desh Sevikas in Bombay, when the Desh Sevika Sangh was declared illegal.
*Source*: Mani Bhavan Gandhi Sangrahalaya.

about 20 women volunteers arrived on the scene at about 7.30 am and started picketing at the foot of the steps leading to the Town Hall. Several Congress volunteers also came along with cloth placards bearing inscriptions such as 'don't vote at the election', 'stop your vote and save your country's soul', and 'councils are bureaucracy's talk-shops'. The women pickets shouted at the voters as they got down from cars to vote, so the latter had to be escorted by the police until the steps. After the arrest of the first batch of women pickets, another batch was brought from the Sassoon building opposite the Town Hall where they had established their headquarters. They also followed the same tactics and were arrested. A total of 382 women volunteers were arrested and sent to the Esplanade Police Station. The polling and picketing both continued until 6 pm. Thereafter, the women marched to the meeting at the Esplanade Maidan. The 382 women detained at the Esplanade Police Station were released and they also marched to the meeting.[22]

## Political Developments

The political atmosphere was uneasy due to the repressive measures by the government and curbs on people's civil liberties. According to the Congress leaders, the government's fiscal policy was responsible for growing unemployment and swaraj was the only solution. People, fired with new aspirations, were prepared to face obstacles in their non-violent struggle.

The viceroy suggested a round-table conference as a conciliatory measure and reiterated readiness to discuss the goal of dominion status. The British prime minister expressed hope that the Congress would participate in it. Gandhi was released unconditionally on 25 January. The first anniversary of Independence Day—26 January 1931—was celebrated with great gusto in Bombay. Gandhi's release added to people's enthusiasm. The momentous day was observed all over the country by holding mass meetings, which confirmed the resolution of independence and passed a similar resolution called the 'Resolution of Remembrance'. Gandhi celebrated the day at Mani Bhavan and hurried to Allahabad to see Motilal Nehru, who was seriously ill.[23]

After prolonged deliberations, the CWC authorized Gandhi to initiate discussions with the viceroy that resulted in the Gandhi–Irwin Pact on 5 March 1931. The terms included some concessions such as release of all political prisoners not convicted for violence and remission of all fines not yet collected. In turn, Gandhi, on behalf of the Congress, agreed to discontinue the Civil Disobedience Movement. The pact was a surprise to the leaders in Bombay and other places. The feeling of dissatisfaction against the pact among the people, especially the youth, was fuelled by the executions of the celebrated revolutionaries Bhagat Singh, Sukhdev, and Rajguru.

Gandhi was in Bombay in the third week of March. Bombay, the 'cradle and storm centre of the current nationalist liberation movement', gave him a tumultuous welcome on his return from his peace negotiation with Irwin. 'A forest of humanity', estimated at 250,000, was present.[24] Gandhi had extensive discussions and meetings with his colleagues. The BPCC convened two meetings in the mill area on 16 March 1931. Gandhi addressed a meeting at Parel. About 20,000 people attended the meeting and prominent amongst them were K.F. Nariman, Jamnadas Dwarkadas, Mukund Malaviya, B.T. Ranadive, G.L. Kanadalkar, Miss Slade, Kasturba Gandhi, V.H. Joshi, Sundar Kabadi, R.M. Jambhekar, Vasant Khale, V.H. Kulkarni, S.B. Mahadeshwar, and A.A. Shaikh.[25]

The two days' crowded programme kept him incessantly busy, and even on Monday, his day of silence, he could get no rest or sleep, having to listen to numerous interviewers. He called on Muljibhai Sikka, had discussions with Jawaharlal Nehru, and managed to find some time to go and see Nagindas Amulakhrai and Kishorlal on 16 March.[26] He also had an important interview with Subhas Chandra Bose in the night that lasted until half-past-two the next morning. After about an hour's sleep, he was up again for the morning prayer.[27] Meetings and interviews kept him busy the next day too. On 17 March, he addressed a meeting of volunteers and another of desh sevikas and also met Shaukat Ali. In addition, he held discussions with industrialists at the office of the Mill Owners' Association and with workers at the Congress House. There was a public meeting at Azad Maidan presided over by Jawaharlal Nehru. He also went to the party hosted by Hussenbhai Lalji, the president of the municipal corporation, and went to see Maharani Gaikwad.[28]

Gandhi went to Vile Parle on 18 March 1931 and visited the Bhagini Seva Mandir. He held discussions with the women

**Figure 6.3**   Gandhi greeting the people from the balcony of Mani Bhavan, Bombay, in 1931.

*Source*: Vithalbhai Jhaveri Collection/Dinodia Photos.

**Figure 6.4**   Gandhi addressing the volunteers at the Congress House, Bombay, on 17 March 1931.

*Source*: Vithalbhai Jhaveri Collection/Dinodia Photos.

workers of the suburbs for about an hour and then attended the meeting in the church compound just before the conclusion of Vallabhbhai J. Patel's address. After the meeting, he went to the *chhawani* (camp) and spoke to the Maharashtrian leaders for a couple of hours. Around noon, he motored to the Andheri railway station to catch the Frontier Mail and left for Delhi with Jamnalal Bajaj by 1 pm. The Frontier Mail especially stopped for about two minutes at the Andheri railway station to pick up Gandhi who was garlanded on behalf of the railway staff. Among those present on the platform included leaders such as Jivraj Mehta and Jankidevi Bajaj. Some leaders including Kasturba Gandhi, Vallabhbhai Patel (the president-elect of the Karachi Congress), Jawaharlal Nehru, Subhas Chandra Bose, Mahadev Desai, Devdas Gandhi, and several other members of the Sabarmati Ashram left for Delhi by the same train. There was a large gathering of about 8,000–10,000 people at Vile Parle to see Gandhi. The president of the meeting was K. Natarajan, and the speakers were Vallabhbhai J. Patel, Jamnalal Bajaj, Swami Anand, and Sakinabai Lukmani. Kamalabai Sonawala presented a sum of Rs 25,465 to Gandhi. Jamnalal Bajaj auctioned a gold *takli* (spindle) which Gandhi had been working on during the meeting. It was bought by Ram Narayan Harichandrai and fetched Rs 5,000. A sandalwood box given to Gandhi by the chhawani leaders was also auctioned for Rs 1,000.[29]

Gandhi came to Bombay on 16 April 1931 and bade farewell to Lord Irwin, the retiring viceroy. During his short stay in the city, he met the governor of Bombay regarding the question of land revenue and return of confiscated property of the peasants in Gujarat. He also spoke with the Congress workers and mill owners such as Sir N. Wadia, H.P. Mody, and Ambalal Sarabhai. The same evening, he received an address from the municipal corporation for the second time at the BMC hall. People in Bombay were very excited. A huge crowd had assembled outside the BMC building. The hall was full to the capacity, although the admission had been restricted to those having tickets. The address was inscribed in silk khadi and enclosed in a beautifully carved rosewood box. Boman Behram paid a tribute to Gandhi's 'invaluable work in the cause of India' and read the address. In his reply, Gandhi emphasized the importance of the villages and the need to take care of the poor. He said, 'Handsome is that handsome does, and Bombay the beautiful must do beautiful things for the poor.'[30] In addition, he had a discussion with Emerson (the secretary to the home department of the Indian government) and was also present in the meeting of the trustees of the Bhagini Samaj. He also met Shaukat Ali and the nawab of Bhopal.[31]

Prabhat pheris, a powerful medium to instill the spirit of nationalism in people, were resumed on 10 June 1931. About 50 members assembled at Chowpatty at 5.30 am, led by K.F. Nariman, the president of the Bombay Congress Committee, and walked to

**Figure 6.5** Gandhi addressing the people after receiving the civic address from the BMC on 18 April 1931.
*Source*: Vithalbhai Jhaveri Collection/Dinodia Photos.

Mani Bhavan, Gandhi's residence, to receive his blessings. Gandhi addressed the procession from a balcony. He said that they should finish their daily rounds before sunrise, singing selected songs of prayer and devotion to God and the motherland. He said no objectionable songs, inconsistent with the Congress creed, should be sung.[32] For Gandhi, the pheris were not only beautiful and part of a religious heritage but also very much a part of the immediate political struggle, a struggle whose tone he defined and whose mode of expression was typically his own.[33]

On 9 June 1931, the CWC met at Mani Bhavan to discuss the general situation in the country. Gandhi was against proceeding to London to attend the Second Round Table Conference unless the Hindu–Muslim question was resolved in India. (The First Round Table Conference convened in London on 12 November 1930 could not lead to any outcome, as neither the Congress nor Gandhi was a party to it.) He felt that if the conference became entangled in the communal issue right at the beginning, the real political and economic issues would not get adequate consideration. The working committee decided that if other conditions were favourable, Gandhi should represent the Congress at the Round Table Conference. He accepted the verdict but took the public into confidence. The committee also passed many other resolutions, important among them being 'Congress and Communal Settlement', 'The National Flag', 'The Labourers', and 'Condemnation of Political Murders'.[34]

Various assignments in Bombay kept him busy: meetings of the working committee on 9, 10, and 11 June, and one of the Akhil Bharat Charkha Sangh on 9 June. On 11 June, Gandhi addressed desh sevikas, distributed certificates to members of the Hindustani Seva Dal, and also visited the Swadeshi Electric Clock Manufacturing Company. He clarified to around 30 Europeans who had come to see him that '[o]ur attitude will be impartial to all'.[35] On 25 June, he had discussions with the representatives of a company exporting foreign cloth, had a meal with young

**Figure 6.6** Gandhi in the balcony of Mani Bhavan, Bombay, in 1931 with Kamala Nehru, Jawaharlal Nehru, and other leaders.
*Source*: Mani Bhavan Gandhi Sangrahalaya.

progressive Europeans at the Taj Mahal Hotel, and talked about the issues in the context of the discussion of 11 June. He paid a condolence visit to the family of Pannalal in Bhuleshwar. On 9 June 1931, Pannalal was stabbed when he and his father attended a meeting addressed by Khan Abdul Ghaffar Khan at Dongri.[36] On 26 June 1931, Gandhi addressed a women's meeting at Madhav Baug. Balu, a well-known cricketer, also met him the same day with a deputation of the depressed classes and presented an address. A deputation of the Rashtriya Stree Sabha also called in.[37]

July again was a busy month in Bombay. Gandhi met Shaukat Ali and attended the meeting of the working committee on 7 and 8 July. The meeting continued on 9, 10, 11, and 12 July. On 9 June, he sent a telegram to the viceroy mentioning his 'difficulty about attending Federal Structure Committee owing continuing breaches of settlement by several provincial authorities'.[38] Complaints were pouring in from all over India that the officials were breaking the Gandhi–Irwin Pact. On 7 July, the CWC met in Mani Bhavan to consider the situation. Gandhi wrote about the state of affairs in *Young India* dated 9 July 1931. Correspondence including telegrams was exchanged between the government and Gandhi on various issues arising out of the pact and his participation in the Round Table Conference. Through his letter dated 14 August 1931, Gandhi informed the viceroy that he would not attend the Round Table Conference. However, he also conveyed that the working committee had passed a resolution that morning that non-participation by the Congress in the Round Table Conference should not be construed as ending the Delhi settlement.[39]

In August, Gandhi attended the meetings of the working committee on 5, 6, 9, 11, and 12 August, and of the A.I.C.C. on 6, 7, and 8 August. On 7 August, he also attended a public meeting under the aegis of the Parsi Rajkiya Sabha at Cowasji Jehangir Hall. There was also a meeting at Swadeshi Market. On 11 August, he wrote to the viceroy that he could not go to London. The nawab of Cambay, Prabhashankar Pattani, and K.T. Shah also called in. He also went to see Abid Ali who was beaten up while picketing near a liquor shop.[40] On 14 August, he held discussions with Sapru, Jayakar, Pattani, and Ambedkar.[41] In his telegram to the viceroy dated 11 August, he had expressed that the government was 'both prosecutor and judge with reference to matters arising out of a contract to which they and the complainants are parties. This is an impossible position for Congress to accept.'[42]

On 9 August 1931, a special conference of the Hindustani Seva Dal was held in the People's Jinnah Hall to consider the question of acceptance of the CWC resolution, which brought the organization under the direct control of the Congress. Gandhi opened the proceedings of the conference and Vallabhbhai J.

Patel presided over it. About 50 delegates, including 30 female delegates, and 250 visitors attended. Prominent among those who attended the conference were Jawaharlal Nehru, K.F. Nariman, S.V. Sovani, N.S. Hardikar, B. Sambarmurti, Kamaladevi, D.D. Sathaye, Khan Abdul Ghaffar Khan, Avantikabai Gokhale, Baba Saheb Deshmukh, Babu Rajendra Prasad, Chandulal Desai, Mohanlal Saxena, and Abidali Jafferbhai.[43] He laid emphasis on non-violence. He said that when there was mass awakening and no discipline, 'many evils are sure to creep in'.[44]

The talks between Gandhi and the Congress on the one hand and with the government on the other continued. Following the meeting between Lord Willingdon and Gandhi at Simla, a communiqué, sometimes called the 'Second Settlement', was published on 28 August. It provided that the Congress would be

**Figure 6.7** People congregating at Ballard Pier to bid farewell to Gandhi, who was sailing by *S.S. Rajputana* from Bombay to London on 29 August 1931 to attend the Round Table Conference.
*Source*: Vithalbhai Jhaveri Collection/Dinodia Photos.

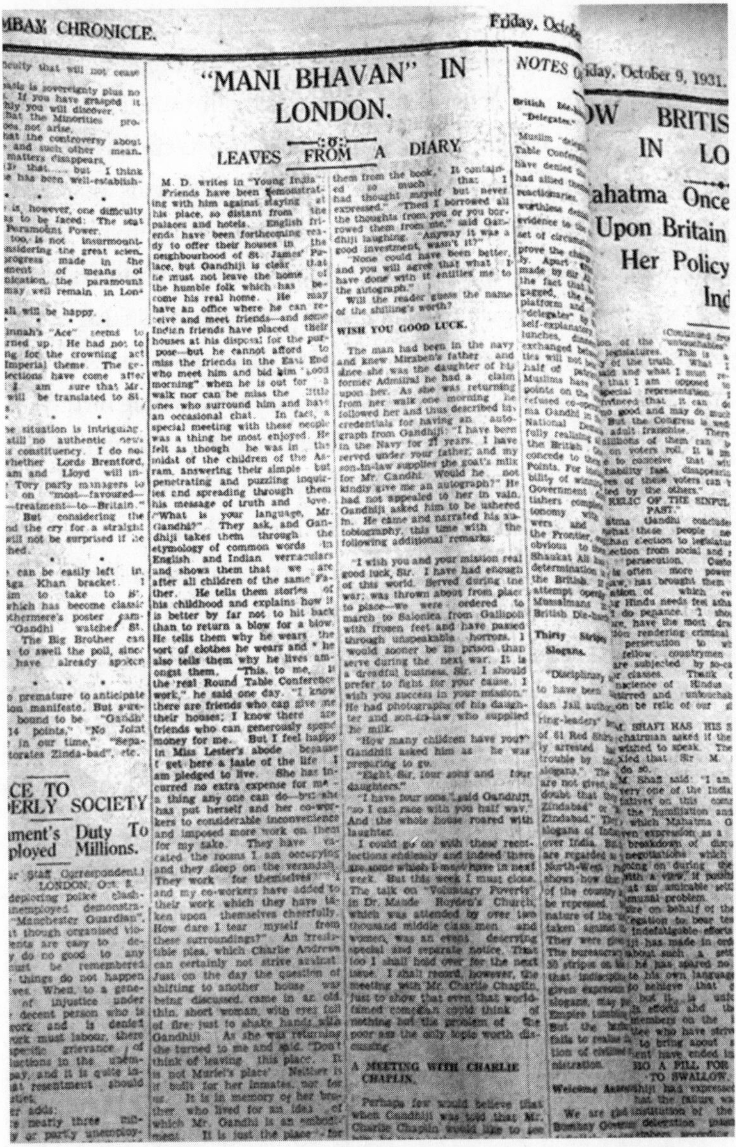

BOMBAY CHRONICLE. Friday, October 9, 1931.

# "MANI BHAVAN" IN LONDON.

## LEAVES FROM A DIARY.

M. D. writes in "Young India":

Friends have been remonstrating with him against staying at his place, so distant from the palaces and hotels. English friends have been forthcoming ready to offer their houses in the neighbourhood of St. James' Palace, but Gandhiji is clear that he must not leave the home of the humble folk which has become his real home. He may have an office where he can receive and meet friends—and some Indian friends have placed their houses at his disposal for the purpose—but he cannot afford to miss the friends in the East End who meet him and bid him "good morning" when he is out for a walk nor can he miss the little ones who surround him and have an occasional chat. In fact, a special meeting with these people was a thing he most enjoyed. He felt as though he was in the midst of the children of the Asram, answering their simple but penetrating and puzzling inquiries and spreading through them his message of truth and love. "What is your language, Mr. Gandhi?" They ask, and Gandhiji takes them through the etymology of common words in English and Indian vernaculars and shows them that we are after all children of the same Father. He tells them stories of his childhood and explains how it is better by far not to hit back than to return a blow for a blow. He tells them why he wears the sort of clothes he wears and he also tells them why he lives amongst them. "This, to me, is the real Round Table Conference work," he said one day. "I know there are friends who can give me their houses; I know there are friends who can generously spend money for me. But I feel happy in Miss Lester's abode because I get here a taste of the life I am pledged to live. She has incurred no extra expense for me—a thing any one can do—but she has put herself and her co-workers to considerable inconvenience and imposed more work on them for my sake. They have vacated the rooms I am occupying and they sleep on the verandah. They work for themselves ... I and my co-workers have added to their work which they have taken upon themselves cheerfully. How dare I tear myself from these surroundings?" An irresistible plea, which Charlie Andrews can certainly not strive against. Just on the day the question of shifting to another house was being discussed, came in an old thin, short woman with eyes full of fire just to shake hands with Gandhiji. As she was returning she turned to me and said. "Don't think of leaving this place. It is not Muriel's place. Neither is it built for her inmates, nor for us. It is in memory of her brother who lived for an idea of which Mr. Gandhi is an embodiment. It is just the place for them from the book." It contained so much that I had thought myself but never expressed." "Then I borrowed all the thoughts from you or you borrowed them from me," said Gandhiji laughing. "Anyway it was a good investment, wasn't it?"

"None could have been better, and you will agree that what I have done with it entitles me to the autograph."

Will the reader guess the name of the shilling's worth?

### WISH YOU GOOD LUCK.

The man had been in the navy and knew Mirabehn's father and since she was the daughter of his former Admiral he had a claim upon her. As she was returning from her walk one morning he followed her and thus described his credentials for having an autograph from Gandhiji: "I have been in the Navy for 21 years. I have served under your father, and my son-in-law supplies the goat's milk for Mr. Gandhi. Would he not kindly give me an autograph?" He had not appealed to her in vain. Gandhiji asked him to be ushered in. He came and narrated his autobiography, this time with the following additional remarks:

"I wish you and your mission real good luck, Sir. I have had enough of this world. Served during the war; was thrown about from place to place—we were ordered to march to Salonica from Gallipoli with frozen feet and have passed through unspeakable horrors. I would sooner be in prison than serve during the next war. It is a dreadful business, Sir. I should prefer to fight for your cause. I wish you success in your mission." He had photographs of his daughter and son-in-law who supplied the milk.

"How many children have you?" Gandhiji asked him as he was preparing to go.

"Eight, Sir, four sons and four daughters."

"I have four sons," said Gandhiji, "so I can race with you half way." And the whole house roared with laughter.

I could go on with these recollections endlessly and indeed there are some which I must have in next week. But this week I must close. The talk on "Voluntary Poverty" in Dr. Maude Royden's Church which was attended by over two thousand middle class men and women, was an event deserving special and separate notice. That too I shall hold over for the next issue. I shall record, however, the meeting with Mr. Charlie Chaplin, just to show that even that world-famed comedian could think of nothing but the problem of the poor as the only topic worth discussing.

### A MEETING WITH CHARLIE CHAPLIN.

Perhaps few would believe that when Gandhiji was told that Mr. Charlie Chaplin would like to see ...

**Figure 6.8** Mahadev Desai continued to write his daily dairy from London where he accompanied Gandhi for the Round Table Conference in 1931. The *Bombay Chronicle* dated 9 October 1931 gave an apt headline to one of his diary entries: 'Mani Bhavan in London'.

*Source*: The Asiatic Society of Mumbai.

solely represented at the Round Table Conference by Gandhi. The document was signed on 27 August. A special train from Simla to Kalka was arranged to enable Gandhi to reach Bombay in time to catch *S.S. Rajputana*. The police commissioner of Bombay received a telegram from Simla on 27 August that said: 'Gandhi will arrive at Bombay on Saturday morning to catch the mail steamer leaving for England that day he has no passport will you kindly arrange that he has no difficulty in getting one— Home.' A special passport was issued to Gandhi within 24 hours. A noteworthy feature of this passport was that a wrong birth year was entered in it due to the rushed circumstances. Gandhi wrote from Mani Bhavan before his departure, 'I must go to London with God as my only guide.... The horizon is as black as it possibly could be. There is every chance of my returning empty-handed.'[45] In a public meeting on 29 August 1931, he said, 'I am a cripple, but it is not only natural that a crippled nation should have a crippled delegate who alone can understand the difficulties and miseries of the millions.'[46]

## On Return from the Round Table Conference

Gandhi arrived in Bombay on 29 August. He went to a public meeting at the Azad Maidan and received address from the National Christian Party. He sailed to London on 29 August 1931 by *S.S. Rajputana* to attend the Second Round Table Conference. Those who came to wish him bon voyage were Kasturba, Vallabhbhai Patel, Maniben Patel, K.M. Munshi, Jivraj Mehta, Ibrahim Rahimtullah, H.P. Mody, and Kasturbhai Lalbhai. During Gandhi's absence, the city celebrated his birthday with great enthusiasm. Programmes celebrating his birthday included those related to khadi and flag salutation. An interesting highlight was an intercommunity event at

**Figure 6.9**  Gandhi arrived in Bombay from Simla to travel to London to attend the Round Table Conference. The *Bombay Chronicle* dated 29 August 1931 reports about the preparations made by Gandhi and others to travel to London.

*Source*: The Asiatic Society of Mumbai.

the Congress House attended by 500 people including those belonging to the depressed classes.[47]

The city was delighted on his return in December. A good deal of enthusiasm was noticed on the morning of 28 December when large crowds of people were seen thronging the route of the procession by which Gandhi was to pass. By 6 am, the route from Laburnum Road to the Mole Station was lined by the reception volunteers who also included children below the age of 12. The route was decorated, particularly at Sheikh Memon Street, Bhuleshwar, and Bazar Gate. About 500 female volunteers in saffron saris were in attendance from Central Hall to the Green Gate. At 8.25 am, the *S.S. Pilsna* came alongside the Mole and a large number of members of the working committee, including Vallabhbhai Patel, M.A. Ansari, Abdul Kalam Azad, K.F. Nariman, Sardar Sardul Singh, M.S. Aney, Jairamdas Daulatram, Alimchandani, Syed Mahmood, and other prominent people such as C. Rajagopalachari, Abbas Tyebji, Pattabhi Sitaramayya, Subhas Bose, Pandit Sunderlal, B. Samba Murti, K.M. Munshi, Kasturba, Reverend Elwin, N.S. Hardikar, Lilavati Munshi, Perin Captain, and Manilal Kothari boarded the steamer. After Lilavati Munshi had garlanded Gandhi, the party disembarked and proceeded to the Central Hall for the reception on behalf of various associations. From there, Gandhi and the members of the working committee drove in procession along the route prescribed.[48]

On his return, Gandhi was received very warmly by the people. The road from Ballard Pier to Mani Bhavan was decorated and people thronged the streets to welcome him. Throughout the route, rows of Congress volunteers tried to keep order in the crowds awaiting his arrival. According to Sitaramayya, 'That day the men-folk of Bombay were on the roads and the women-folk were gathered on the balconies of the sky-scrapers of the city.'[49] On the evening of 28 December, he was given a public welcome by Vallabhbhai Patel on behalf of the BPCC on the Esplanade Maidan. The whole maidan from Dhobitalao to Waudly Road was packed with people. Loudspeakers were installed to enable the crowds to listen to the speeches. A large number of volunteers, both men and women, maintained order at the meeting that lasted only for half an hour. Almost all the members of the working committee and those of the BPCC were present.[50]

Gandhi had returned home full of frustration. The government repression was continuing and the country was burdened with many ordinances. Winston Churchill, the right-wing leader in England, was opposed to the British government negotiating with Gandhi on equal terms. In India, the government reverted to its repressive policy. Abdul Ghaffar Khan was arrested on 24 December and Jawaharlal Nehru on 26 December, two days before Gandhi's arrival in India.

Gandhi gave a detailed account of his work in England and Europe to the CWC members and listened to the representatives from Bengal and UP. The working committee demanded an impartial public inquiry into the ordinance question. Gandhi lost no time and sat with the CWC at Mani Bhavan to discuss the situation. Some members were of the view that the government policy meant a complete breach between the Congress and the government, and further negotiations were useless. Gandhi advised the committee to defer its decision until he had a chance to ascertain the government's view before renewing the struggle.[51]

**Figure 6.10** Gandhi in a meeting with Rajendra Prasad, Maniben, Rajgopalachari, Sardar Patel, and others at the CWC in Mani Bhavan, Bombay, on 29 December 1931.
*Source*: Mani Bhavan Gandhi Sangrahalaya.

Within a few hours of his arrival on 28 December, Gandhi addressed a mass meeting at Azad Maidan; it was 'the biggest that any public speaker in Bombay had ever dreamt of'.[52]. He concluded by saying:

What I have to tell you now is that, if there is to be a fight, be prepared for every sacrifice, but take a pledge that you will not do harm to others. I will do all that lies within the power of a human being to prevent another fiery ordeal, but if I find that there is no other way out, I will not hesitate to call upon you to go through it, whatever the magnitude of sufferings may be. May God give us the strength to suffer and sacrifice in the cause of freedom.[53]

Gandhi was the guest of honour at a meeting of the Welfare of India League held on Monday night, 28 December, at the Hotel Majestic and presided over by Sir Stanley Reed. Prabhashankar Pattani, Pheroz Sethna, Nassarvanji Choksy, Vallabhbhai Patel, and some members of the CWC were present in the meeting. He explained the situation in the country and concluded by saying that 'I appeal to you, Englishmen and women, to ponder over the facts I have placed before you tonight and do your bit for creating an atmosphere of love and peace in this country.' [54]

On 29 December, Gandhi sent a telegram from Mani Bhavan to the viceroy:

I was unprepared on landing yesterday to find Frontier and U.P. Ordinances shootings in Frontier and arrests of valued comrades in both on top of the Bengal ordinance awaiting me. I do not know whether I am to regard these as an indication that friendly relations between us are closed or whether you expect me still to see you and receive guidance from you as to the course I am to pursue in advising the Congress. I would esteem a wire in reply.[55]

An address was presented to Gandhi on behalf of over 50 depressed classes associations from all over the Presidency, on the terrace of Mani Bhavan after the evening prayers on 28 December.[56] In reply, Gandhi said, 'I am conscious of the great harm the Hindu society has done by keeping you out. Adult suffrage and joint electorates would facilitate social life between you and the caste Hindus, and the day will not be far away when all these distinctions would cease to exist.'[57] On 29 December 1931, he addressed the Hindustan Seva Dal women and held discussions with Subhas Chandra Bose.[58]

On 30 December, he addressed women volunteers at Matunga, held a discussion with Jayaprakash Narayan, and went to see the ailing Sir Chinubhai. He also hurried the work of buying good English watches for Rogers and Evans (members of the British secret service who were with Gandhi from 4 November 1931 to 14 December 1931) and sending them as gifts before getting arrested.[59]

In the evening of 31 December 1931, a prayer meeting was held in the public garden near Gandhi's camp. Gandhi spoke in Gujarati, his mother tongue. Earlier the working committee had considered the viceroy's telegram (justifying the harsh steps taken by the government), which was received at 4 pm. Gandhi said, 'During one or two days more of freedom that I have left, let us say our prayers in peace.'[60] He continued with his activities. On the same day, he also visited the Lady Northcote Orphanage and went to see the ailing Sarladevi Sarabhai. The working committee decided to restart the satyagraha.[61]

When the viceroy's reply to Gandhi's telegram (of more than 1,200 words and emphasizing his creed of non-violence) dated 1 January 1932 was handed over to him on the evening of 2 January at Mani Bhavan, he smiled and remarked, 'Now I am preparing to go to jail.' Kasturba and Vallabhbhai Patel were seated around him.[62] On 1 January 1932, the resolution of the CWC, drafted by Gandhi, calling upon the nation to resume civil disobedience was adopted. Gandhi had sent his rejoinder to the government that if the viceroy refused to discuss with him the Frontier, UP, and Bengal ordinances, the nation would resort to civil disobedience. The Gandhi–Willingdon correspondence was also released. On 2 January, Gandhi had talks with the deputation of the Welfare of India League. The viceroy rejected Gandhi's request for an interview. On 3 January, Gandhi wired to the government regretting the government's decision and assuring a non-violent struggle. He sent messages to America and Indian Christians. In an interview with the *Bombay Chronicle*, he outlined the plan of action to be followed after his arrest and spoke about the utility of prayer.[63]

The day was full of interviews, messages, and meetings with people. Gandhi sent a message to Kheda farmers and dictated a note on the temple-entry satyagraha.[64] At about 2 am on 3 January 1932, Gandhi told the following to a reporter from the Associated Press of India on telephone:

The nation must now respond to the challenge of the Government. It is hoped, however, that whilst the people belonging to all classes and creeds will courageously and in all humility go through the fiery ordeal considering no price too dear and no suffering too great, they will observe strictest non-violence in thought, word and deed, no matter how great the provocation may be. I would also urge them not to be angry with the administrators. It is not easy for them to shed the habit handed down from generation to generation. Our quarrel is not with men but with measures.[65]

In his message to America conveyed through Mills, an American press correspondent, he expressed, 'This Indian struggle is more than national. It has international value and importance.'[66] Leading liberals and merchants continued to come and see Gandhi. Some non-Congress leaders including Sir Purshotamdas, Sir Cowasji, Pheroz Sethna, and Jayakar came to see Gandhi on 3 January and requested him to be in Bombay since 'we are in correspondence with the Viceroy'.[67]

It is interesting to note that in January 1932 a huge crowd used to join the prayers at Mani Bhavan. Gandhi feared that the terrace and the staircase of Mani Bhavan would collapse with the weight of so many people. He requested the trustees of the Lady Northcote Orphanage to allow him to have his prayers in their large compound. The trustees obliged, and thousands would join him in the evening prayers there.[68]

## Gandhi's Arrest

Under the circumstances, the government was gearing up to suppress people's movement and Gandhi's arrest seemed imminent. Sensing danger from Gandhi and his movement, the Indian government sent secret instructions to the Bombay government for his 'imminent arrest'. A warrant of Gandhi's arrest was prepared on 3 January 1932: 'Whereas the Governor in Council, for good and sufficient reasons, has, under the powers vested in him by Bombay Regulation XXV of 1827 resolved that Mr. Mohandas Karamchand Gandhi shall be placed under restraint in the Yervada Central Prison during the pleasure of Government.'[69]

Despite being under heavy pressure, Gandhi was unruffled and unperturbed. On the evening of 3 January, he wrote to Tagore, 'I want you to give your best to the sacrificial fire that is lighted.'[70]

His message to the people was unambiguous. In an interview to the *Bombay Chronicle* on 3 January 1932, he said:

What I would ask the nation to do after my arrest, is to wake up from its sleep; and 1. to discard at once all foreign cloth and take to khaddar; 2. to discard all drugs, narcotics, and intoxicating drinks; 3. to discard every trace of violence and give absolute protection to every Englishman,

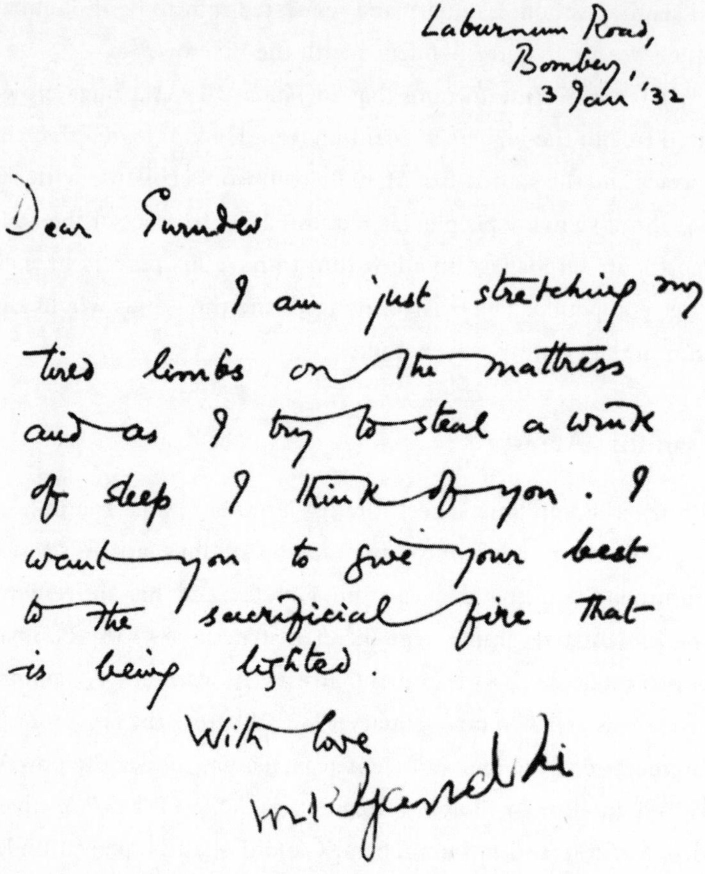

Laburnum Road,
Bombay,
3 Jan '32

Dear Surnder

I am just stretching my
tired limbs on the mattress
and as I try to steal a wink
of sleep I think of you. I
want you to give your best
to the sacrificial fire that
is being lighted.

With love
MKGandhi

Figure 6.11  Gandhi's letter to Tagore, 'I am just stretching my tired limbs', written from Mani Bhavan, Bombay, on 3 January 1932.
*Source*: Mani Bhavan Gandhi Sangrahalaya.

woman or child whether official or otherwise, no matter how provocative the action of officials may be; 4. to withdraw from Government every form of co-operation that is possible for every individual; and 5. to study the resolution of the Working Committee and carry it out to the letter and in the spirit and in that process suffer all hardships that they may be put to, including loss of life and property.[71]

He further added:

It is difficult to lay down one rule for the whole of India. But it seems to me that, since the Congress has adopted the method of self-purification through non-violence, I should begin by *hartal*, that is, voluntary suspension of all works for profit and undergo a prayerful fast and then begin simultaneously civil disobedience in such manner as may be possible in each locality such as (*a*) unlicensed manufacture of salt, (*b*) picketing of liquor and foreign-cloth shops, (*c*) breach of orders under Section 144 and the like when there is no likelihood of breach of peace and where orders have been issued not out of any legal necessity but manifestly for the sake of crushing the spirit of the people of what is the same thing as suppressing the Congress.[72]

As to what particular items of programme Bombay should follow, he left to K.F. Nariman and his council. When questioned that whether the work of carrying on the commands of the Congress would prove difficult if all the listed Congress workers were removed from the field of action, Gandhi commented that the resolution of the working committee was framed to cover the difficulty raised. After an experience of nearly 12 years of satyagraha in a more-or-less acute form, individuals were expected to know what the change in circumstances would require. The recent experience had showed that in spite of the imprisonment of almost all the leaders, the nation had showed marvellous resourcefulness in the emergency as it arose and kept up the spirit of civil defiance.[73]

Mani Bhavan was vibrant with all the political activities around. Gandhi had many visitors and guests and had managed to say and write important messages. Verrier Elwin, the renowned anthropologist and tribal activist, has given a touching description of the situation. He was invited by Gandhi to stay at Mani Bhavan. Elwin says:

There was great excitement in the city; the Viceroy had finally rejected the Congress offer of peace; Nehru was already in jail, and the arrest of other national leaders was expected at any moment. But when we reached Mani Bhuvan and climbed to the roof, we found a great serenity in astonishing contrast to the crowds and turmoil outside. The roof was a very pleasant place. Low tents had been erected, and there were palms and plants: at least 300 people could gather there. It was cool and you could see the stars. Bapu was sitting at the wheel quietly spinning. He had already begun his weekly silence. I carried on a one-sided conversation with him, and he wrote down his questions and replies on a scrap of paper.... Then Shamroa and I retired to the smaller tent and Bapu lay down about three yards from us, while some thirty others lay on the roof under the canvas shelter. Mrs. Gandhi and Mirabehn gave us a surprisingly satisfying supper of dates, nuts and fruit. But I could not sleep. As I wrote at the time, 'I felt I had to keep vigil, and for hours I was under those splendid stars that rose, tier upon tier above me, while beside me Bapu slept like a child committed to his Father's hands. I thought of Christ going up to Jerusalem, his eyes filled with determination and courage: and I seemed to see the Spirit of Christ travelling the centuries like a bright sword turned against all wrong and injustice. Among those sleeping friends so dear to us, brave, pure-hearted, sincere, the spirit of Love was manifest and unconquerable.'[74]

Thereafter, at 3 am on 4 January, the police arrived to arrest Gandhi. G.S. Wilson, the police commissioner, and the police force had made the required preparations for their important assignment. He had written its exhaustive account. In his words:

[S]ome half a dozen of us, got into the car destined for Gandhi's conveyance to Poona, and drove the few hundred yards distance which had to be covered between the Police Station and Mani Bhuwan, Mr. Gandhi's house. As we turned into the road where the house is situated we observed a sleepy group of five Congress volunteers in spotless Khaddar and caps sitting at the corner. These immediately grasped the situation but made no demonstration. The watchman at the gate opened it and let us in. Our arrival, I think, was not unanticipated for as we went up the staircase passing the entrances to the two flats we found the doors open and groups of people looking out eager to witness what to them was one of the great events of the Indian drama. Mr. Gandhi and his immediate entourage live and have their being on the damp by nigh roof of the block the flats known as Mani Bhuwan. A tent is pitched for protection from sun by day and damp by night and the floor of the roof is carpeted with mattresses and cushions. On the landing below the staircase leading to the roof Devdas Gandhi, Mr. Gandhi's second son met me and took me to the roof. Mr. Gandhi was sleeping on a mattress surrounded by both men and women among whom was Miraben alias Miss Slade. On being awakened Mr. Gandhi sat up but uttered no word as it was his silence day. I said to Mr. Gandhi 'it is my duty to arrest you' and showed him the warrant to take him to Yervada Jail under the old Bombay Regulation of 1827, I read out the warrant to him and touched his shoulder in token of having arrested him and told him that I would give him half an hour to get ready. Asking for paper and pencil he wrote 'I will be ready in exactly half an hour'.[75]

Mirabehn collected Gandhi's kit and made preparations for the morning prayer. His jail kit contained a portable charkha, a mattress, two handbags, a fruit basket, a pair of sandals, and a bottle of milk. The prayer was held on the terrace of Mani Bhavan. '*Vaishnav jan to tene kahiye je peer parai jane re*' was sung by all those present who touched his feet to bid him farewell and receive his blessings. Gandhi wrote out farewell messages and instructions to his associates. Gandhi's message to his people, in a note to Vallabhbhai Patel, read: 'Infinite is God's mercy. Never swerve from truth and non-violence, never turn your back, and sacrifice your lives and all to win swaraj.'[76] He did not know then that Vallabhbhai was also arrested. He emerged out of Mani Bhavan, walked arm in arm with Devdas to the police car, and quietly took his seat. He was cheered by the large crowd which had by then collected outside Mani Bhavan.[77] This was his fifth imprisonment.[78]

The city had observed a complete hartal on Gandhi's arrest. A procession of thousands of men and women proceeded from the Congress House in the afternoon, and after going through the important roads in the city, it ended as a mass meeting at Azad Maidan. K.F. Nariman presided over the meeting. He exhorted the people of Bombay to carry on the non-violent struggle until freedom was won. Meetings were also held by the different ward committees condemning Gandhi's arrest.[79]

Oppressive ordinances were promulgated on 4 January 1932, and from that date the Congress and its allied organizations were declared illegal. Between January 1932 and April 1933, as many as 14,101 people including 939 women were convicted in the Bombay Presidency.[80]

The women of the Desh Sevika Sangh were very active after Gandhi's arrest. Sarojini Naidu, Kamaladevi, Hansa Mehta, Perin Captain, Avantikabai Lilavati Munshi, and others were busy picketing in favour of swadeshi and boycott of foreign cloth and liquor. The Mulji Jetha cloth market was paralysed for more than three months until Sarojini Naidu inaugurated the Swadeshi Wing in the market on 7 April 1932.[81] The Mulji Jetha Market observed a hartal for three months in 1932, and after 7 April, during the National Week, the dealers opened a swadeshi wing to deal in Indian piece-goods approved by the Congress. The *Bombay Chronicle* of 8 April 1932 reported: 'A fervent exhortation to the merchants of Bombay to stand by the creed of Swadeshi and help the country to achieve freedom was made by Mrs. Sarojini Naidu in declaring open the Swadeshi Wing of the Mulji Jetha Market on Thursday.' She said amidst cheers, 'You the merchants of Bombay, I am glad to say, have fully shown that you are solidly behind the patriots who have sacrificed everything in the cause of the country.[82]

The favourite venues of picketing of foreign cloth were the Mulji Jetha Market, the Mangaldas Market, the Lakshmidas Market, Hornby Road, Esplanade Road, and Masjid Bunder Road. Areas such as Princess Street, Lohar Chawl, and Sheikh Memon Street were also the sites for agitation.

After Gandhi's arrest, the emergency councils of the BPCC became very active in the city. 'Dictators' were appointed for each ward and each District Congress Committee in the city. Bombay City was divided into seven wards, each with the local organizing 'dictator', and by the end of March 1932, 20 emergency councils had been arrested.[83] However, the intensive nationalist campaign and picketing continued despite the police raids. It was not easy for the police to suppress these activities because of their diffused nature. The Bombay Congress Bulletin, the *Congress Prabhat Patrika*, the Kamgar Bulletin, and the Students' Bulletin were circulated occasionally for dissemination of information and messages.

Several occasions and days were especially celebrated. The fourth day of every month was celebrated as Gandhi Day until he was released. Hartals were observed on these days. At some places, salt was manufactured and sold in packets in public meetings. The National Week was celebrated from 6 to 13 April. It assumed a different significance in 1932 in view of the intensity of the movement and the atrocities by the administration. Each day was symbolic of the various aspects of the movement. The first day was celebrated as the Ladies Day in recognition of their contribution. Then there were the Flag Day and the Swadeshi Day. The fourth day was devoted to the boycott of foreign cloth. The fifth thrilling event of the next day or the Workers' and Peasants' Day was the arrest of Achyut Patwardhan, who was working secretly in Bombay. This day was followed by the No Tax to Government Day. The last day was the Jallianwala Bagh Day. Throughout the week, many men and women were arrested and convicted.[84]

According to a report from Bombay, while it was not yet possible to examine statistically the effect of Mahatma Gandhi's boycott, the official trade return for April showed that the imports of piece goods were 165,000,000 yards compared to 215,000,000 yards in April 1929 and 188,000,000 yards in April 1928.[85] The middle class of Bombay remained a strong base of the movement; many Gujarati and Marwari merchants were with Gandhi. Gandhi and his movement received support from associations such as the Cotton Brokers' Association, the Grain Merchants' Association, the Bombay Shroffs' Association, the Indian Merchants' Chamber, and the Bombay Native Piece-goods Merchants' Association. According to A.D.D. Gordon, as was the case with the 1918–22 agitations, the predominantly Gujarati petty traders and marketers formed the backbone of the Congress civil disobedience campaign of boycott and hartal in Bombay. There was also a marked degree of overlap between leaders of merchant groups and the Congress, two outstanding examples being Hirachand Vanechand Desai and Virchand Panachand Shah. Desai was the president of the Bombay Shroffs' Association during 1928–9 and played an important role as a Congressman in 1930 when he roused the shroffs by using economic arguments and by directing his attack against the hated Imperial Bank. Shah, also a prominent shroff, became the Congress 'dictator' or the head of the War Council in 1930. In 1930, Begraj Gupta was another Congressman who led the merchants, especially those of the cotton and bullion bazaars. Mathuradas Matani, Mathuradas

Tricumji, Mulraj Kasondas, Vithaldas Jerajani, Vithaldas Govindji, C.B. Mehta, and Velji Napoo were all prominent merchants and leading Congressmen.[86]

Pointing out the inputs of the Parsis, Aloo Dastur comments:

One contribution of the Parsis to nationalism is worth recording. At [the] Round Table Conference when leaders vied with each other to seek benefits and advantages for their respective religious groups and begged for reservations, the three Parsis nominated or invited by the British Government were Sir Pheroze Sethna, Sir Cowasji Jehangir and Sir Homi Mody. They were tempted to ask for reservation. Their attempt was failed by Burjorji Bharucha, who under the auspices of the Parsi Rajkiya Sabha convened public meetings of Parsis in several parts of Bombay and moved resolutions against reservations or any other privileges for the community. He cabled these resolutions to Lord Sankey, the Chairman of the Round Table Conference, Ramsey MacDonald, the Prime Minister, Mahatma Gandhi and the three Parsi members. Thus was the move was foiled.[87]

However, this time the Muslims of the city, by and large, could not be drawn into the movement, as there was dissatisfaction in certain sections of Muslims. On his return from England on 29 January 1932, Shaukat Ali had put the responsibility of the disappointment of the Round Table Conference on Gandhi. A little later the relations between Hindus and Muslims also became tense and a riot broke out on 14 and 15 May 1932. As pointed out by A.D.D. Gordon, some industrialists, elites, and liberals in Bombay, such as Thakurdas, Ness Wadia, F.E. Dinshaw, Sir Pheroze Sethna, Jehangir, and Setalvad, believed that the boycott was damaging the city's economy.[88]

Despite the disturbances and disquiet, Gandhi's spell continued. Gandhi's leadership had certainly made a difference to the political atmosphere of Bombay. In the words of K.M.

Munshi, 'Political consciousness, so far confined to a section of the highly educated in the city, began to filter down to the middle class, both upper and lower. Flowering during the Gandhian movement of 1930, it made Bombay the citadel of national movement.'[89]

## Notes and References

1. Kumar, 'From Swaraj to Purna Swaraj', pp. 267–8.
2. 'Bombay Presidency Police Abstracts of Intelligence' cited in K.K. Chaudhari (ed.), *Source Material for a History of the Freedom Movement in India, Civil Disobedience Movement (April>September 1930)*, Vol. XI, e-Book edition (Bombay: Gazetteers Department, Government of Maharashtra, 2007), p. 573.
3. Kumar, 'From Swaraj to Purna Swaraj', p. 268.
4. 'Daily Reports of the Police Commissioner of Bombay', Confidential No. 1582/H, Head Police Office, Bombay, 8 April 1930 cited in Chaudhari, *Source Material for a History of the Freedom Movement in India*, Vol. XI, pp. 11–12.
5. Kumar, 'From Swaraj to Purna Swaraj', p. 269.
6. 'Daily Reports of the Police Commissioner of Bombay', Confidential No. 1611/H, Head Police Office, Bombay, 9 April 1930; Confidential 1627/H/3717, Head Police Office, Bombay, 10 April 1930; and Confidential No. 1641/H/3717, 11 April 1930 cited in Chaudhari, *Source Material for a History of the Freedom Movement in India*, Vol. XI, pp. 13–16.
7. Confidential No. 1682/H/3717, Head Police Office, 14 April 1930; Confidential No. 1703/H/3717, Head Police Office, 15 April 1930; Confidential No. 1730/H/3717, Head Police Office, 16 April 1930; Confidential No. 1758/H/371, Head Police Office, 17 April 1930; Confidential No. 1762/11/3717, Head Police Office, 18 April 1930; Confidential No. 1777/H/3717, Head Police Office, 19 April 1930; *The Bombay Chronicle* dated 19 April 1930; and Confidential No. 1784/11/3717, Head Police Office, 21 April 1930 cited in Chaudhari,

*Source Material for a History of the Freedom Movement in India,* Vol. XI, pp. 19–31.

8. *Young India* dated 12 March 1930 cited in *CWMG*, Vol. 43, p. 37.

9. Sitaramayya, *History of the Indian National Congress,* Vol. I, p. 400.

10. *The New York Times,* 2 June 1930.

11. Confidential No. 2427/H/3717, Head Police Office, Bombay, 22 May 1930 cited in Chaudhari, *Source Material for a History of the Freedom Movement in India,* Vol. XI, p. 121.

12. Chaudhari, *Source Material for a History of the Freedom Movement in India,* Vol. XI, p. 196.

13. Chaudhari, *Source Material for a History of the Freedom Movement in India,* Vol. XI, pp. 196–8.

14. *Mahasabha Suvarna Mahotsava,* p. 30; Jim Masselos, 'Controlling the Prabhat Pheris', in *The City in Action: Bombay Struggles for Power* (New Delhi: Oxford University Press, 2007), pp. 223–4.

15. Chaudhari, *Source Material for a History of the Freedom Movement in India,* Vol. XI, p. 270.

16. Chaudhari, *Source Material for a History of the Freedom Movement in India,* Vol. XI, p. 449.

17. *The New York Times,* 6 June 1930.

18. *The Times of India,* 2 September 1930.

19. *The Times of India,* 23 September 1930.

20. Rashtriya Stree Sabha, *Report of Desh Sevika Sangh, Bombay, 1930–1931,* p. 13.

21. Kunjlata Shah, 'Desh Sevika Sangh: A Troop of Women Warriors of Bombay in the Non-violent Struggle of 1930–31' (unpublished); Rashtriya Stree Sabha, *Report of Desh Sevika Sangh;* Geraldine Forbes, *Women in Modern India,* The New Cambridge History of India, Vol. 2, Part 4 (Cambridge University Press; New Delhi: Foundation Books, 1998), pp. 130–5; Gail Pearson, 'Women in Public Life in Bombay City with Special Reference to the Civil Disobedience Movement', PhD thesis, Jawaharlal Nehru University, New Delhi, 1979; *The New York Times,* 22 June 1930; *The Times of India,* 22 July 1930.

22. Confidential No. 4956/H/3717, Head Police Office, Bombay, 18 September 1930 cited in Chaudhari, *Source Material for a History of the Freedom Movement in India*, Vol. XI, pp. 516–17.

23. *Gandhiji and Mani Bhavan, 1917–1934* (New Delhi: Gandhi Smarak Nidhi, 1959), p. 25.

24. *The Sun*, 18 March 1931.

25. 'Bombay Secret Abstract', 1931, p. 668, para 940 (3)(4)(5)(6) cited in Kunte, *Source Material for a History of the Freedom Movement in India*, Vol. IX, p. 199.

26. Dalal, *Gandhijini Dinwari*, p. 289.

27. *Gandhiji and Mani Bhavan*, p. 25.

28. Dalal, *Gandhijini Dinwari*, pp. 289–90.

29. 'Bombay Secret Abstract', 1931, p. 668, para 940 (3)(4)(5)(6), Bombay Suburban District, March 21 cited in Kunte, *Source Material for a History of the Freedom Movement in India*, Vol. IX, pp. 200–1.

30. *Young India* dated 23 April 1931 cited in *CWMG*, Vol. 46 (New Delhi: Publications Division, Ministry of Information and Broadcasting, Government of India, 1971), p. 13; *The Times of India*, 20 April 1931.

31. Dalal, *Gandhijini Dinwari*, p. 294.

32. *The Hindu* dated 10 June 1931 cited in *CWMG*, Vol. 46, p. 356.

33. Masselos, 'Controlling the Prabhat Pheris', p. 238.

34. *Gandhiji and Mani Bhavan*, p. 26.

35. Dalal, *Gandhijini Dinwari*, p. 298.

36. Dalal, *Gandhijini Dinwari*, pp. 298–9.

37. Dalal, *Gandhi*, p. 89.

38. *Young India* dated 27 August 1931 cited in *CWMG*, Vol. 47 (New Delhi: Publications Division, Ministry of Information and Broadcasting, Government of India, 1971), p. 121.

39. *Young India* dated 20 August 1931 cited in *CWMG*, Vol. 47, pp. 290–1.

40. Dalal, *Gandhijini Dinwari*, p. 304.

41. Dalal, *Gandhi*, p. 91.

42. *Young India* dated 20 August 1931 cited in *CWMG*, Vol. 47, p. 281.

43. 'Bombay Secret Abstract', 1931, p. 1683, para 4093, Bombay, August 10 cited in Kunte, *Source Material for a History of the Freedom Movement in India*, Vol. IX, p. 205.

44. *The Bombay Chronicle* dated 10 August 1931 cited in *CWMG*, Vol. 47, p. 279.

45. *Gandhiji and Mani Bhavan*, p. 29.

46. *The Hindu* dated 29 August 1931 cited in *CWMG*, Vol. 47, p. 384.

47. *The Times of India*, 5 October 1931.

48. 'Bombay Secret Abstract', 1931, p. 110, para 164 cited in Kunte, *Source Material for a History of the Freedom Movement in India*, Vol. IX, pp. 210–11.

49. Sitaramayya, *History of the Indian National Congress*, Vol. I, p. 509.

50. 'Bombay Secret Abstract', 1931, p. 110, para 164 cited in Kunte, *Source Material for a History of the Freedom Movement in India*, Vol. IX, p. 211.

51. *Gandhiji and Mani Bhavan*, p. 30.

52. *CWMG*, Vol. 48, p. 446.

53. *The Bombay Chronicle* dated 29 December 1931 cited in *CWMG*, Vol. 48, pp. 449–50.

54. *The Hindu* dated 31 December 1931 cited in *CWMG*, Vol. 48, p. 458.

55. 'India in 1931–32' cited in *CWMG*, Vol. 48, p. 459.

56. Dalal, *Gandhi*, p. 96.

57. *Gandhiji and Mani Bhavan*, p. 32.

58. Dalal, *Gandhi*, p. 96.

59. Dalal, *Gandhi*, p. 96.

60. *The Hindustan Times* dated 3 January 1932 cited in *CWMG*, Vol. 48, p. 459.

61. Dalal, *Gandhi*, p. 96.

62. *Gandhiji and Mani Bhavan*, p. 33.

63. *CWMG*, Vol. 48, p. 513.

64. *The Hindu* dated 4 January 1932 and *Young India* dated 14 January 1932 cited in *CWMG*, Vol. 48, pp. 481–4.

65. *The Hindu* dated 3 January 1932 cited in *CWMG*, Vol. 48, p. 488.

66. *The Hindu* dated 3 January 1932 cited in *CWMG*, Vol. 48, p. 492.

67. Dalal, *Gandhi*, p. 97.

68. Dalal, *Mahadevbhaini Diary* (in Gujarati) [The Diary of Mahadevbhai], Vol. 15, 30 August 1931 to 9 March 1932 (Ahmedabad: Sabarmati Ashram Suraksha Ane Smarak Trust, 1976), p. 542.

69. *Gandhiji and Mani Bhavan*, p. 36.

70. *CWMG*, Vol. 48, p. 489. This letter was dictated to Mahadev Desai on 3 January at 4 am and signed the next day, 'a few moments after his actual arrest', according to a covering letter Desai sent along with it.

71. *The Bombay Chronicle* dated 4 January 1932 cited in *CWMG*, Vol. 48, pp. 490–1.

72. *The Bombay Chronicle* dated 4 January 1932 cited in *CWMG*, Vol. 48, pp. 490–1.

73. *The Bombay Chronicle* dated 4 January 1932 cited in *CWMG*, Vol. 48, p. 491.

74. Verrier Elwin, *The Tribal World of Verrier Elwin: An Autobiography* (New Delhi: Oxford University Press, 1988), pp. 65–6.

75. G.S. Wilson, 'Story of My Arrest of Gandhi on 4th Jan 1932 During the Civil Disobedience Troubles in Bombay'. We are grateful to David Wilson for giving this document to the Mani Bhavan Gandhi Sangrahalaya and his permission to take this extract in this book.

76. *Gandhiji and Mani Bhavan*, p. 38.

77. *Gandhiji and Mani Bhavan*, p. 38.

78. Dalal, *Gandhi*, p. 97.

79. Gopalswami, *Gandhi and Bombay*, p. 280.

80. Judith Brown, *Gandhi and Civil Disobedience: The Mahatma in Indian Politics, 1928–1934* (Cambridge: Cambridge University Press, 1977), p. 284.

81. Chaudhari, *Maharashtra State Gazetteers: History of Bombay—Modern Period* (Bombay: Gazetteers Department, Government of Maharashtra, 1987), p. 215.

82. Extract from the *Bombay Chronicle* dated 8 April 1932 cited in K.K. Chaudhari, *Source Material for a History of the Freedom Movement in India: Civil Disobedience Movement (October 1930–December*

*1941)*, Vol. XII, e-Book edition (Mumbai: Gazetteers Department, Government of Maharashtra, 2007), pp. 207–8.

83. Brown, *Gandhi and Civil Disobedience*, p. 287.

84. Chaudhari, *Maharashtra State Gazetteers*, p. 219.

85. *The New York Times*, 28 June 1930.

86. Gordon, *Businessmen and Politics*, p. 232.

87. Aloo J. Dastur, *Parsis and Nationalism in the Role of Minorities in Freedom Struggle*, Asghar Ali Engineer (ed.) (Delhi: Ajanta Publications, 1986), p. 156.

88. Gordon, *Businessmen and Politics*, pp. 217–18.

89. K.M. Munshi, *Pilgrimage to Freedom (1902–1950): Indian Constitutional Documents*, Vol. 1 (Bombay: Bharatiya Vidya Bhavan, 2012 [1967]), p. 9.

# 7

## PRELUDE TO THE QUIT INDIA
## MOVEMENT: 1932–41

PROCESSIONS AND MEETINGS IN THE CITY OF BOMBAY CONTINUED
much to the discomfort of the British government. The activities
related to the bonfire of foreign cloth and picketing outside the
stores that sold British goods also persisted. In 1932, Sir Frederick
Sykes wrote to the viceroy:

I see that the people at home are finding some difficulty in understanding
why it is that the Ordinances appear to have been less effective with
the civil disobedience movement in Bombay City than in other places.
Although the situation here is developing on lines which to us on the
spot were not unexpected, I have no doubt that the people at home,

understanding the position.[1]

He emphasized the connection between economic policy and the economy on the one hand and the merchants' cultural affinity with Gandhi on the other.[2] The programme of Gandhi and the Congress against intoxicating drinks made an impact on the lives of the people. It was reported that the government's receipts from liquor were the lowest in 10 years. It was also estimated that drunkenness decreased in 1931 by nearly 60 per cent and the sale of opium in Bombay Presidency decreased by 2,356 pounds in 1931.[3]

In tune with its policy of 'divide and rule', the British government had announced the Communal Award in August 1932. It allotted to each minority a number of seats in the legislatures to be elected on the basis of a separate electorate. In addition to Muslims, Sikhs, and Christians, the award also recognized the Depressed Classes as a minority community entitled to have a separate electorate, thus separating them from the Hindus. Gandhi was in Yerwada jail at that time, and from there, he strongly protested against it, as he considered it detrimental for Indian unity and nationalism. He went on a fast unto death on 20 September 1932 against the award and this gave a jolt to the people. There were discussions with B.R. Ambedkar and other leaders. Finally, on 26 September, Gandhi broke the fast in Tagore's presence in Yerwada jail. An understanding, known as the Poona Pact, was arrived at, which increased the number of seats reserved for the Depressed Classes in the provincial and central legislatures while withdrawing the provision of separate electorates for them.

The news of the award was received well in the city. At a public meeting in Bombay on 30 September 1932, the All-India

Anti-Untouchability League was formed with G.D. Birla as the president and Amritlal Thakkar (known as Thakkar Bapa) as the secretary. This was the early stage of the formation of the Servants of Untouchables Society (Harijan Sevak Sangh).[4]

## Constructive Work

Gandhi had stirred the hearts of the Indians not only by his non-violent agitation against the unjust British rule but also by his vision of a regenerated and revitalized social and economic order. Gandhi presented the humane face of development. Some basic objectives of the Gandhian scheme of holistic development were human development (including moral development) for capability expansion; development in a balanced way through manual and intellectual labour (development of body, mind, and soul); development with social justice, rights and freedom; attainment of self-sufficiency and self-reliance through rural development; and reduction in poverty through the generation of additional income and employment.[5]

Gandhi's emphasis on decentralization, community-based economics, self-sufficiency, spinning, promotion of khadi and handicrafts, village industries, Hindu–Muslim unity, national education, and removal of untouchability and other harmful social practices outlined his vision for a self-sufficient economy and a just society. Concerted efforts to initiate constructive activities were of vital importance for him, especially during the lean period of protests and agitations. He often talked and wrote about it. He had said at a prayer meeting held in the Congress House, 'I am told that there is despair and depression everywhere, that there is disappointment all round as the gateway to jail is closed. People, I am told, do not know what to do. I do not know why, when there is the whole of the constructive programme of work to do.'[6] According to Bipan Chandra, 'Constructive work was basic to a war of position. It played a crucial role during the "passive phase" in filling the political space left vacant by the withdrawal of civil disobedience, thus solving a basic problem that a mass movement faces, i.e., how to sustain a sense of activism in the non-mass movement phases of the struggle?'[7] While mass movements were sporadic, constructive work was to be carried on at all times.[8]

Gandhi's going to the jail was a familiar phenomenon to the government as well as the people. Soon after his release on 8 May 1933, the movement for individual civil disobedience started at Ahmedabad on 31 July 1933 and he was arrested the next day. He was taken to the Sabarmati jail and soon thereafter to the Yerwada jail. This was his seventh imprisonment.[9] He commenced fasting on 16 August as a protest against the government's decision not to grant him the facilities for the Harijan work that were provided to him previously. His condition deteriorated and he was therefore released on 23 August 1933 on medical grounds. He decided to devote the remaining period of his sentence to the service of Harijans and other constructive activities.

The public response to Gandhi's call for the removal of untouchability did undoubtedly affect the progress of the Civil Disobedience Movement.[10] The tempo of the movement was slowing down and the government was adamant. There were some leaders who wanted to enter the legislatures by getting elected. Many felt frustrated that the social issue of the removal of untouchability was taking precedence over political issues. The situation, however, did not dampen Gandhi's spirit. Explaining the difference between individual civil resistance and mass civil resistance, Gandhi wrote to Nehru on 14 September 1933, 'I have no sense of defeat in me and the hope in me that this country of ours is fast marching towards its goal is burning as bright as in 1920; for I have an undying faith in the efficacy of civil resistance.'[11]

Gandhi and the Congress decided at Patna to withdraw the Civil Disobedience Movement on 18 May 1934 after much deliberation on the political situation.[12] Gandhi toured the country extensively for the Harijan and Bihar earthquake campaigns and collected funds.

Gandhi was in Bombay from 14 to 17 June 1934 in connection with the Harijan work. The Bombay board of the Harijan Sevak Sangh, at a meeting held on 31 May in the office of the Indian Merchants' Chamber and Bureau, appointed a reception committee consisting of the board members and other prominent citizens including Congressmen to collect funds for presentation to Gandhi and make his visit a success.[13] Gandhi's days were packed with meetings and discussions pertaining to the Harijan work. On the morning of 14 June 1934, Gandhi reached Bombay with Miraben and others. There were around 150 people including prominent Congressmen on the platform, and outside, a crowd of around 1,000 of his admirers had gathered. He stayed at Mani Bhavan. There he met some members of the provincial board of the Harijan Sevak Sangh in the morning, and in the afternoon, about 40 members of the Gandhi Seva Sena, consisting mostly of women, visited him. He advised them to strive hard for the removal of untouchability and collect as much money as possible for the Harijan cause.[14]

Gandhi had a wonderful rapport with women. He sought the support of the women of Bombay for the cause of Harijans, which was dearer to him than anything else. He emphasized that his battle would be more than half-won if he could enlist their wholehearted support.[15] He said this to an audience of 1,000 women (mostly Gujaratis) in the Royal Opera House on 15 June 1934. Women did not disappoint him; he was presented with a sum of Rs 50,000 as well as ornaments. Gandhi praised the women for their generosity and also remarked that the amount was nothing for a city like Bombay. He concluded by saying that by contributing to the Harijan cause, they were purging themselves of their past sins. On 16 June, he addressed a huge meeting of about 2,500 people and spoke in Gujarati. The meeting was held under the auspices of the Bombay provincial board of the Harijan Sevak Sangh. There he was presented an amount of Rs 47,000 on behalf of the citizens of Bombay.[16]

The poor working conditions of Harijans troubled him. At a meeting held at the Azad Maidan on 16 June, he said, 'My heart wept within me when I observed the housing conditions of the Harijan employees of Bombay Municipality. Bombay is beautiful, indeed, but wherein does its beauty consist—in Malabar Hill or in the Kacharapatti at Mahalaxmi?'[17] The speech was published in *Harijan* with an introductory note by Valji Desai, informing that despite the rain Gandhi had come punctually to address the public meeting, and that Mathuradas Vissanji, the chairman of the Harijan Sevak Sangh, had presided over the meeting.[18]

Ambedkar, Solanki, G.V. Naik, Amritrao Khambe, and Baburao Gaekwad came to see him and discussed the issue of untouchability on 16 June 1934. Gandhi asked Ambedkar for a criticism of the Harijan Sevak Sangh's work. Ambedkar suggested that the sangh might economize on education and medical relief, as these were attended to by the government and there was a possibility of duplication of work. Again, education benefited only the individual: whether it would benefit society or not would depend upon what attitude the educated individual adopted towards society. He preferred that the sangh concentrated on the primary objective of securing full civic rights for Harijans, such as the right to draw water from public wells and send children to public schools without facing any discrimination. As regards cases of maltreatment of Harijans by villagers, such as those adduced by Ambedkar, Gandhi said that the sangh was bound to deal with them. In fact, steps had actually been taken in numerous cases. Gandhi further said that he had, in the course of his tours of villages, noticed a change for the better. Progress in that direction would be accelerated if he had Ambedkar's valued cooperation.[19] He also attended the meeting of the parliamentary board of the Congress and visited Walpakhadi, a thickly populated area of Bombay mostly inhabited by Harijan families.[20] At Walpakhadi, he had a friendly conversation with the untouchable families and discussed their problems with them. He was accompanied by Kasturba, Mathuradas V. Khimjee (the president of the Harijan Sevak Sangh), Solanki Kajrolkar, V.L. Mehta, and Dahanukar. The party visited Tadwadi, Love Lane, Kamathipura, Stable Street, Mahalakshmi Kachrepatti Chawls, and the slums at Prabhadevi. Wherever Gandhi went, he was received cordially by the Harijan families.[21]

On 17 June 1934, Gandhi visited Santacruz in the Bombay Suburban District, where he was to address a meeting. Around 2,000 Hindus attended the meeting. The proceedings opened with the offering of a sum of Rs 8,050 and a gold necklace. He auctioned the necklace and his own photograph and got Rs 1,011. He then addressed the meeting and spoke about the removal of untouchability and also advocated the elevation of Harijans.[22]

For Gandhi, rebuilding villages, in accordance with the principles of self-sufficiency and decentralization, was very important. He insisted on regulation of wants and use of indigenous goods and material. His swadeshi, a dynamic concept of self-reliance, was closely connected with swaraj, political freedom. When he was in Bombay on 17 June 1934, a deputation of the All-India Swadeshi Sangh waited upon Gandhi to know his views about swadeshi industries. The deputation was headed by Sir Lalloobhai Samaldas Mehta.[23]

It was in Bombay that the INC passed a resolution on 28 October 1934 to start the All-India Village Industries Association. Pattabhi Sitaramayya moved the resolution:

Whereas organisations claiming to advance Swadeshi have sprung up all over the country with and without the assistance of Congressmen and whereas much confusion has arisen in the public mind as to the true nature of Swadeshi and whereas the aim of the Congress has been from its inception progressive identification with the masses and whereas village re-organisation and reconstruction is one of the items in the constructive programme of the Congress and whereas such reconstruction necessarily implies revival and encouragement of dead or dying village industries besides the central industry of hand spinning, and whereas this work like the reorganisation of hand-spinning is possible only through concentrated and special effort unaffected by and independent of the political activities of the Congress, Shri J.C. Kumarappa is hereby authorised to form, under the advice and guidance of Gandhiji, an association called the All-India Village Industries Association as part of the activities of the Congress. The said Association shall work for the revival and encouragement of the said industries and for the moral and physical advancement of the villages, and shall have power to frame its own constitution; to raise funds and to perform such acts as may be necessary for the fulfilment of its objects.

The resolution was seconded by Khan Abdul Ghaffar Khan.[24]

Whenever he was in Bombay, his associates and followers accompanied him. In 1935, when he reached Bombay from Wardha on the morning of 22 May accompanied by Mahadev H. Desai, Kasturba Gandhi, Ceresole, and Wilkinson, they were received at the Victoria Terminus by Vallabhbhai J. Patel, K.F. Nariman, K.M. Munshi and Lilavati Munshi, Ganpati Shankar N. Desai, S.K. Patil, and about 50 Congress workers. He stayed at Mani Bhavan and visited the All-India Village Industries Association's centre started by the members of the Gandhi Seva

Sena in Nair Building, Lamington Road. He also met some people interested in the spread of Hindi language and the workers of the All-India Village Industries Association led by Shoorji Vallabhdas and Perin Captain.[25]

At a meeting of the Parsis in 1934, Gandhi said that while amongst the Parsis he was amidst members of his own family. Gandhi spoke against the habit of drinking and the practice of untouchability. He advised to wear khadi, as buying khadi provided work to the villagers. He added that there were 75 Parsi women in Bombay,

who maintain themselves by doing khadi embroidery. Dadabhoy's granddaughters have engaged them for that work. Mithubehn Petit also does similar work. She has gone to the villages. In Bombay the women earn (daily) wages of one, two and even three rupees out of this kind of work. These women print designs and embroider khadi and thereby make it acceptable to the women who are fond of these things. You can help these women.[26]

Gandhi's focus on the constructive work never wavered. Advising the Congress workers on the importance of the National Week in 1941, he observed: 'Civil resistance is merely lawful and obligatory only in some cases, whereas constructive work is obligatory on all who belong to a non-violent organization. And civil resistance can be effective only when it is backed by constructive effort on mass scale. Success of civil resistance can be measured by success of constructive work.[27]

## Prohibition

Gandhi valued the resolution aiming at total prohibition that was passed by the working committee at Wardha in August 1937. For Gandhi, prohibition was one of the chief Congress planks since the inauguration of the Non-Cooperation Movement in 1920.[28] He was pained to find that there was nothing but the liquor revenue to fall back upon in order to give education to the children.[29] Gandhi made it clear that the prohibition move sponsored by him was not calculated to injure Parsi interests or, for that matter, any legitimate interests. It was directed as much against opium, ganja, charas, and every narcotic as it was against liquor drinking.[30]

Gandhi and the Parsis continued their dialogue regarding the policy of prohibition. Most of the liquor merchants in Bombay were Parsis. They would request the leaders of their community to meet Gandhi and discuss the issue of prohibition. Someone had described the prohibition programme of the Bombay ministry as a 'madcap scheme'.[31] A deputation of the merchants and representatives of liquor dealers/manufacturers visited him on 2 June. According to Mahadev Desai, the deputation was headed by Sir Cowasji Jehangir and its other members were J.C. Koyaji, H.P. Mody, Khareghat, A.D. Shroff, and Saklatwala. They pleaded that that the prohibition policy was tantamount to coercion since the community had, for centuries, indulged in drinking without being harmed by it. There was also the argument of the dislocation of trade and the financial and economic structure of the province, the hardships it would cause to traders and tappers, and the interference with the religious rites of the people. Some of them had been Gandhi's friends for years, especially Cowasji. Gandhi patiently argued that it was Dadabhai Naoroji who taught him prohibition and the difference between prohibition and temperance. Individual liberty was allowed to humans only to a certain extent. They could not forget that they were social beings and that their individual liberty had to be curtailed at every step. He had seen families being ruined because of drinking; there was the tragic case of his own son.[32]

When prohibition was introduced in Bombay on 1 August 1939, a delighted Gandhi wrote in *Harijan* with the heading 'Well Done Bombay!': 'The great Parsi community deserves congratulations for the restraint it observed in spite of its bitter opposition to the measure.... The demonstration of 1st August shows that they had and have practically the whole of Bombay behind them. No constructive measure promoted by the Congress has had such enthusiastic support as this great moral reform.'[33]

## Navigating the Congress

The road before the Congress had many turns and twists after the Civil Disobedience Movement. People's aspirations were rising and so were the oppressive measures of the British rule. The Communal Award was a complex issue, and the Congress had to deal with it carefully. Important discussions took place when Gandhi was in Bombay. Gandhi had consultation with Malaviya, M.S. Aney, and some other members, who pleaded for the rejection of the Communal Award by the Congress Parliamentary Board that met in Mani Bhavan on 15 and 16 June 1934. The nationalist Muslims had been supporting the view of the Ranchi Conference that the award should be neither accepted nor rejected until an agreement was brought about between Hindus, Muslims, and Sikhs. The board, therefore, sought Gandhi's advice. After the consultation, Gandhi addressed the board in a speech. The *Bombay Chronicle* described it as one of the most moving and earnest speeches that he had ever delivered. The main trend of the speech was that the Congress claimed to stand for Muslims as well as Hindus, Sikhs, and other communities and that, therefore, nothing should be done that would have the effect of making the Muslims feel that the Congress had departed from that position. The majority of Muslims had accepted the Communal Award. It was their duty to bring about such a voluntary settlement of

the Communal Award as would satisfy all the communities. The
CWC, which met in Mani Bhavan on 17 June at the parliamentary
board's request, accepted Gandhi's view.[34]

**Figure 7.1**  Gandhi standing in the balcony of Mani Bhavan, Bombay, on
15 June 1934.
*Source*: Vithalbhai Jhaveri Collection/Dinodia Photos.

Malaviya and Aney resigned from the Congress Parliamentary Board and summoned a conference of Congressmen and others at Calcutta on 18 and 19 August 1934 under the presidentship of Malaviya, which announced the formation of the Nationalist Party with the objective of carrying on agitation in the legislatures and outside against the Communal Award and the White Paper, and putting up candidates for the legislative assembly to promote that objective.[35]

Mani Bhavan remained an important place for the Congress meetings. The CWC met there on 17 and 18 June 1934.[36] The Congress had to evolve a strategy as the government announced elections for the new assembly. Gandhi had argued strongly for constructive work that would consolidate people's energy, while a group of Congressmen favoured entry into the legislature. On 17 June, he participated in the CWC meeting and approved the election manifesto of the Congress. He was also present in the meeting of the Harijan Board at Santacruz. Furthermore, he addressed some members of the All-India Swadeshi League and even found time to visit the famous Gujarati litterateur Narsinhrao Divetia. He met Malaviya and Shaukat Ali on 18 June.[37]

Gandhi was back in Bombay in October 1934. He arrived by Nagpur Mail from Wardha on 20 October to attend the A.I.C.C. meeting. He alighted at the Matunga railway station and drove straight to Worli where a special hut had been erected for him near the subjects committee pandal of the Congress. Abul Kalam Azad and Jamnalal Bajaj came with him. Immediately after Gandhi's arrival, Vallabhbhai Patel, K.F. Nariman, K.M. Munshi, Nagindas T. Master, Bhulabhai J. Desai, and I.S. Patel met him.[38]

Under the auspices of the BPCC and the Congress Parliamentary Board, a public meeting was held on the Esplanade

Maidan on 22 October 1934 to observe the first death anniversary
of the late V.J. Patel. About 10,000 people attended the meeting
and M.A. Ansari presided over it. The president, Gandhi, Abdul
Ghaffar Khan, C. Rajagopalachari, Syed Mahmood, and Sardul
Singh Kaveeshver made speeches eulogizing the services of the
late V.J. Patel to the cause of India's freedom. They appealed to
the audience that as a mark of appreciation and tribute to his
memory, they should return the Congress candidates to the
legislative assembly where he had fought for India's freedom.
Gandhi, in the course of his speech, said that Patel was a tough
fighter and a great patriot. He appealed to the audience to
contribute liberally to his memorial fund in appreciation of the
great services rendered by him for the country's cause.[39]

K.F. Nariman, as the chairman of the reception committee
of the INC's 48th session (26–8 October 1934), had made special
efforts to make the session in Bombay a huge success. He paid
rich tributes to the people of Bombay for their impressive
contribution in organizing processions, raids, boycott, and
picketing. He referred to Bombay as 'this commercial capital of
India and this centre of Congress politics'.[40] Recalling the city's
contribution to the Civil Disobedience Movement, he pointed out
that the quiet assertion of popular strength had developed into a
brilliant, non-violent offensive where it was quickly transformed
into a test between the police's capacity to inflict physical injury
and the capacity of the Congress volunteers to bear it. While
processions and raids inflicted the more spectacular defeats on
the government forces, it was the organization of boycott and the
intensification of picketing that kept up a steady and crushing
pressure on them. Bombay—with her hundreds of thousands
of men, women, and children, of Hindus, Muslims, Christians,
Sikhs, Parsis, and Jews—felt moved and acted like a single being.
She prided herself in the purity of her struggle; she was glorified

in the martyr's strength and sacrifice. He also acknowledged the glorious role played by the women in the freedom struggle and pointed out that the organization of the Vanar Sena was another special feature of the 1930 struggle.[41]

Gandhi made an important announcement in Bombay at the subjects committee of the INC's 48th session presided over by Rajendra Prasad on 23 October 1934. Before the regular business of the meeting, Gandhi spoke both in Hindi and English on the question of his retirement. He said that he wished to retire from the Congress and invited blessings from the members of the A.I.C.C. He assured them that he was not leaving in a huff but was going out of the Congress only to enable the party to grow to its full and natural height and stature.[42]

K.F. Nariman voiced the feeling of many: 'With an ideal hitched to freedom, with a life dedicated to service, Gandhiji cannot in any accepted sense of the term "retire". Inside or outside the Congress he will be the living challenge to all oppression and tyranny and the guiding star to the Congress, to every votary of freedom.'[43]

Gandhi had deep faith in the power of prayer. While delivering a public discourse in Hindi at the Congress House on 22 May 1935, he said that the people had no cause for despair. If the public followed the Congress programme, the portals of freedom or swaraj would be open to them. He advised people to invoke the assistance of God when they were overcome by feelings of despair and weakness. He then led the prayer by reciting verses from the Bhagavadgita and his favourite 'Raghupati raghav rajaram' (a prayer song praising Lord Rama). About 5,000 people had assembled for this public prayer (3,000 inside the Congress compound admitted by tickets and 2,000 collected on the road).[44] He further said, 'Swaraj is our birth right. No one can deprive us of it, unless we forfeit ourselves. It does not depend on going to the jails, but it depends on every one doing his or her own task.'[45]

**Figure 7.2**   Gandhi at a prayer meeting at the Congress House, Bombay, on 22 May 1935.
*Source*: Vithalbhai Jhaveri Collection/Dinodia Photos.

Elections to provincial legislatures under the Government of India Act 1935 were announced in early 1937. The Congress had decided to take the plunge after much discussion. During July 1937, it formed ministries in six provinces including Bombay. The new ministry in Bombay assumed office on 19 July 1937, marking the inauguration of provincial autonomy. B.G. Kher became the chief minister (at times called the prime minister) of Bombay Presidency. It was a good experiment with positive results. Gandhi was happy to know about the introduction of prohibition in Bombay. In his message from Abbottabad to the Bombay Government Prohibition Board on 23 July 1939, he wrote, 'I hope that good sense for which Bombay is famous will ultimately prevail and all will combine to make the brave reform undertaken by the Bombay Ministry the success it deserves to be. I am quite sure that the removal of the curse of intoxicating drinks and drugs will confer lasting benefit on the country.'[46]

Gandhi had discussions with the members of the working committee in Bombay on 2 and 3 January 1938.[47] Keen to find a solution for the agonizing issue of Hindu–Muslim differences, Gandhi was in touch with Jinnah. He expressed his concern to Jinnah, emphasizing his wish to retain peace between the two communities.[48]

The communal situation had been deteriorating; the riots did not stop. The situation required urgent attention. There was a long correspondence first between Nehru and Jinnah and then between Gandhi and Jinnah, culminating in two meetings between Gandhi and Jinnah on 28 April and 20 May 1938. In reply to Jinnah's telegram of 16 April, Gandhi had written that he would visit Jinnah's home on 28 April. He later wrote to C. Rajagopalachari on 21 May from Shegaon that 'the talk was cordial but not hopeful, yet not without hope'.[49]

**Figure 7.3** Gandhi's meeting with Jinnah on 28 April 1938 at the latter's residence at Mount Pleasant Road, Bombay, to solve the communal problem.

*Source*: Vithalbhai Jhaveri Collection/Dinodia Photos.

Subhas Bose, the then Congress president, also deliberated with Jinnah between 12 to 16 May. Jinnah was firm that only the Muslim League could speak for the Muslims and the Congress should accept it. The prevailing political atmosphere and differences within the Congress also caused anguish in Gandhi's heart, but his faith in non-violence did not waver. It was expressed in a letter on 16 May 1938, 'The violence that I see running through speeches and writings, the corruption and selfishness among Congressmen, and the petty bickering fill one with dismay. In the midst of this, we who know must be unyielding and apply the golden rule of non co-operation.'[50] However, the rift between the Congress and the Muslim League continued to widen.

Gandhi's views on the Hindu–Muslim unity had earned respect as well as criticism from both the communities. Often he had to face criticism and emotional outbursts. On 2 June 1939, he arrived in Bombay accompanied by Kasturba, Sushila Nayar, and his two secretaries from Rajkot. As he alighted from the Kathiawar Mail at the Bombay Central station, leaders like Vallabhbhai Patel, K.M. Munshi, and Bhulabhai Desai received him and a crowd that had gathered from an early hour welcomed him. However, some people from the Hindu Mahasabha had raised anti-Congress slogans and waved black flags in front of Gandhi's compartment at the Dadar station.[51]

On a special invitation, Gandhi attended the CWC on 21 and 22 June 1939 in Bombay. He was staying at Birla House. His advice was that any amendment to the constitution that was being given effect to should find favour with the general body of Congressmen in the country. Changes of far-reaching importance should not be decided by a mere majority vote.[52] Some resolutions drafted by Gandhi were passed by the A.I.C.C. at its session held in Bombay from 24 to 27 June 1939. One of

**Figure 7.4** Mahatma Gandhi walking with Rajendra Prasad, Mahadev Desai, and others at Birla House, Bombay, in June 1939.
*Source*: Vithalbhai Jhaveri Collection/Dinodia Photos.

the resolutions was that the A.I.C.C. regretted the attitude of the union government towards the Indian settlers. The policy recently initiated by them was in direct breach of the Smuts–Gandhi Agreement of 1914, the Cape Town Agreement of 1927, the Feetham Commission, and the subsequent undertakings on the behalf of the union government.

There was also a resolution that no Congressman should offer or organize any form of satyagraha in the administrative provinces of India without the previous sanction of the provincial Congress committee concerned.[53] The ideological differences between Gandhi and Nehru were becoming obvious by this time despite their strong personal bond, and Gandhi was aware of it. He wrote about it candidly in a letter dated 23 June 1939, from Birla House, to Amrit Kaur (interestingly addressing her as 'My dear idiot' and signing as 'Tyrant'). He also mentioned that '[t] here is no coolness between us. Perhaps we have come nearer for the discovery of the wide divergence of views.'[54]

When the Second World War broke out on 1 September 1939, the British government declared India a 'belligerent country' without her consent. The Congress did not approve of this. There were intense deliberations and meetings. The A.I.C.C. met at Wardha on 9 and 10 October and demanded that India should be declared an independent nation. Moreover, it urged an extension of democracy to all colonial countries and application of the principle of self-determination to them so as to eliminate imperialist control. The working committee called upon the Congress provincial governments to tender their resignation. Accordingly, they all, including the ministry headed by B.G. Kher in Bombay, resigned.[55]

Gandhi arrived in Bombay on 12 September 1940 and had informal discussions with Abul Kalam Azad, Sardar Patel, Pandit Nehru, and the other CWC members. He attended the CWC meeting on 13, 17, and 18 September and addressed the A.I.C.C. meeting on 15 and 16 September.[56]

The British government had rejected the Congress offer of conditional cooperation. The Congress insisted that India had been dragged into war against the will of a vast body of the Indian people. The Congress was pledged under Gandhi's leadership to non-violence for the vindication of India's freedom. And at this grave crisis in the movement for national freedom, the A.I.C.C.

**Figure 7.5** Gandhi, Kasturba, and Abdul Ghaffar Khan at Birla House, Bombay, in September 1940. Khan had been invited to attend the CWC meeting.

*Source*: Vithalbhai Jhaveri Collection/Dinodia Photos.

requested Gandhi to guide the Congress with regard to the action to be taken.[57] Gandhi was once again established as the general of the Congress.[58]

Gandhi's passion for non-violence ruled his speech at the A.I.C.C. meeting in Bombay in September 1940. It was a long powerful speech not prepared beforehand. He was confident of the principle of non-violence and himself. He stated his position clearly:

I do not want England to be defeated or humiliated. It hurts me to find St. Paul's Cathedral damaged. It hurts me as much as I would be hurt if I heard that the Kashi Vishvanath Temple or the Jama Masjid was damaged. I would like to defend both the Kashi Vishvanath Temple and the Jama Masjid and even St. Paul's with my life, but would not take a single life for their defence.'[59]

He also said, 'Freedom of speech and pen is the foundation of swaraj. If the foundation-stone is in danger, you have to exert the whole of your might in order to defend that single stone.'[60]

K. Gopalaswami cites an interesting anecdote in the context of this A.I.C.C. meeting at Bombay. The reception committee had to find a suitable venue for the meeting. Places such as the Sir Cowasji Jehangir Hall were out of the question as the government would not lend them for a hostile Congress demonstration. Bhulabhai Desai persuaded the authorities of the Sundarabai Hall to allow the use of their premises, but they would not permit any flags or portraits. Bhawanji Arjan Khimji (the leading city Congressman and president of the Cotton Merchants' and Muccadams' associations) would not accept any such restriction. As Bombay's cotton trade had always stood by Gandhi, he tried to get the Survey Hall at the Cotton Green, Sewri. Despite knowing that the meeting would revive civil disobedience under Gandhi's leadership, Purshottamdas Thakurdas, the president of the East India Cotton Association, agreed to Bhawanji's request to not only allow the A.I.C.C. meeting in the Cotton Green but to also house the delegates in the spare rooms. Furthermore, Thakurdas arranged for a tea party for the A.I.C.C. members and invited the elite of Bombay, about 500 in number, including some British judges of the high court. He went along with Vallabhbhai to invite Gandhi to attend the tea party. With a broad smile on his face, Gandhi told Thakurdas: 'You are a Bania, and so am I. If you want me to attend your tea party, let us make a deal— you give a donation of Rs. 20,000 to the Harijan Sevak Sangh.' Though generally believed to be close-fisted, Thakurdas agreed. Unfortunately, the session did not conclude by the time fixed for the tea party. Gandhi began to speak and went on for 45 minutes. Then it was time for his evening meal. He forgot all about the tea party. The important guests waited for some time and then left. Later Gandhi remembered his promise, apologized to Thakurdas, and offered to return the donation, but the latter waived it.[61]

Gandhi had friends and admirers all over the world. He was given an American medal for service to humankind by the Community Church of New York on 24 April 1932. Haridas Majumdar, Gandhi's colleague of the Dandi March, accepted it on the latter's behalf.[62] A special correspondent of the Associated Press of America interviewed him at Juhu on 20 May 1938.[63]

It is interesting that in mid-July 1940, a statue of Gandhi donated by Clare Sheridan was exhibited at the Prince of Wales Museum in Bombay. Sheridan had requested Gandhi for a sitting for the statue during the latter's stay in Great Britain in 1931.[64]

Gandhi's visits to Bombay brought him nearer to his coworkers and followers. People close to him, such as Kasturba, Mahadevbhai Desai, and Maniben Patel, often travelled with him. He was always surrounded by people; there were consultations on topics ranging from personal to political. When he was in

Bombay in September 1933, some political leaders and notable persons including Nehru, Sarojini Naidu, G.D. Birla, and Cowasji Jehangir (Jr), had discussions with him on 16 September. This day was Gandhi's birthday according to the Hindu calendar. Most probably, this day came to be celebrated as *Rentio Baras* from then onwards. On 19 September, the representatives of the Ahmedabad Mill Owners' Association and the Ahmedabad Labour Union (Majur Mahajan) discussed their issues with Gandhi in Bombay.[65]

It is amazing to find instances about Gandhi's qualities of social grace as well as inquisitiveness about new innovations that came naturally to him. On 22 May 1935, he went with Vallabhbhai Patel to see Kamala Nehru (who was going to Europe for convalescence) at J.A.D. Nowroji's bungalow, Nepean Sea Road, and wished her bon voyage. On the same day, despite his hectic schedule, he found time to visit the Haffkine Institute at Parel. He was accompanied by Vallabhbhai and Bhaskar Patel (who was in charge of the non-official plague camp at Borsad in Kheda) and had a long talk with S.S. Sokhey, the institute's director, on the question of adopting measures to prevent the spread of plague and rooting it out.[66]

When King George V died in London, Gandhi sent on 21 January 1936 a cable to Her Majesty the Queen Mary and members of the royal family, expressing deep regret over the passing away of His Majesty the King and conveying his sincere condolences.[67]

During his visit to Bombay in 1939, he was present at the convocation of the SNDT Women's University on 1 July.[68] On 4 July 1939, he went to see Gujarati poet Ardeshar Faramji 'Khabardar' who had been ill. Accompanied by Vallabhbhai Patel, Devdas Gandhi, and Sushila Nayar, he also visited the Chemical Industrial and Pharmaceutical Laboratories (Cipla) Ltd. the same day and was delighted to visit 'the Indian enterprise'.[69] He also wrote tender letters from Birla House in June 1939 to Manilal Gandhi and Chhaganlal Gandhi enquiring after his near and dear ones and expressing concern over Kasturba's health.[70]

Revolutionaries also, at times, sought Gandhi's guidance. It is touching to find that Prithvi Singh went to see Gandhi on 17 and 18 May 1938. He was a revolutionary involved in the Lahore Conspiracy Case and was sentenced for life in 1915. He had, however, escaped in 1922 and worked for 16 years as a physical instructor in many schools and, probably during this time, assumed the name 'Swamirao'. With the passing of time, he moved towards non-violence and Gandhi. Gandhi wrote to the government in Bombay that he was going to request the government of India to release Singh. If the government allowed, Singh could stay with him; otherwise the government could take him. The Bombay government took charge of Singh on 19 May and sent him to the jail in Rawalpindi.[71]

**Figure 7.6** Gandhi with Sushila Nayar and others at Juhu Beach, Bombay, in 1939.
*Source*: Vithalbhai Jhaveri Collection/Dinodia Photos.

In the latter half of the 1930s, Gandhi remained busy travelling and spreading the message of non-violence and constructive work. His health was now under stress and demanded attention. He stayed at Bhulabhai Desai's home during his visit to Bombay in 1936 from 17 to 21 January. (His teeth were extracted on 19 January.) He was again in Mumbai from 7 December 1937 to 7 January 1938. He stayed in Juhu for a few days to recuperate. He continued to receive visitors such as Aga Khan and his son Ali Khan and the ruler of Rewa. Pagnis also came to see Gandhi and sang bhajans. He had played the titular role in a blockbuster Marathi film titled *Sant Tukaram* (Saint Tukaram). The film was based on the life of Tukaram, a revered saint of Maharashtra.[72]

During this period he wrote tender letters to his son Manilal and daughter-in-law Sushila, to Vijaya Patel and J.P. Bhansali on 20 December 1937, to Ramdas Gandhi on 21 December, and to Amrit Kaur on 24 and 27 December 1937.[73] In his letter to Sharda C. Shah dated 30 December 1937, he even drew a sketch to show how one should sit in a bathtub for hot and cold water.[74]

As the British attitude became tougher, Gandhi announced the programme of individual satyagraha on the issue of freedom to preach non-cooperation with the government in its war effort and to make anti-war speeches. He chose Vinoba Bhave as the first individual satyagrahi, who started satyagraha on 17 October 1940. This policy, however, could not generate much enthusiasm among the people. People under Gandhi's leadership were instead getting prepared for the great struggle ahead.

A special correspondent met Gandhi for an answer to the appeal made by the *Times of India* for the withdrawal of the Civil Disobedience Movement. Gandhi said:

When I launched out, I had no foolish illusion about a sudden miracle happening. It was conceived to be, and it remains, a silent declaration of unquenchable faith in the power of non-violence even in the midst of circumstances so terrible and so baffling as face the world today.... It [the movement] was never intended that it would create an appreciable impression upon the war effort, but it is a moral, and from that standpoint a grand protest against the conduct of the war in the name of a free people.[75]

Though disturbed by increasing communal tension in the country, Gandhi insisted on strict adherence to non-violence and constructive work. In his words, the '[m]ere filling of jails can bring us no nearer our freedom than we are now. The virtue lies in the people learning through restricted civil disobedience the necessity of discipline, suffering and self-sacrifice.' He further said, 'I have said repeatedly that constructive work is the foundation for civil disobedience. It promotes discipline and conduces to the growth on non-violence in the worker.'[76]

The political winds in the 1940s were affecting the country's political equilibrium. Gandhi and the Congress had to take important decisions that would affect the course of history.

## Notes and References

1. Gordon, *Businessmen and Politics*, p. 238.
2. Gordon, *Businessmen and Politics*, p. 238.
3. *The New York Times*, 16 April 1932.
4. Dalal, *Gandhi*, p. 99.
5. B.N. Ghosh, *Gandhian Political Economy: Principles, Practice and Policy* (Aldershot: Ashgate Publishing, 2007), p. 213.
6. *Harijan* dated 1 June 1935 and *The Bombay Chronicle* dated 23 May 1935 cited in *CWMG*, Vol. 61 (New Delhi: Publications Division, Ministry of Information and Broadcasting, Government of India, 1975), pp. 88–9.
7. Chandra, *Indian National Movement*, p. 37.
8. Chandra, *Indian National Movement*, p. 37.

9. Dalal, *Gandhijini Dinwari*, pp. 350, 353–4.

10. Sitaramayya, *History of the Indian National Congress*, Vol. I, p. 555.

11. 'Bombay Secret Abstracts', Home Department, Special Branch, File No. 800 (40), (14), pp. 153–61 cited in *CWMG*, Vol. 55 (New Delhi: Publications Division, Ministry of Information and Broadcasting, Government of India, 1973), p. 430.

12. Dalal, *Gandhi*, p. 108.

13. 'Bombay Secret Abstract', 1934, p. 308, para 580 cited in B.G. Kunte (ed.), *Source Material for a History of the Freedom Movement in India: Mahatma Gandhi*, Vol. III, Part VII: 1934–1945 (Bombay: Gazetteers Department, Government of Maharashtra, 1975), p. 9.

14. 'Bombay Secret Abstract', 1934, p. 339, para 627 cited in Kunte, *Source Material for a History of the Freedom Movement in India: Mahatma Gandhi*, Vol. III, Part VII, p. 11.

15. *Harijan* dated 29 June 1934 and *The Bombay Chronicle* dated 16 June 1934 cited in *CWMG*, Vol. 58 (New Delhi: Publications Division, Ministry of Information and Broadcasting, Government of India, 1974), pp. 81–2.

16. 'Bombay Secret Abstract', 15 and 16 June 1934, p. 340 cited in Kunte, *Source Material for a History of the Freedom Movement in India*, Vol. III, Part VII, pp. 11–12.

17. *Harijan* dated 29 June 1934 cited in *CWMG*, Vol. 58, p. 85.

18. *Harijan* dated 29 June 1934 cited in *CWMG*, Vol. 58, pp. 84–6.

19. *Harijan* dated 29 June 1934 cited in *CWMG*, Vol. 58, p. 82.

20. Dalal, *Gandhi*, p. 109.

21. Gopalaswami, *Gandhi and Bombay*, p. 289.

22. 'Bombay Secret Abstract', 1934, p. 340 cited in Kunte, *Source Material for a History of the Freedom Movement in India*, Vol. III, Part VII, pp. 12–13.

23. 'Bombay Secret Abstract', 1934, p. 340 cited in Kunte, *Source Material for a History of the Freedom Movement in India*, Vol. III, Part VII, p. 13.

24. Zaidi and Zaidi, *The Encyclopaedia of the Indian National Congress*, pp. 330–4.

25. 'Bombay Secret Abstract', p. 202, para 458 cited in Kunte, *Source Material for a History of the Freedom Movement in India*, Vol. III, Part VII, p. 48.

26. *Harijanbandhu* dated 22 July 1934 cited in *CWMG*, Vol. 58, p. 176.

27. 'Congress Bulletin No. 6', 1942, File No. 3/42/41-Poll. (I) and *The Bombay Chronicle* dated 22 March 1941 cited in *CWMG*, Vol. 73 (New Delhi: Publications Division, Ministry of Information and Broadcasting, Government of India, 1978), p. 388.

28. *Harijan* dated 28 August 1937 cited in *CWMG*, Vol. 66 (New Delhi: Publications Division, Ministry of Information and Broadcasting, Government of India, 1976), p. 81.

29. *Harijan* dated 21 August 1937 cited in *CWMG*, Vol. 66, p. 59.

30. *Harijan* dated 9 October 1937 and *Harijanbandhu* dated 19 September 1937 cited in *CWMG*, Vol. 66, pp. 147–50.

31. Letter to Sikandar Hyat Khan dated 9 July 1939 cited in *CWMG*, Vol. 69 (New Delhi: Publications Division, Ministry of Information and Broadcasting, Government of India, 1977), p. 409.

32. *Harijan* dated 10 June 1939 cited in *CWMG*, Vol. 69, pp. 320–2.

33. *Harijan* dated 12 August 1939 cited in *CWMG*, Vol. 70 (New Delhi: Publications Division, Ministry of Information and Broadcasting, Government of India, 1977), p. 60.

34. *The Bombay Chronicle* dated 17 June 1934 cited in *CWMG*, Vol. 58, p. 83.

35. Sitaramayya, *History of the Indian National Congress*, Vol. I, pp. 576–7; *CWMG*, Vol. 58, p. 317.

36. *Gandhiji and Mani Bhavan*, p. 39.

37. Dalal, *Gandhijini Dinwari*, p. 374.

38. 'Bombay Secret Abstract', 1934, p. 570, para 999 cited in Kunte, *Source Material for a History of the Freedom Struggle in India*, Vol. III, Part VII, p. 35.

39. 'Bombay Secret Abstract', 1934, p. 607, para 1027 (5) cited in Kunte, *Source Material for a History of the Freedom Struggle in India*, Vol. III, Part VII, pp. 38–9.

40. Zaidi and Zaidi, *The Encyclopaedia of the Indian National Congress*, p. 341.

41. Zaidi and Zaidi, *The Encyclopaedia of the Indian National Congress*, pp. 345–7.

42. 'Bombay Secret Abstract', p. 576, para 1002 cited in Kunte, *Source Material for a History of the Freedom Struggle in India*, Vol. III, Part VII, p. 35.

43. Zaidi and Zaidi, *The Encyclopaedia of the Indian National Congress*, p. 358.

44. 'Bombay Secret Abstract', p. 202, para 458 cited in Kunte, *Source Material for a History of the Freedom Struggle in India*, Vol. IX, pp. 244–5.

45. *Harijan* dated 1 June 1935 and *The Bombay Chronicle* dated 23 May 1935 cited in *CWMG*, Vol. 61, p. 89.

46. *Harijan* dated 5 August 1939 and *The Bombay Chronicle* dated 31 July 1939 cited in *CWMG*, Vol. 70, p. 19.

47. Dalal, *Gandhi*, p. 121.

48. *The Hindustan Times* dated 16 June 1938 cited in *CWMG*, Vol. 66, p. 257.

49. *CWMG*, Vol. 67 (New Delhi: Publications Division, Ministry of Information and Broadcasting, Government of India, 1976), p. 90.

50. *Harijan* dated 21 May 1938 cited in *CWMG*, Vol. 67, p. 85.

51. *The Bombay Chronicle*, 3 June 1939.

52. *The Bombay Chronicle* dated 23 June 1939 cited in *CWMG*, Vol. 69, p. 365.

53. *Harijan* dated 1 July 1939 cited in *CWMG*, Vol. 69, pp. 366–8.

54. *CWMG*, Vol. 69, p. 369.

55. Sitaramayya, *History of the Indian National Congress*, Vol. II, pp. 124–44.

56. *CWMG*, Vol. 73, p. 475.

57. *Harijan* dated 22 September 1940 cited in *CWMG*, Vol. 73, pp. 1–3.

58. Sitaramayya, *History of the Indian National Congress*, Vol. II, pp. 215–16.

59. *Harijan* dated 22 September 1940 cited in *CWMG*, Vol. 73, p. 16.

60. *Harijan* dated 29 September 1940 cited in *CWMG*, Vol. 73, p. 21.

61. Gopalaswami, *Gandhi and Bombay*, p. 339.

62. Dalal, *Gandhi*, p. 97.

63. *The Hindu* dated 23 May 1938 cited in *CWMG*, Vol. 67, p. 90.

64. Dalal, *Gandhi*, pp. 95, 134.

65. Dalal, *Gandhijini Dinwari*, p. 357.

66. Gopalaswami, *Gandhi and Bombay*, p. 301.

67. *The Hindustan Times* dated 22 January 1936 cited in *CWMG*, Vol. 62 (New Delhi: Publications Division, Ministry of Information and Broadcasting, Government of India, 1975), p. 180.

68. Dalal, *Gandhi*, p. 129.

69. *The Bombay Chronicle* dated 5 July 1939 cited in *CWMG*, Vol. 69, p. 394; Dalal, *Gandhijini Dinwari*, p. 446.

70. *CWMG*, Vol. 69, pp. 373–4.

71. Dalal, *Gandhijini Dinwari*, pp. 425–6.

72. Dalal, *Gandhijini Dinwari*, pp. 396–7, 417–18.

73. *CWMG*, Vol. 66, pp. 320–3.

74. *CWMG*, Vol. 66, pp. 326–7.

75. *The Times of India* dated 20 April 1941 cited in *CWMG*, Vol. 74 (New Delhi: Publications Division, Ministry of Information and Broadcasting, Government of India, 1978), pp. 2–3.

76. 'Statement to the Press', 6 July 1941 and 'Congress Bulletin No. 6', 1942, File No. 3/42/41-Home Department, Pol. (I) cited in *CWMG*, Vol. 74, p. 150.

## 8

# 'The Volcanic Eruption of a People's Indignation': 1942

THE BEGINNING OF THE 1940S BROUGHT MAJOR UPHEAVALS IN THE Indian political scene. Individual civil disobedience, inspired by Gandhi, had been orderly but was tried on a limited scale. The Muslim League, at its annual convention in Lahore in March 1940, had emphatically voiced its demand for the creation of a Muslim state. Currents at the international level were strong and swift as nations were embroiled in the Second World War. India, under the British rule, was dragged into the war and its tribulations were felt intensely as the Japanese army marched forward. In this background, the mission headed by Sir Stafford Cripps, which arrived in India from England in March 1942, brought new hopes. The proposals promised India a dominion status and a body to frame the constitution after the war, whose members would be elected by the provincial assemblies and nominated by the rulers in case of the princely states. There was also a provision that any province that was not prepared to accept the new constitution would have the right to sign a separate agreement with Britain regarding its future status. These proposals were incommensurate with the Indian demands.[1] The proposals were rejected by all the parties in India, each for its own reasons. The situation was getting tense: the advance of the Japanese forces had already sent shock waves through the economy and politics of the country and the British attitude towards the Indian demand continued to be rigid and insensitive. Discontent in the people against the foreign rule, economic and political changes resulting from the war, and rising prices demanded immediate and effective action. The Congress and Gandhi were getting prepared for it.

'Quit India' was a masterstroke by Gandhi not only due to the directness and force of words but also because of its power to energize people. However, according to Pyarelal, Quit India 'was an apocryphal and much misunderstood phrase fathered upon Gandhiji; it was really coined by an American press correspondent in the course of an interview with Gandhiji and caught on. The actual expression used by Gandhi was "orderly British withdrawal".'[2]

## The Genesis

The idea of a strong protest against the British rule had started taking concrete shape by July 1942. In the same month, the CWC met in Wardha. The atmosphere was tense. Neither the pursuit of the policy of non-embarrassment of Britain in this war (September 1939 to October 1940) nor the studied moderation of India's protest through a campaign of individual civil disobedience (October 1940 to October 1941) had stirred Britain's conscience. There was 'a continuity of thought coursing the steps and stages through which the Congress had taken its campaign, now of silent waiting, and now of anxious inquiry, now of gentle protest and now of stern revolt'.[3] A decision had to be taken now that would lead the country to the destination of freedom.

The resolution passed by the working committee at Wardha on 14 July was a bold resolve asking that the British rule in India must end immediately and inevitably placing the widespread struggle under the leadership of Gandhi. It stressed India's need to feel 'the glow of freedom'. The A.I.C.C. that met in Bombay in August endorsed this resolution in substantially the same language. While C. Rajagopalachari had resigned over political differences with the Congress and Gandhi, prominent leaders such as Sardar Patel, Jawaharlal Nehru, and Abul Kalam Azad were with Gandhi and leading socialists such as Ashok Mehta and A. Patwardhan supported him in this struggle.

The BPCC had decided to organize propaganda meetings in different parts of the city to popularize the working committee's resolution passed at Wardha before the A.I.C.C. session at Bombay. This would build the tempo of the movement in the city. The first such meeting of about 5,000 people was held in Chowpatty on 26 July under the presidentship of Nagindas T. Master.[4] Among other such meetings was one organized in Chowpatty on 2 August. Vallabhbhai Patel spoke in Gujarati about 'the task before the country' to an audience of about 50,000 people. He said that it was the last movement to be launched by Gandhi and he was undertaking to lead it at an advanced age knowing its implications fully. He appealed to the people of Bombay to wholeheartedly support the movement that was based on complete non-violence and justify the past history of the city regarding such issues.[5]

Sir Roger Lumley, the governor of Bombay, admitted that Vallabhbhai Patel was successful in inspiring the Congress followers in Bombay. After his first enormous meeting in Bombay, which was attended possibly by 100,000 people, the atmosphere changed completely and became definitely revolutionary in outlook. The other leaders who were prominent in whipping up enthusiasm were Shankarrao Deo and Yusuf Meherally, the mayor of Bombay, who spent much time inciting students. The general effect of this propaganda by the Congress was to create a feeling of tension and excitement so that by the time the A.I.C.C. met, an atmosphere for a civil disobedience movement had been prepared at any rate in Bombay and Gujarat.[6] An official document also records that Patel, Deo, and others prepared the people for the fight to the finish through public meetings and exhorted students to take an active part in the movement.[7]

Gandhi was in Bombay on 10 and 11 May to collect funds for the Andrew Memorial and had received a warm response. However, his visit to the city in August was epoch-making. He arrived in Bombay on 3 August and stayed at Birla House. The CWC met on 4, 5, and 6 August at Birla House. On 5 August, it deliberated for three hours in the morning and three hours in the evening. Jaimatram Daulatram was appointed to fill the position left vacant by the resignation of C. Rajagopalachari. Acharya Narendra Deo replaced Khan Saheb upon the latter's resignation, and Bhulabhai Desai was replaced by Harekrishna Mehtab. Gandhi addressed the members for nearly an hour on the reactions to the Wardha resolution and the criticisms levelled against the Congress by the press in India and abroad. He conveyed that the prestige of the Congress would not in any way suffer from such criticism. The committee then considered the Wardha resolution and made necessary alterations in the draft. All members unanimously approved the new draft resolution for the A.I.C.C. 'to show that there was no difference among them'.[8]

## The Historic Session

The A.I.C.C. session on 7 and 8 August left its indelible mark on history. It commenced on 7 August under the presidentship of Abul Kalam Azad.[9] The gathering was attended by prominent national leaders and notable people from Bombay and was held in a specially erected pandal on the Gowalia Tank Maidan opposite the Goculdas Tejpal House where the INC was established in 1885. Excellent preparations were made by S.K. Patil, a competent leader in the city. On 7 August, about 10,000 people attended the meeting, including about 250 members of the A.I.C.C. from different provinces. About 3,000 volunteers of the Bombay National Guards, the Bombay Seva Dal, and the People's Volunteer Brigade, including 500 desh sevikas, were there to keep order. Besides the aforementioned, there were about 5,000 people who heard the proceedings from outside the pandal with the help of loudspeakers that were specially installed for them.[10] The CID report mentions that on 8 August the proceedings with Abdul Kalam Azad commenced at about 2.30 pm. About 10,000 people were in the pandal and about the same number of people had collected outside it.[11] Those who had assembled were excited to see their favourite leaders, especially Gandhi, amidst them. Gandhi was taken to the A.I.C.C. by the front gate of the pandal. Bhawanji Khimji recalled that a huge crowd hemmed in on him and the situation became critical. About half a dozen hefty Sikhs linked their arms and, forming a human fence around Gandhi, rescued him from the melee and conducted him inside.[12]

**Figure 8.1**   Gandhi arriving in Bombay to attend the A.I.C.C. session in
August 1942. To his right is Sardar Patel.
*Source*: Mani Bhavan Gandhi Sangrahalaya.

The words of the historic resolution, chosen after deep
deliberation and debate, convey indomitable and indivertible
determination to fight for the freedom of the country. It was
stated that:

The All India Congress Committee has given the most careful
consideration to the reference made to it by the Working Committee in
their resolution dated July 14, 1942, and to subsequent events, including
the development of the war situation, the utterances of responsible

spokesmen of the British Government, and the comments and criticisms made in India and abroad. The Committee approves of and endorses that resolution, and is of the opinion that events subsequent to it have given it further justification, and have made it clear that the immediate ending of the British rule in India is an urgent necessity, both for the sake of India and for the success of the cause of the United Nations. The continuation of that rule is degrading and enfeebling India and making her progressively less capable of defending herself and of contributing to the cause of world freedom.[13]

The committee further resolved

to sanction, for the vindication of India's inalienable right to freedom and independence, the starting of a mass struggle on non-violent lines on the widest possible scale, so that the country might utilize all the non-violent strength it has gathered during the last twenty-two years of peaceful struggle. Such a struggle must inevitably be under the leadership of Gandhiji and the Committee requests him to take the lead and guide the nation in the steps to be taken.[14]

The committee appealed to the Indian people to face with courage and endurance the dangers and hardships that would befall them and to hold under Gandhi's leadership. Further:

A time may come when it may not be possible to issue instructions or for instructions to reach our people, and when no Congress Committee can function. When this happens, every man and woman, who is participating in this movement must function for himself or herself within the four corners of the general instructions issued. Every Indian who desires freedom and strives for it must be his own guide urging him on along [the] hard road where there is no resting place and which leads ultimately to the independence and deliverance of India.[15]

The A.I.C.C. resolution was moved by Jawaharlal Nehru and seconded by Sardar Patel on 7 August. It was passed but with

13 voting against it. Nehru explained that the communists were wrong and the stand taken by them had no popular support. The real need of the hour was to shift the emphasis from the physical to the moral plane. The flame that would be kindled by passing the resolution of the day would illuminate the darkened horizon right from the Caucasus to Chungking. The resolution represented the voice of India—of the oppressed humanity. In his final speech after the resolution was passed, Abul Kalam Azad, the president, counselled patience and said that if they did not hasten mass civil disobedience, it was only to strengthen the ground under their feet. He himself intended writing to President Roosevelt and the generalissimo in Chungking. People heard these speakers as well as others such as A. Patwardhan, Ram Manohar Lohia, T. Prakasam, and Pandit Nekiram with rapt attention.

**Figure 8.2** Gandhi and Sardar Patel with Jawaharlal Nehru, Mahadev Desai, and Acharya Kripalani at the A.I.C.C. meeting in Bombay in August 1942.

*Source*: Vithalbhai Jhaveri Collection/Dinodia Photos.

Gandhi spoke after the resolution was passed. To quote Sitaramayya:

Verily Gandhi spoke like a prophet in a moment of inspiration, full of fire, purifying by its flames, but consuming by its contact, rising from the sordid depths of politics to the sublime heights of humanity, fellowship on earth and of peace and goodwill to mankind—in a world-full of the spirit Divine. Indeed he spoke as the great leveller up of the nations, the friend of the poor, the uplifter of the depressed and the emancipator of the enslaved.[16]

In his speech at the A.I.C.C. on 7 August, Gandhi had stressed the importance of non-violence.

At a time when I am about to launch the biggest fight in my life there can be no hatred for the British in my heart.... Non-violence is a matchless weapon which can help everyone.... When I raised the slogan 'Quit India' the people in India who were then feeling despondent felt I had placed before them a new thing. If you want real freedom you will have to come together and such coming together will create true democracy— democracy the like of which has not been so far witnessed nor have there been any attempts made for such type of true democracy.... There are people who may call me a visionary but I tell you I am a real bania and my business is to obtain swaraj. Speaking to you as a practical bania, I say, if you are prepared to pay full price (of non-violent conduct), pass this resolution, otherwise do not pass it.... I want you to adopt non-violence as a matter of policy. With me it is a creed, but so far as you are concerned I want you to accept it as policy. As disciplined soldiers you must accept it in toto and stick to it when you join the struggle.[17]

Gandhi clarified his and the Congress position vis-à-vis the British government. In his interview to the press on 8 August, he maintained that '[i]f the resolution goes through this evening, I shall be the chief actor in the tragedy; it is therefore dreadful if any responsible Englishman considers me to be guilty of hatred of the British and admitted partiality for appeasement ... I own no enemy on earth. That is my creed.'[18]

On 8 August, he congratulated all who passed the resolution and stressed:

In satyagraha, there is no place for fraud or falsehood, or any kind of untruth. Fraud and untruth today are stalking the world. I cannot be a helpless witness to such a situation. I have travelled all over India as perhaps nobody in the present age has. The voiceless millions of the land saw in me their friend and representative, and I identified myself with them to an extent it was possible for a human being to do so. I saw trust in their eyes, which I now want to turn to good account in fighting this Empire upheld by untruth and violence.... Nevertheless, the actual struggle does not commence this moment. You have only placed all your powers in my hands. I will now wait upon the Viceroy and plead with him for the acceptance of the Congress demand. That process is likely to take two to three weeks. What would you do in the mean while? What is the programme, for the interval, in which all can participate? As you know, the spinning wheel is the first thing that occurs to me.... What more should you do? I will tell you. Every one of you should, from this moment onwards, consider yourself a free man or woman, and act as if you are free and are no longer under the heel of imperialism.... The bond of the slave is snapped the moment he considers himself to be a free being.... Here is a *mantra*, and a short one, that I give you. You may imprint it on your hearts and let every breadth of yours give expression to it. The *mantra* is 'Do or Die'. We shall either free India or die in the attempt; we shall not live to see the perpetuation of our slavery.... Let every man and woman live every moment of his or her life hereafter in the consciousness that he or she eats or lives for achieving freedom and will die, if need be, to attain that goal. Take a pledge with God and your own conscience as witness, that you will no longer rest till freedom is achieved and will be prepared to lay down your lives in the attempt to achieve it. He who loses his life, will gain it; he who will seek to save it shall lose it. Freedom is not for the coward or the faint-hearted.[19]

Gandhi further said that he was called the leader or the commander of the people. However, he did not see his position in that light. To quote him:

I have no weapon but love to wield my authority over anyone. I do sport a stick which you can break into bits without the slightest exertion. It is simply my staff with the help of which I walk. Such a cripple is not elated, when he is called upon to bear the greatest burden. You can share that burden only when I appear before you not as your commander but as a humble servant. And he who serves best is the chief among equals.... [M]y wisdom is not such a treasure which I cannot afford to lose; but my honesty is a precious treasure to me and I can ill afford to lose it.... [L]et me say without fear of challenge that throughout my career never have I asked for any personal favour.... I must not suppress the voice within, call it 'conscience', call it the 'prompting of my inner basic nature'.... Believe me, friends, I am not anxious to die. I want to live my full span of life. According to me, it is 120 years at least. By that time India will be free, the world will be free.... I trust the whole of India to launch upon a non-violent struggle on the widest scale.... Even if my eyes close and there is no freedom for India, non-violence will not end.... There are representatives of the Foreign Press assembled here today. Through them I wish to say to the world that the United Nations, who say that they have need for India, have the opportunity now to declare India free and prove their *bona fides*.[20]

Gandhi's words were evocative and powerful without any rhetoric or rancor. The British government, however, was in no mood to loosen its grip over India. Oppressive steps were continuously taken to put down any voice of protest. It is interesting here to mention a particular circular. Immediately after the resolution of the CWC dated 14 July, Frederick Puckle, the Indian government's director-general of Information, had issued, on 17 July, a circular to the chief secretaries of all the local governments to mobilize public opinion against the Congress resolution, which he described as a party manifesto opposed by other communities and organizations. He made a number of suggestions for publishing cartoons and posters, among which one was to show Hitler, Mussolini, and Tojo each with microphones saying 'I vote for the Congress resolution'. Gandhi received a copy through friends and thought it necessary to make it public. Commenting on it, Gandhi wrote under the title 'How to Crush National Movements! Amazing Disclosures':

[I]t is good for the public to know to what lengths the Government can go in their attempt to suppress national movements, however innocent, open and above board they are. Heaven knows how many such secret instructions have been issued which have never seen the light of the day. I suggest an honourable course. Let the Government by all means influence public opinion in an open manner and abide by its verdict. The Congress will be satisfied with a plebiscite or any other reasonable manner of testing public opinion and undertake to accept its verdict. That is real democracy. *Voxpopulivoxdei*.[21]

Referring to Puckle's secret circular he had said in his speech on 8 August, 'It is a suicidal course that he has taken. It contains an open incitement to organizations which crop up like mushrooms to combine to fight the Congress. We have thus to deal with an Empire whose ways are crooked.'[22]

Explaining his position to American friends, Gandhi wrote about the kind feelings of Dr Holmes and Bishop Fischer towards him; his indebtedness to Thoreau, Ruskin, and Tolstoy; and his own claim to be a votary of truth since his childhood. He requested them to read his formula of withdrawal or, as it had been popularly called, 'Quit India' in this context. To quote him, 'I assert that I would not have asked my country to invite Great Britain to withdraw her rule over India, irrespective of any demand to the contrary, if I had not seen at once that for the sake of Great Britain and Allied cause it was necessary for Britain boldly to perform the duty of freeing India from bondage.'[23]

It was announced on 8 August that a flag salutation would take place on Sunday, 9 August, at the Gowalia Tank Maidan in the morning, followed by an address by Jawaharlal Nehru to the students in the Congress pandal. It was also announced that Gandhi would address a public meeting at Shivaji Park, Dadar, the same evening with Nagindas T. Master as the president.[24]

Events, however, took a different turn. Gandhi's arrest was in the air. Journalists waited outside Birla House to keep a check on what was happening. And just when they thought the crisis might have been postponed, they realized that it was not so. To quote G.N. Acharya:

Hardly were we ensconced in the cosy warmth of the waiting taxi and it got going, when I peered out and sighted a beam of light coming down the Mount Pleasant Road. During the black-out days, only the police cars could have such headlights. Galvanized into action, all of us jumped out without waiting to ask the taxi to stop or back up, and sprinted. We were at the gates of Birla House, where the Mahatma slept peacefully, just as the police party arrived—in time to be witness to the beginning of the 1942 revolution.[25]

On 9 August, Harold Edwin Butler, the commissioner of police, went personally to effect the arrest of Gandhi. Accompanied by two police officers, the commissioner drove to Birla House at about 5 am. They were received by Mahadev Desai. The commissioner informed Desai that he had warrants for the arrest of Gandhi, Miraben, and Desai as well. He also told that although he had no warrants for Kasturba Gandhi and Pyarelal, they could accompany Gandhi to the police station, if they so wished. Both of them, however, preferred to stay behind for a moment.[26]

In reply to Gandhi's enquiry, the police commissioner informed Desai that they had half an hour to get ready. Gandhi had his breakfast of goat milk and fruit juice as usual. His favourite hymn 'Vaishnav jan' was then sung by his party, members of the Birla family, and his host. Verses from the Quran were recited by Amtusalam. He then left with a few of his personal belongings including his copy of the Gita, the ashram hymn book, a copy of the Quran, and his *dhanushtakli* for spinning.[27]

According to a report of a well-placed agent, Gandhi's arrest was in the air. Sushila Nayar had managed to obtain from Delhi a copy of the Indian government's letter to the government of Bombay conveying instructions about action against the Congress leaders, the disposal of Gandhi, and his immediate entourage. Nayar took this letter to Bombay from Delhi on 5 August 1942. Devdas Gandhi knew about it and had tried to communicate it to Bombay on telephone.[28]

Gandhi was driven to the Victoria Terminus where a special train had been drawn up. The members of the working committee and a number of Bombay Congress leaders had already been rounded up and taken to the special train. The Bombay group was sent to the Yerwada jail. The members of the working committee were sent to the Ahmednagar Fort.

When the Congress leaders were whisked away by the government on 9 August, Aruna Asaf Ali, a young firebrand leader, emerged like a lightning in the morning, unfurled the national flag at the Gowalia Tank Maidan, and went underground. She talked about it later: 'The meeting was declared illegal under Section 144. A white sergeant gave two minutes for the crowd to disperse. I quickly scrambled up to the dais, announced to the people the arrest of the leaders, and pulled the cord to hoist the national flag. Hardly had the flag been unfurled when the police lobbed tear-gas shells into the crowd.'[29] The police took charge of the pandal of the

**Figure 8.3** *The Bombay Chronicle* dated 10 August 1942 headlines the protests and demonstrations in the city after the arrests of Gandhi and other leaders.
*Source*: The Asiatic Society of Mumbai.

A.I.C.C. meeting and the Congress House. Curfew was imposed; tear gas and lathi charge were used to stop the rally of protesters.

On 9 August, Gandhi, Miraben, and Mahadev Desai were taken to Aga Khan's bungalow in Poona. Kasturba, Pyarelal, and Nayar were given the option to accompany Gandhi, but they declined. They were arrested on 9 August for breach of the order prohibiting them from leaving the house. They intended to attend the banned meeting in Shivaji Park, which was to be addressed by Gandhi. They were taken to the Bombay jail and were sent to join Gandhi. Picketing was declared illegal in Bombay and Ahmedabad. The commissioner of police recommended immediate promulgation of the emergency-powers ordinance as he anticipated further trouble. But the government proposed to wait.[30]

It is interesting to note that in midst of his preoccupations Gandhi had time to visit the aged and ailing among his friends and coworkers. K.P. Khadilkar (a devoted spinner who used to invariably present hanks of yarn to Gandhi, and the wife of the well-known Gandhian of Bombay), whose leg had been amputated, was bedridden in her home. Gandhi called on her to console and encourage her.[31]

## Course of the Movement

Gandhi's arrest marked the launch of the movement in a spontaneous way. The city plunged into hartals, processions, demonstrations, and outburst of popular unrest. The government took recourse to arrests and firing, leading to further chaos and disorder. Unrest spread to the interiors of Bombay Presidency like the other provinces. Attempts were made to set post offices, railways stations, and political stations on fire. The youth diverted to violent methods such as exploding bombs and going underground.

There was no definite programme for the movement. However, the British secret reports state the contrary. The statement of Rajindra Nath is interesting in this context. He was told by Pyarelal on 9 August at about 9 am after the arrest of Gandhi and other leaders that Gandhi had received a message on telephone from the *Bombay Chronicle* at about 11 pm the previous night that he and other important leaders would be arrested in the early hours of the following morning. On receiving this information, Gandhi got instructions drafted and prepared overnight about the programme to be followed by the people after the arrest of the leaders, and that was why Pyarelal and others, who had been given by the police the option to accompany Gandhi in jail if they wanted, had chosen to stay behind with a view to pass the instructions to the masses. Pyarelal further told Rajindra Nath that Gandhi had made it clear this time that he would not call off his movement even if the masses were to resort to violence.[32]

A secret evidence of 25 July 1942 cites Vallabhbhai Patel talking to some people that the struggle would start soon after the A.I.C.C. meeting was over. It would not stop even if there was a civil war or anarchy in the country and would shake the whole world. It would be carried on by masses, even if all the leaders were arrested by the government at the end of A.I.C.C. meeting. The Congress would not interfere if some people lost their temper and took dangerous and drastic steps against the government during the struggle, nor would Gandhi show his disapproval in that connection. Congressmen would certainly observe non-violence during the struggle, but others were not bound by that rule.[33]

Gandhi's instructions for civil resisters that were discussed in the working committee were an outline of the programme of the Quit India Movement. Gandhi told that every Congressman was his own leader and every Indian who desired freedom for the entire India should regard himself as a Congressman and act as such. All students above the age of 16 should come out of their schools and colleges and should not return to them until independence. The people should refuse to submit to the government's coercion or orders. They should also refuse to pay taxes, land revenue, and other government dues. 'The object of the struggle was to secure the withdrawal of the British rule and attainment of independence for the whole of India.'[34] He was clear that '[t]he programme covers every activity included in a mass movement... I would not hesitate to go to the extreme limit, if I find that no impression is produced over the British Government or the Allied Powers.... [It will be] my biggest movement.... [With the arrest of the leaders] it should gain strength, if it has any vitality.'[35]

A secret report mentions that Yusuf Meherally, at a meeting of the Bombay Congress on 31 July 1942, said:

The Congress may be declared illegal even before the A.I.C.C. meeting and the Government may resort to repression. But repression will not be able to crush the movement. On the contrary, it will fan the flames. Out of the repression will emerge a great revolution which would create a new World Order.... Even if all the leaders are arrested, the movement cannot be stopped. Every man in the country will be a Congressman and every house a Congress house.[36]

Supporters of Gandhi in Bombay included leaders such as Yusuf Meherally, B.G. Kher, S.K. Patil, Shankarrao Deo, Achyutrao Patwardhan, Ashok Mehta, Purshotam Tikamdas, Khurshed Naoroji, Hansa Mehta, and Nagindas T. Master. The young people of the city such as Minoo Masani, M.L. Dantwala, G.G. Parikh, Shanti Patel, and Prabhakar Kunte were also active. As is recorded, Bombay became not only the venue of the historic A.I.C.C. session, but also the important site where the discontent and protest of the people were expressed. Huge crowds had gathered on 9 August at the Gowalia Tank Maidan and later at Shivaji Park to protest against the arrest of the leaders. There was firing at the maidan, resulting in eight deaths and wounding 169, according to an official version. Students took the lead; schools, colleges, and even the markets remained closed for about two weeks. Markets also did not open. Soon the element of violence and destruction entered the movement. Government buildings such as post offices were attacked, means of communication were tampered with, telegraph and telephone lines were cut, and roads and lanes were blocked. The GIP, BB, and CI railway lines were tampered with. The Matunga railway station was attacked and demonstrations were held at Parel. Firings were reported from several parts of the city. In September the first bomb burst in the city, and thereafter a number of government buildings were burnt.[37]

The official version of the happenings in the city during the week from 9 to 15 August gives an indication about the situation prevailing at that time. According to it:

Disorderly crowds, among whom students were prominent, gathered simultaneously at several places and threw stones and soda water bottles at trams, buses and cars and at the police. They ripped open tyres of several buses and burnt a few buses. Two post offices were broken into and one was looted and the papers of the other were burnt. Five grain shops and two sugar depots were looted. Some Government servants in uniform such as peons of the postal and telegraph department, railway employees and policemen were assaulted and a police constable was stabbed. Municipal property, street lamps, lamp-posts, refuge carts, hydrants etc. was destroyed or damaged. Telephone wires were cut. Several police *chowkies* and one B.E.S.T. *chowky* were burnt. Trees were uprooted and several letter boxes damaged or destroyed. Stones, soda water bottles, fallen trees and debris were thrown on the streets in attempts to stop vehicular traffic. An electric wire box of the B.E.S.T. and several fuse boxes were burnt. A lorry loaded with bags of grain was looted. Unauthorized Congress bulletins were distributed. To disperse the crowds the police had to make lathi charges several times, use tear smoke six times and open fire on 35 occasions. As a result of firing 32 persons were killed, and 60 persons were injured.[38]

The report for the week ending on 29 August 1942 contains news of disturbances. It mentions that on the BB and CI railway lines much of the railway property was damaged by unruly mobs at Dadar, Matunga, and Marine Lines stations and obstruction was caused by prostrating on the railway tracks.[39] The official report of casualties in the city from 9 August to 24 September shows 36 dead and 472 injured.[40]

**Figure 8.4** Demonstrations in Bombay during the Quit India Movement in August 1942.
*Source*: Mani Bhavan Gandhi Sangrahalaya.

It is important to note that people's protest contained methods of Gandhian agitation also. They included peaceful processions, spinning, and programmes to spread Gandhi's message. Women played a remarkable role in this context. Undaunted by the fear of arrest or police repression, the women of Bombay removed the shackles of traditions and customs and participated in political activities with rare courage. They organized processions; distributed Congress bulletins and other nationalist leaflets; spread the message of nationalism; continued spinning, teaching Hindustani, and bringing Gandhi's message in the precincts of homes.

Students from various institutions such as Elphinstone College, Sydenham College, Ramnarain Ruia College, Khalsa College, and the VJTI were active during the movement. A police report of incidents on 9 September 1942 records six girl students at the main entrance of Elphinstone College preventing other students from entering, two girl students distributing a leaflet 'Carry on' among the college students, and some women organizing processions.[41]

The Congress bulletin carried reports of the past events and information about the coming programmes. A particular incident is important in this context. It was announced that a women's procession would be taken out from C.P. Tank to Chowpatty at 2.30 pm on 9 September 1942 in observance of the completion of a month since the arrest of the Congress leaders. At the scheduled time, a batch of five women led by Jaishri Raiji came out with a Congress flag from the side of Hira Baug to C.P. Tank. They were followed by about 50 women who were dispersed after the arrest of the five leading women. At 2.45 pm, a batch of four women attempted to form a procession at Vithalbhai Patel Road; about 50 women followed. However, the leaders were arrested and the group dispersed. At 3.10 pm, a batch of 24 girls who refused to give their names was arrested at Kandewadi for forming a procession. Another batch of 30 girls was arrested at 3.25 pm at the same place for forming a procession. In the meanwhile, about 40 desh sevikas (34 of them clad in saffron-coloured saris) carrying small Congress flags tried to march in procession near Prarthana Samaj. They were arrested. When they were being taken to the police station, stones were thrown from all directions, injuring the police escorts. After the desh sevikas were removed, some students shouted Congress slogans and tried to form processions. The police chased them away, but they repeatedly tried to form processions. Several times lathi charges were made to disperse them. Thirty-four female and eleven male students were arrested. About this time a procession of women and men numbering about 34 was intercepted near the Congress House at Lamington Road. A batch of 20 girl students from the Seva Sadan School shouted Congress slogans in front of the Lamington Road police station; they were arrested. Two BEST buses were damaged in that area due to stone pelting. Girl students made an attempt to form a procession in the Gamdevi area at about 3.30 pm. About 300 students in batches marching down from Sandhurst Bridge converged in Chowpatty. They were dispersed by cane and lathi charges. The crowd, however, stopped a passing bus and threw stones at it, breaking the glass panes. The situation was calmer in the evening after the enforcement of a curfew order.[42] Such incidents highlighted the determined efforts of women to participate in the struggle.

The Bombay Congress bulletin of 11 September called the day as 'Stree Shakti Din' and offered 'respectful congratulations to the Women of Bombay for the fighting manner in which they celebrated the beginning of the second month of our great revolution'. Further, 'people were expecting starting developments during the day and their wildest expectations came true due to the inestimable courage and resourcefulness of the women of Bombay'. It also reported:

the police resorted to innumerable lathi charges and releasing of tear gas. They opened fire five times and five people were wounded. They arrested nearly 250 ladies. And yet more than 600 women took part in the procession, [a] large number of which succeeded in reaching the Chowpatty sands and shouted to the world that the Government has left no weapon in their armoury and the day of retribution is fast approaching.[43]

The wary government continued its repressive measures, constraining the movements of the people. On 9 September, an order was issued by the presidency magistrate in view of rioting and disturbance in public peace in the city of Bombay. Exercising the powers under Section 144 of the Code of Criminal Procedure, the order restricted the movements of people between 7.30 pm and 6 am in some areas such as Girgaum Road, Kalbadevi

**Figure 8.5** The procession of women volunteers in Bombay during the Quit India Movement, 1942.
*Source*: Vithalbhai Jhaveri Collection/Dinodia Photos.

Road, Sheikh Memon Street, Sandhurst Road, Masjid Bunder Road, Narsi Natha Street, and Samuel Street.[44] Such measures, however, did not dampen the awakened spirit of the people.

The city had chalked out a special programme to celebrate the birthday of its special leader Gandhi. The programme for the celebration of the Gandhi Week in the city of Bombay was as follows:

2 October 1942: complete hartal, stoppage of traffic, and complete deadlock.

3 October 1942: prayers at 6 o'clock at Prarthana Samaj. It is to be observed as 'Tri-Colour Day' by wearing a dress of white, green, and orange colour.

4 October 1942: 'Do or Die Day'. At 7 am, there should be prabhat pheris in all wards. There should be spinning between 12 noon to 2 pm.

5 October 1942: 'Quit India Day'

6 October 1942: 'Azad Day'

7 October 1942: 'Flag Day'. There should be flag salutations in all wards at 9.30 am.

8 October 1942: complete hartal. At 5 pm, there should be general prayers in all wards.

9 October 1942: the programme for 9 October will depend on the response given by the public during the week. On this day, two months of Gandhi's arrest will be completed.[45]

The letter from the police commissioner to the secretary to the government of Bombay reported on 26 arrests on 3 October, closing of shops and markets in the Congress localities, police action to frustrate flag salutation ceremonies or processions, and some incidents of stone pelting and normal working of the mills.[46]

Efforts were made by leaders to spread the message of Gandhi and the movement. The Congress bulletins, other leaflets, and cyclostyled weeklies and fortnightlies such as Ninth August and Inqilab disseminated the progress of the movement, suppressive measures taken by the government, and inspiring messages of Gandhi and other leaders. The Quit India bulletin dated 27 September 1942 carried news of barbarism at Chimur, a village in the Chanda district, by the military on villagers expressing their spirit of nationalism.[47] A booklet entitled Quit India by Gandhi was compiled by R.K. Prabhu and U.R. Rao and edited by Yusuf Meherally. It was printed at the Associated Advertisers and Printers Ltd., Bombay, and published by Padma Publication, Bombay.

People expressed their resolve in many ways. Women shed their inhibition and social taboo and expressed their political views. An interesting letter to 'Every Government Officer and

by almost 500 women from different areas of Bombay such as
Marine Drive, Sandhurst Road, Girgaum, Vithalbhai Patel Road,
Bhuleshwar, Matunga, and Khar 'in sisterly love'. It spelled the
resolve to celebrate the Gandhi Week with greater zest and
zeal, as Gandhi was behind the prison bars. It further conveyed
that the Congress exhorted them to shed all fear and observe a
complete hartal on 8 October and asked them to respond to the
call for the national cause of freedom in token sympathy.[48]

Peaceful protests and sabotage of government property
continued. Government records show incidents of holding of
buses by the students in Khar; stopping of a student procession
in Santacruz; uprooting of road signs; an attempt to burn the Vile
Parle post office; an explosion in a compartment of a Kurla local
train that was shunted in the car shed; as well as an effort by some
men, women, and children to hold a flag salutation ceremony in
Vile Parle.[49]

The highlight of the Quit India Movement in Bombay was
the Congress Radio that gave regular updates of national and
international news. This bold and unusual initiative was taken
soon after the A.I.C.C. Congress session in Bombay in August
1942 to disseminate information about the movement and other
important national and international news. The courageous
core group of Vithaldas (Babubhai) Madhavji Khakkhar, Usha
Mehta, Vithaldas Kanthabhai Jhaveri, Nanak G. Motwane and
Chandrakant Babubhai Jhaveri was helped by leaders such as
Ram Manohar Lohia and others. They worked with single-
minded dedication, driven by deep patriotism. They kept on
changing their places of transmission, avoided getting caught by
the police for some time, and created waves in the country. The
radio appealed that '[a]ll Indians should be determined to play
their part in the present movement and should request others to

join hands with them'. Usha Mehta remembered that she and her colleagues were convinced that

a transmitter of our own is perhaps one of the most important requirements for the success of the movement. When the press is gagged and the news is banned, a transmitter helps a good deal in furnishing the public with the correct news of happenings. The Congress Radio was not a radio only in name. It had its own transmitter, transmitting station, recording station, its own call sign and a district wave-length. We started broadcasting with the announcement 'This is the Congress Radio calling on 42.34 meters from somewhere in India'.[50]

The Congress Radio managed to be on air from the second half of August and did an excellent job until 12 November when the police raided the place of the then transmission; Usha Mehta and Chandrakant Jhaveri were arrested on the spot. The charges against them included working illegally and disturbing the government. The case attracted the nation's attention. Ultimately, Khakkhar was sentenced to rigorous imprisonment for five years; Usha Mehta and Chandrakant Jhaveri were sentenced for a period of four years and one year respectively. Vithaldas Jhaveri and Motwane were acquitted of charges and discharged. N.S. Lokur, a special judge, mentioned in the beginning of his verdict dated 14 May 1943 that '[t]his case has brought to light the daring with which a broadcasting station was illegally established and worked in different populated localities in Bombay, and the cunning which, for nearly three months, baffled the attempts of the Police to trace it'.

Bombay always responded enthusiastically to causes dear to Gandhi. In 1942, Gandhi had issued an appeal for collections for the Deenbandhu (C.F. Andrews) Memorial. After some time, he found that only a small sum had been collected. He was naturally worried about the matter; thereafter, he came to Bombay. He wrote to the readers of *Harijan*:

[T]he efforts of Sardar Vallabhbhai Patel and Sheth Ghanshyamdas Birla, who had asked me to go to Bombay for eight days for the purpose of finishing the Deenbandhu Memorial collections, have been crowned with full success. Only over Rs. 60,000 were collected in response to the appeal through the papers. The whole of the balance of five lacs was collected during the eight days' strenuous labour. Bombay has never disappointed me whenever I have gone there for collections.[51]

The movement of 1942 was a massive tumultuous wave engulfing the people in the country, and the city of Bombay was a nerve centre drawing people from all sections. Recollecting those times, Aruna Asaf Ali had said later, 'I was but a splinter of the lava thrown up by the volcanic eruption of a people's indignation.'[52] The year 1942 in Bombay was spectacular in its scope of awakening and protest, unleashing of the energy, and opening up of new avenues of freedom.

## Notes and References

1. According to Pyarelal, the expression 'a post-dated cheque on a crashing bank' was wrongly ascribed to Gandhi in reference to the Cripps proposals of March 1942. Gandhi never used it in that form or even in substance. See 'Chapter 2', note 1, in Pyarelal, *Mahatma Gandhi: The Last Phase*, Vol. I (Ahmedabad: Navajivan Publishing House, 1956), p. 707.

2. Pyarelal, *Mahatma Gandhi*, Vol. I, p. 707.

3. Sitaramayya, *History of the Indian National Congress*, Vol. II, p. 338.

4. Home Department (Special), File 1110 (1), Maharashtra State Archives, Bombay (hereafter MSA).

5. Home Department (Special), File 1110 (1), MSA.

6. Sir R.L. Lumley (Bombay) to the Marquess of Linlithgow (Extract), Mss. Eur. F. 125/56, Confidential, Govt. House, Bombay, 24–7 August 1942, Report No. 110 cited in Nicholas Mansergh and E.M.R. Lumby (eds), *Constitutional Relations between Britain and India: The Transfer of Power, 1942–47, Vol. II, Quit India, 30 April–21 September 1942* (London: Her Majesty's Stationary Office, 1971), p. 806.

7. *Congress Responsibility for the Disturbances, 1942–43* (Delhi: Manager of Publications, 1943), p. 17.

8. Home Department (Special), File 1110 (1), Bombay City, S.B. (I) 6 August 1942, secret letter no. S.A. 32/A-23, 11-8-42, MSA.

9. 'Bombay Secret Abstract', p. 271, para 770 cited in Kunte, *Source Material for a History of the Freedom Struggle in India*, Vol III, Part VII, p. 68.

10. Home Department (Special), File 1110 (1), Confidential Spl. Br. I, CID, 5739/H/3035 dated 8 August 1942, MSA.

11. Home Department (Special) 1110 (1), 9 August 1942, MSA.

12. Gopalaswami, *Gandhi and Bombay*, p. 371.

13. Sitaramayya, *History of the Indian National Congress*, Vol. II, p. 343; *CWMG*, Vol. 76 (New Delhi: Publications Division, Ministry of Information and Broadcasting, Government of India, 1979), p. 458.

14. Sitaramayya, *History of the Indian National Congress*, Vol. II, p. 345; *CWMG*, Vol. 76, p. 461.

15. Sitaramayya, *History of the Indian National Congress*, Vol. II, p. 345.

16. Sitaramayya, *History of the Indian National Congress*, Vol. II, p. 348.

17. *The Hitavada* dated 9 August 1942 and *The Bombay Chronicle* dated 8 August 1942 cited in *CWMG*, Vol. 76, pp. 377–81.

18. *The Bombay Chronicle* dated 9 August 1942 cited in *CWMG*, Vol. 76, p. 383.

19. *CWMG*, Vol. 76, pp. 391–2. He first spoke in Hindi and then in English.

20. *CWMG*, Vol. 76, pp. 396–401.

21. Sitaramaiyya, *History of the Indian National Congress*, Vol. II, pp. 373–4.

22. *Mahatma*, Vol. VI, cited in *CWMG*, Vol. 76, pp. 154–64, 391.

23. *Harijan* dated 9 August 1942 cited in *CWMG*, Vol. 76, pp. 358–9.

24. Home Department (Special), File 1110 (1), 9 August 1942, MSA.

25. G.N. Acharya, 1947, 'The 1942 Revolution', *Sound Magazine*, VI(8).

26. *The Times of India* dated 10 August 1942; Home Department (Special) File 1110 (61) II, 1942, MSA.

27. *Harijan*, 16 August 1942.

28. 'Secret Evidence', Part I, 101, extract from the statement of Rajindra Nath quoted in P.N. Chopra (ed.), *Quit India Movement: British Secret Report* (Faridabad: Thomson Press, 1976), p. 258. Nath was a Punjab Congress worker who did secretarial work in Sevagram Ashram. He was the son of Gauri Shankar Khatri of Batala, Gurdaspur District. He was arrested on 23 December 1942.

29. G.N.S. Raghavan, *Aruna Asaf Ali* (New Delhi: National Book Trust, 1999), p. 43.

30. Home Department (Special), File 1110 (6) B 1942, Confidential telegram, 10 August 1942 to Home, New Delhi from Bombay, MSA.

31. Gopalaswami, *Gandhi and Bombay*, p. 359.

32. 'Secret Evidence', Part II, 55, extracts from the statement of Rajindra Nath quoted in Chopra, *Quit India Movement*, p. 285.

33. 'Secret Evidence', Part I, 60, Kanji Dwarkadas's notes dated 5 August 1972, to Sir Frederick Stone, E.D. Sassoon Mills, Bombay quoted in Chopra, *Quit India Movement*, p. 245.

34. Gandhi's correspondence with the government quoted in *CWMG*, Vol. 76, pp. 364–7.

35. *Harijan*, 26 July 1942.

36. 'Secret Evidence', Part I, 78, copy of an intercepted letter dated 30 July 1942, from Bhola Nath Prasad 'Vimal', 73, Broacha Hostel, B.H.U. Banaras to Gopal Krishna Sahay, sub-registrar, P.O. Village Mahanar, Muzaffarpur District cited in Chopra, *Quit India Movement*, pp. 251–2.

37. Sanjiv P. Desai (ed.), *Calendar of the Quit India Movement in the Bombay Presidency* (Bombay: Department of Archives, Government of Maharashtra, 1985), pp. viii–ix.

38. Desai, *Calendar of the Quit India Movement*, pp. vii–viii.

39. Home Department (Special), File 1110 (6) E, MSA.

40. Home Department (Special), File 1110 (6) A (1) I, MSA.

41. Home Department (Special), File 1110 (6) A (1) I, MSA.

42. Home Department (Special), File 1110 (6) A (1) I, MSA.

43. Home Department (Special), File 1110 (6) A (1) I, MSA.

44. Home Department (Special), File 1110 (6) A (1) I, MSA.

45. Home Department (Special), File 1110 (6) E, MSA. The police commissioner forwarded a copy of the programme for Bombay City during the Gandhi Week from 2 to 9 October 1942 and a copy of the programme for the Gandhi Week for the whole of India together with instructions purporting to have been issued by the A.I.C.C. to the secretary to the government of Bombay, Home Department (Special), and the assistant to the deputy inspector general of police, intelligence branch, CID, Province of Bombay, Poona.

46. Home Department (Special), File 1110 (6) A (1) I, 1942, MSA.

47. Home Department (Special), File 1110 (6) A (1) I, 1942, MSA.

48. Home Department (Special), File 1110 (6) A (1) I, 1942, MSA.

49. Home Department (Special), File 1110 (6) A (2), express letter reg. no. S.D.V./362, dated 15 August 1942; weekly confidential report dated 26 September 1942; daily report dated 8 December 1942, MSA.

50. Personal communication.

51. *Harijan*, 24 May 1942.

52. Raghavan, *Aruna Asaf Ali*, p. 41.

## 9

# THE TESTING TIMES: 1943–8

THE FERMENT AND STIR GENERATED BY THE 1942 MOVEMENT
continued in the city. On 26 January 1943, declared as 'Independence
Day', the BPCC announced a pledge stating:

We pledge ourselves anew to the Independence of India and solemnly
resolve to carry on the struggle, no matter what odds may face us and
what sufferings be our lot, till Purna Swaraj is attained. We declare
ourselves 'Open Rebels' against the usurper British administration and
resolve to disobey its laws. We further resolve to adopt all legitimate and
non-violent ways to bring about a complete paralysis of the machinery of
administration through which the British Rule operates.[1]

It called for hartals in the city, town, or village; hoisting of
the national flag in every house; strikes in schools and colleges;

wearing by students and others of suitable badges; strikes in mills and factories; and processions and meetings in the evenings at all public places and buildings where people should assemble in thousands to repeat the pledge and declare their determination to act upon it.[2] Activities on these lines continued in the city.

Gandhi was imprisoned and kept in the Aga Khan Palace in Poona. Kasturba stayed with him, and so did some others such as Sushila Nayar and Mahadev Desai. The sudden death of Mahadev Desai, who was very close to Gandhi apart from being his secretary for years, on 15 August 1942 was a cruel blow of destiny that hit the latter severely. Meanwhile, the British government continued to blame Gandhi and the Congress for the violence following the Quit India Movement. Gandhi emphatically denied it. He fasted in protest against the government propaganda that the responsibility for disturbances after the arrest of leaders lay at the Congress's door. He observed a fast from 10 February 1943 for 21 days.[3] Its purpose was to draw the world's attention to India's cause.

## 1944

Gandhi suffered an irreparable loss when Kasturba, his life partner of 62 years, breathed her last in his lap on 22 February during confinement at the Aga Khan Palace. The city of Bombay was with its leader in his grief. Prayer meetings were held at several places in Bombay. In response to the appeal made by Madan Mohan Malaviya, Bombay observed 5 March as 'Kasturba Gandhi Day'. The day being Sunday, most of the Indian markets remained closed. Seven mills stayed closed as a mark of respect for the deceased and a few shops in the mill area were also shut down. Devotional songs were sung at a meeting held under the auspices of the Freedom Group in the building of the Indian Merchants' Chamber.[4] Again, it was decided to observe 14 March

as 'Kasturba Day' at all the production centres and sales depots
of the All-India Spinners' Association throughout the country.
The Bombay Charkha Sangh had chalked out a programme to
mark the occasion: all the *bhandars* in the city would be closed
on 14 March with non-stop spinning at each bhandar from 9 am
to 5 pm, offering of prayers at each bhandar, and an appeal to the
people to spin on this day and contribute their quota of spinning.[5]

The city remembered Kasturba warmly at a public meeting
held at Sunderbai Hall. Glowing tributes were paid to her by
various speakers including Purushottamdas Thakurdas, Hansa
Mehta, Shantidas Askuran, M.C. Chagla, Rustom Masani,
Premlila Thackersey, Bhulabhai Desai, John McKenzie, Sultan
Chinoy, Sorab Saklatvala, Ramdeo Podar, Y.K. Khadilkar, and
Jamnadas Dwarkadas. In his remarks from the chair, M.R. Masani
emphasized that the distinguished citizens present showed that
the citizens of Bombay, whether they were political opponents of
Gandhi or those who owed him allegiance, were one in offering
their condolences to him in his loss.[6]

The Bombay committee of the Kasturba Gandhi National
Memorial Fund was appointed to make collections for the
fund. Pranlal Devkaran Nanjee was its president and other
office-bearers included Mrs G.M.S. Captain and Professor
P.A. Wadia, Ratilal M. Gandhi, C.C. Shah, Mahomed Hussain
Hasham Premji, Jaishri Raiji, Ramnath A. Podar, and Motichand
G. Kapadia. Trustees of the fund who belonged to Bombay
included Purushottamdas Thakurdas, J.R.D. Tata, K.M. Munshi,
Shantikumar N. Morarji, and Lady Premlila Thackersey. V.L.
Mehta and Swami Anand, the secretaries of the central fund,
were ex officio members.[7] Gandhi was elected the chairman of
the first executive committee. Bombay contributed to the fund
with generosity and affection. A.V. Thakkar, the secretary of
the fund, Bombay, announced that the total amount collected at

the Bombay headquarters had already reached the figure of Rs 10 million by the evening of 6 October.[8] The Kasturba Gandhi National Memorial Fund was established for the welfare and education of women and children of all communities in India.

Gandhi was released from detention on 6 May 1944. He reached Bombay from Poona on 11 May and went to the shack built by Jahangir Patel in the compound of Narottam Morarji in Gandhigram, Juhu. He decided on 14 May to enter a fortnight's silence to ensure uninterrupted rest. It was discovered by now that he had contracted hookworm infection.[9]

Although Gandhi was out of detention, the British government kept a close watch on his activities and maintained a record of his routine. It was reported that his camp followers, namely Sushila Nayar, Pyarelal, Miraben, and D.D. Gilder, attended to him. He went for a morning walk on the Juhu sands and attended the prayers in the evening at about 7.30 pm daily. On 14 May, a large gathering of about 12,000 people attended the prayers in the evening and people contributed to the Harijan Fund after the prayers. On 19 May 1944, Gandhi, accompanied by Mayor Nagindas T. Master and others, visited the areas of the docks and Mandvi, which were devastated by the recent fires in the Bombay docks. On his way back to Juhu, Gandhi saw the ailing Mangaldas Pakwasa, the president of the Bombay Legislative Council. During the week, he was visited by some prominent people of Bombay, including K.T. Gajjar, S.A. Brelvi, P.C. Bharucha, Harendranath Chattopadhyaya, Jivraj Mehta, G.P. Hathisingh, Mathuradas Trikamji, D.G. Tendulkar, V.S. Dongre, and Dahyabhai Vallabhbhai Patel. Visitors from other places included Vijaya Laxmi Pandit from Allahabad, Jhaverchand Meghani from Ahmedabad, Premlila Thackersey from Poona, Swami Anand from Thane, Kamaladevi Chattopadhyaya, and Chang Sun, the editor-in-chief of *Ta-Kung-Pao* of Chungking.[10]

A stream of visitors such as Kanji Dwarkadas and others continued to pour in to see Gandhi. On 21 May 1944, he watched the film *Mission to Moscow*. He also made time to see his near and dear ones who were not well, such as Umaben, G.L. Mehta's daughter, on 21 May and Yusuf Meherally on 30 May. It is interesting that some time was set aside from 15 to 30 May to hear soothing bhajans from renowned singers such as Manohar Barve, Hirabai Barodekar, Lala Ghorpade, Bade Ghulam Ali Khan, Chimanlal Shastri, Padmavati Shaligram, and Vishnu Pant Pagnis. On 26 May, he listened to Bade Ali Khan's rendering of bhajans. On 29 May, his silence ended but he still observed partial silence.[11] Political matters, however, weighed heavily on his mind. He wrote to M.R. Jayakar on 20 May 1944, 'The country expects much from me ... I cannot withdraw the August resolution.'[12]

Gandhi stayed in Bombay until 14 June; he left for Poona on 15 June. During these days, he had discussions with H.P. Mody, Jayakar, Jamnadas Dwarkadas, Kanji Dwarkadas, and others. He also found some time to hear ghazals from Shayada, a writer in Gujarati, and to watch the film *Ram Rajya*. He appealed to people who would gatecrash in an attempt to see him to disperse quietly. His concern for those involved in the movement did not diminish; his emphasis on non-violence never lost its sheen. In a letter, he advised Aruna Asaf Ali to come out and surrender and not to die underground. In a letter to Annada Babu Chowdhary, he wrote, 'Secrecy is a sin and symptom of violence ... all underground activity is taboo.' He maintained that the government was responsible for the outbursts in 1942, and not him or the Congress as it alleged. On 10 June, he distributed to friends copies of his correspondence with the government, as also his reply to the review report titled *Congress Responsibility for the Disturbances, 1942–43.*[13]

Many Congressmen had asked Gandhi about the manner in which the second anniversary of the Quit India Day could be celebrated on 9 August 1944. Gandhi said that there was a difference between mass civil disobedience and civil disobedience for the defence of individual citizens' rights. On such occasions as 9 August, the people must understand this difference and exercise this right of individual civil disobedience for the defence of civil rights.[14] According to him, '[I]n all places except in Bombay, my advice is not to disregard special police prohibitions for that day.' For him, Bombay was 'most easily accessible' and 'the place where the historic meeting of August 1942 was held'. He had suggested 'the symbolic procedure to see whether those who organize the demonstration have cooperation from the local public. Freedom of 400 million people through purely non-violent effort is not to be gained without learning the virtue of iron discipline, not imposed from without, but sprung naturally from within. Without the requisite discipline non-violence can only be a veneer.'[15] Pyarelal had noted that in accordance with Gandhi's advice, 25 citizens of Bombay sent a notice to the city's police commissioner a week before 9 August, stating their intention to offer silent prayers for five minutes and sing the flag-salutation song before the statue of Tilak at the Chowpatty sands and disperse.[16]

Gandhi made a sincere effort to find a way to solve the communal problem by conducting negotiations with Jinnah. On 9 May, Allama Mashriqi, the leader of Khaksars, asked Jinnah to see Gandhi and explore the possibility of a settlement. He also telegraphed Gandhi similarly.[17] On 15 May, Gandhi responded to Mashriqi's telegram saying that he was ready.[18] Gandhi's aim behind the talks with Jinnah was not to conclude a bilateral agreement with him that would then get implemented through the Congress and the Muslim League. The talks were intended to be the beginning of a search for national consensus in an atmosphere of goodwill created through the purifying effect of non-violence.[19]

Gandhi wrote to Jinnah on 17 July in Gujarati from Panchgani, 'Brother Jinnah, today I venture to write to you in the mother tongue … let us meet whenever you wish. Do not regard me as an enemy of Islam or of Indian Muslims. I have always been a servant and a friend of you and to mankind. Do not disappoint me.' Jinnah replied to Gandhi from Srinagar on 24 July 1944, 'I shall be glad to receive you at my house in Bombay on my return.'[20]

On 9 September when Gandhi reached Bombay, the entire area of Malabar Hill was protected by the police.[21] The Gandhi–Jinnah meeting took place the same day, and the talks lasted for 18 days. The announcement of the failure of the talks on 27 September meant closing the possibility of a peaceful solution to the knotty problem. Jinnah wanted an agreement between Gandhi and himself as representatives of Hindus and Muslims, which would be binding on the Congress and the Muslim League. The main argument of the Muslim League was the two-nation theory. The two-nation theory was based on the premise that Hindus and Muslims are not just two different religious groups but also two distinct and separate nations. Gandhi wrote to Jinnah on 15 September 1945 that he saw 'nothing but ruin for the whole of India' in the practice of the Lahore resolution of the Muslim League. 'Believe me, I approach you as a seeker. Though I represent nobody except myself, I aspire to represent all the inhabitants of India, for I realize in my own person their misery and degradation, which is their common lot, irrespective of caste, class or creed.'[22] After his meeting with Jinnah that lasted for three-and-a-quarter hours, he communicated to C. Rajagopalachari on 9 September that '[i]t was a test of my patience … I am amazed at my own patience. However it was a friendly talk.'[23] In his letters, he addressed Jinnah as 'Quaid-e-Azam'.

Why can you not accept my statement that I aspire to represent all the sections that compose the people of India? Do you not aspire? Should not every Indian? That the aspiration may never be realized is beside the point.... Can we not agree to differ on the question of 'two nations' and yet solve the problem on the basis of self-determination?[24]

**Figure 9.1** Gandhi in the compound of Birla House, Bombay, in 1944.
*Source*: Vithalbhai Jhaveri Collection/Dinodia Photos.

**Figure 9.2** Gandhi at a prayer meeting in the Rungta House compound,
Bombay, in September 1944.
*Source*: Vithalbhai Jhaveri Collection/Dinodia Photos.

In his letter to Jinnah dated 22 September, he wrote, 'We seem to be moving in a circle.'[25] In an interview to the *News Chronicle* (of London, represented by Stuart Gelder) on 29 September 1944, he said that 'I could not accept the two nations theory.... We have parted as friends.'[26] The correspondence between them was released to the press.

**Figure 9.3** Gandhi and Jinnah speaking to the journalists at Jinnah House, Mount Pleasant Road, Bombay, during the Gandhi–Jinnah talks in September 1944.

*Source*: Vithalbhai Jhaveri Collection/Dinodia Photos.

The Second World War ended in May 1945 with the Allied Powers as winners. Gandhi, accompanied by his two secretaries Sushila Nayar and Syed Mahmood, reached Bombay by the Calcutta Mail on 31 March 1945. The party was received by about 300 people including Nagindas T. Master, S.K. Patil, Pakwasa, Dahyabhai Patel, and Maniben Patel. He stayed at Birla House.[27] He also went to see Purushottamdas Thakurdas who was ill.[28]

Since his arrival in Bombay, Gandhi had a number of visitors including M. Pakwasa, Gulzarilal Nanda, Khandubhai Desai, G.V. Mavlankar, Prafulla Chandra Ghosh, Bishwanath Das of Orissa (now Odisha), Shrikrishna Das Jaju, Gangadharrao Deshpande, Syed Mahmood, and Maitreyee Bose. Khan Abdul Ghaffar Khan, who arrived in Bombay on 3 April, was almost a daily visitor. Informal discussions regarding the Kasturba Gandhi National Memorial Fund took place at Birla House on 1, 2, and 4 April, and various schemes put forward by the provinces were considered. Gandhi remained present at the well-attended evening prayers first at Birla House and from 3 April, at Rungta House, where collections were also made for the Harijan Fund.[29]

Gandhi's prayer meeting on 3 April 1945 was attended by about 30,000 people; Khan Abdul Ghaffar Khan was also present in the meeting. The crowd attending the prayer had become unmanageable at one stage, and a number of people including Sushila Nayar and Krishna Hatheesingh suffered injuries in the rush. Gandhi said that it was a matter of shame that they had come to pray to God but failed to conduct the prayer peacefully. He also said that he had been told by a friend that the people of Bombay would derive no benefit from his prayer: they would throw a few rupees for the Harijan Fund, but if Gandhi thought

**Figure 9.4** Gandhi and Sardar Patel greeted by people at the Dadar station, Bombay, in 1945.
*Source*: Vithalbhai Jhaveri Collection/Dinodia Photos.

that it was going to produce any effect on them or that they would embrace the Harijans as their own kith and kin, he was mistaken. Gandhi, however, said that he was not entirely convinced. He could not give up his principles, his trust in the people, and his faith in prayers. If he gave up prayers, the next thing for him to do would be give up the struggle for freedom, the striving for truth and non-violence. He asked the people how they would wield the reins of power if they could not even control themselves. The man with God in his heart would know how to control himself.[30]

In a prayer meeting on 6 April 1945, Gandhi said that the National Week was being observed since the last 26 years. It was meant for purification of thoughts and language. Over the years, he had abandoned fasting and hartal, but the week had not become less holy on that account. The constructive programme such as khadi and Hindu–Muslim unity was very much there. In conclusion, he said, 'Freedom is in our hands. When we breathe, we cannot take other people's help. If we resort to artificial methods of respiration, it means that we are on the brink of death. Freedom is like our breath.'[31]

A meeting of the trustees of the Kasturba Gandhi National Memorial Fund was held at Scindia House on 13 April.[32] It was attended by Gandhi, G.D. Birla, J.R.D. Tata, Shantikumar N. Morarji, V.L. Mehta, Mavlankar, Pakwasa, A.V. Thakkar, and Lady Premlila Thackersey. Several schemes for starting dispensaries in rural areas for the prevention of leprosy and also centres for training nurses and spreading basic education were approved.[33] On 14 April, Gandhi's son Manilal came from South Africa to meet his father. In the evening, prayers were held at Rungta House, collections were made for the Harijan Fund, and a sum of Rs 35,000 was given to Gandhi by the Bullion Exchange for the use of the dependents of the Chimur and Ashti convicts. Gandhi left Bombay for Mahabaleshwar by the Deccan Queen on 20 April. Khan Abdul Ghaffar Khan had left for Peshawar on 15 April.[34]

The BEST workers who had been on strike sought Gandhi's advice on 8 April 1945. As it was Gandhi's silence day, he gave his remarks in writing. Since he was not acquainted with the issue, he advised them to consult their leaders. However, based on his experience he narrated four conditions for a successful strike:

the cause should be clear and just, strikers should not be afraid of starvation or even death, they should never deviate from the path of truth and non-violence, and strikers should have public support behind them.[35] He wrote to G.D. Birla, 'My work has increased. My endeavour now is to see that no one expects any money from me and the institutions I have created become self-supporting.'[36] In another letter to R.K. Karanjia dated 10 April, he wrote, 'I am now tired of meeting people. Even now I have to meet them in the interest of the work but I try to avoid it as far as possible.'[37]

He visited the Women's Training Centre at Borivali on 11 April 1945 with Khan Abdul Ghaffar Khan and Purushottamdas Tandon. He was also present in the evening prayer at Borivali.[38] The camp was organized by Mridula Sarabhai under the auspices of the Kasturba Gandhi National Memorial Fund. In his speech, Gandhi explained the importance of prayers and removal of untouchability. Further, he said that the slavery of evil customs and superstitions was the worst form of slavery. He expected that for the women who want to go and work in villages, the first lesson in the camp was to learn to break all social restrictions that cramped or degraded them. He, however, warned them that this did not mean throwing off of all moral restraints. Uttermost moral purity was the first prerequisite for establishing social freedom. In his speech at the prayer meeting, he emphasized that Hinduism would perish if untouchability lived on.[39]

Gandhi was very much concerned about the events at the international level and the futility of war. On the death of President Roosevelt, he cabled a message of condolence. He also sent a message of congratulations on 16 April to Roosevelt's wife, because the president had died in harness and was spared the humiliating spectacle of being party to a peace that threatened to be a prelude to a war bloodier still if possible.[40] He made an important statement to the press on 17 April 1945 about the San Francisco Conference (convened on 25 April and concluded on 26 June when the charter for the United Nations was adopted). He reiterated his conviction that there would be no peace for the Allies and the world unless they shed their belief in the efficacy of war and the terrible deception and fraud accompanying it and were determined to hammer out real peace based on the freedom and equality of all races and nations. Germany and Japan should not be humiliated. India should be either represented at San Francisco by an elected representative or not represented at all.[41]

On 18 April, the leading members of the Indian Merchants' Chamber headed by its president M.A. Master and vice-president Mahamed Hussein Premji met Gandhi and discussed with him a report published in the British press to the effect that India could only be industrialized by British and Indian cooperation on a 50–50 basis in capital and controlling interests. Gandhi advised the merchants not to cooperate with such industrialization schemes if they found them impracticable in India. On 19 April, Gandhi held his evening prayers at Rungta House before a gathering of about 500 people and once more laid stress on his 15-fold constructive programme in preference to the parliamentary one.[42] He left for Mahabaleshwar on 20 April.

Gandhi came to Bombay on 20 June and stayed at Birla House. He attended the meeting of the CWC on 21 and 22 June.[43]

After a lapse of about three years, the A.I.C.C. met for the first time in Bombay at the Gowalia Tank Maidan under the presidentship of Maulana Abul Kalam Azad on 21 September. About 25,000 people attended and an equal number assembled outside the pandal. About 2,000 volunteers headed by T.R. Naravane and Sofia

**Figure 9.5**   Gandhi with Sardar Patel and others at Birla House, Bombay, prior to his visit to Simla to meet Lord Wavell in June 1945.
*Source*: Vithalbhai Jhaveri Collection/Dinodia Photos.

Khan were posted at the pandal to preserve order. Gandhi did not attend the A.I.C.C. meeting owing to indisposition.[44] However, he spoke at the prayer meeting that day. Asking for contributions to the Harijan Fund, he said that it would please him more if people came forward with hand-spun yarn instead of cash. He said that Bombay was the first city to contribute yarn and hoped that the citizens would continue the practice.[45]

There were some disturbances towards the end of September in the backdrop of the standoff between the A.I.C.C. that had just held a session in Bombay and the Muslim League. The Congress leaders such as S.K. Patil objected to the disturbances being described as communal riots. B.G. Kher, the former prime minister of Bombay, also said that the disturbances 'could not be strictly styled as communal riots; they were not a political but an administrative problem'.[46]

**Figure 9.6** Gandhi with the CWC members Maulana Azad, Sardar Patel, and J.B. Kripalani in Bombay on 21 June 1945.
*Source*: Vithalbhai Jhaveri Collection/Dinodia Photos.

## 1946

Gandhi arrived in Bombay from Poona on 11 March 1946 for a few days. He attended the meetings of the working committee at Birla House, mainly to advise the members on the policy to be adopted regarding the British Cabinet Mission and the food problem. On his advice, the working committee adopted the resolutions that had been reported to the government separately. He also addressed a largely attended public meeting at Shivaji

Park on 14 March and explained the implications of satyagraha and duties of a satyagrahi. He left Bombay for Poona on 16 March.[47] He had many visitors at Birla House during the week.

The situation in the country was tense due to all the political negotiations. Discontent among the people was rising. Revolt by the Indian sailors of the Royal Indian Navy (RIN) was a major jolt to the government. It started with the protest by the ratings at HMIS Talwar on 18 February 1946 and spread the next day to the RIN Depot (Castle Barracks) and to the ships in the Bombay harbour. The situation in the streets of Bombay became alarming as the demonstrations turned violent. The government had to give orders to open fire several times. Kanji Dwarkadas observed that the Congress socialists who did not want a settlement with Britain on any terms whatsoever except on the basis of 'Quit India' saw in this RIN revolt an opportunity to recreate the August 1942 atmosphere and the mentality of sabotage, strikes, disruption, and murder. For a couple of days or so, the Bombay government was hard-pressed to maintain security. Sardar Patel intervened effectively and told the socialist leaders that at a time when there were prospects of a friendly settlement with the British, he would not tolerate any disruptive activities and would not let them succeed through this strike of the RIN in creating panic and confusion in the country.[48]

A mammoth meeting attended by over 100,000 people was held at Chowpatty, Bombay, on 26 February 1946 under the auspices of the BPCC. Sardar Patel presided over and Jawaharlal Nehru addressed the meeting. Both Patel and Nehru condemned the violence and hooliganism in the city during the last four days and emphasized that the Congress, which was fighting for the independence of the country, had not called a hartal and people should not listen to the advice of those who spoke in the name of the Congress and created trouble.[49]

The Muslim League also did not want to aggravate the violence triggered by the RIN mutiny. On 23 February, Jinnah, the president of the Muslim League, appealed 'to all RIN men not to play in the hands of those who want to create trouble and exploit those on strike for their own ends. I urge upon them to restore normal conditions and let us handle the situation, which will surely result in their welfare and will be in their best interests.'[50]

Life in Bombay was disturbed, and Gandhi felt deeply anguished. He wrote with great concern: 'See what is happening in Bombay—the Bombay where I have passed so much time, which has given the public causes so much money, and which I had thought had fairly imbibed something of ahimsa. Will it prove the burial ground of ahimsa?'[51]

In the prayer meeting at Rungta House on 11 March 1946, he said:

The news of the recent events in Bombay has filled me with shame and humiliation as it must have you too. Let me hope that none of those who are here took part in these disgraceful happenings.... Inaction at a time of conflagration is inexcusable.... We have always proclaimed from the house-tops that non-violence is the way of the brave, but there are some amongst us who have brought ahimsa into disrepute by using it as a weapon of the weak. In my opinion, to remain a passive spectator of the kind of crimes that Bombay has witnessed of late is cowardice.... Silence becomes cowardice when occasion demands speaking out the whole truth and acting accordingly. We have to cultivate that courage, if we are to win India's independence through truth and non-violence as proclaimed by the Congress. It is an ideal worth living for and dying for.[52]

In a speech at the prayer meeting on 12 March 1946, he talked about his tour to Bengal, Assam, and Madras (now Chennai), where people donated money and ornaments for the Harijan Fund. In this meeting, Kanu Gandhi auctioned a silver charkha and a silver flask that fetched Rs 250 and Rs 200 respectively.

Gandhi also asked the seekers of his autograph to send their books with a sum of Rs 5 per autograph to him later.[53]

Shah Nawaz Khan and P.K. Sahgal of the Indian National Army (INA) came to see Gandhi on 13 March. Gandhi said that, in his opinion, constructive activity should absorb every INA member who was willing and worthy of his name. There was romance and incitement in fighting but not in civil life. The INA men had physical stamina, discipline, and a feeling of solidarity and oneness, untainted by narrow communalism.[54]

In his speech at Shivaji Park on 14 March, he thanked the gathering for the atmosphere of silence and calm in which the prayers were conducted. He said that 'Ramdhun' was the most important part of the prayer. It was as simple as effective. Emphasizing the importance of prayers, he said that will power and concentration were developed by prayer. He had learnt this through his experience over the years since he started satyagraha. The root of satyagraha was in prayer. The art of dying followed as a corollary from the art of living. The art of dying for a satyagrahi lay in facing death cheerfully in the performance of one's duty. That was an art the people of Bombay apparently had not yet learnt. Referring to the mutiny of the RIN ratings in Bombay and the disturbances that followed, he said that every activity carried out these days was motivated by a desire for freedom. But those who took part in these did not know the art of satyagraha. A satyagrahi must protect even his enemy at the cost of his life. He further pointed out that all were passing through a crisis in our history. But it could be converted into an opportunity if the power of satyagraha was realized. In a brief reference to the impending Cabinet Mission to India, the Mahatma counselled patience. He would indicate the next step if the mission failed to implement the pledges and promises made to India.[55] Among those who were present on the rostrum were Sardar Patel, Shah Nawaz Khan, and P.K. Sahgal of the INA.[56]

Gandhi had come to Bombay accompanied by Amrit Kaur and Pyarelal on 31 March 1946 while on his way to Delhi from Uruli Kanchan and stayed at Harijan was in Worli. Prior to his arrival in Bombay, there was an unsuccessful attempt to burn the hut he was to stay in. There were demonstrations against Gandhi at Dharavi Crossing and Worli.[57] Gandhi was again in Bombay on 5, 6, 7, and 8 July to attend the meetings of the CWC and the A.I.C.C.[58] This was his last visit to Bombay.

Bombay was jubilant on 15 August 1947. Many programmes and meetings were arranged to celebrate the Independence Day. Headlines of the *Times of India* announced 'Frenzied Enthusiasm in Bombay' and 'Crowds in Festive Mood'. The governor gave a message: 'May Bombay Prosper'. However, on this historic day Gandhi was in Calcutta healing the wounds of the suffering humanity.

When Gandhi came to know about the talk of erecting his statue at a public site in Bombay at the cost of Rs 1 million, he expressed his strong disapproval. In his words:

In Bombay, the beautiful, insanitation remains. There is so much overcrowding that poor people are packed like sardines. Wise use of ten lacs of rupees will consist in its being spent on some public utility. That would be the best statue. Money thus wisely spent will make an adequate return. Imagine how many hungry mouths would be filled if the amount was spent on growing more food crops![59]

The people in Bombay were enthusiastic about celebrating his birthday, although Gandhi, tormented by the violence following the Partition, was in Delhi in October 1947. All communities and classes in Bombay joined in the celebrations of his 78th birthday according to the Hindu calendar. The provincial government had declared the day a holiday. Small processions with national flags paraded the streets, later ending with flag salutations in different

**Figure 9.7**  Gandhi in the compound of Birla House, Bombay, in March 1946. Walking along with him are Amrit Kaur, Horace Alexander, Agatha Harrison, and Pyarelal.
*Source*: Vithalbhai Jhaveri Collection/Dinodia Photos.

wards. J.B. Kripalani, the Congress president, presided over a meeting in Chowpatty organized by the BPCC. Rev. Dr J.H. Holmes of New York referred to Mahatma Gandhi as the noblest and purest soul ever born in the world after Jesus Christ.[60]

Soon after India's independence, it was from Bombay Harbour that the British troops left the country. It was reported that at 11.30 am on 17 August 1947, with the lifting of the anchor of *S.S. Georgic,*

India said bon voyage and goodbye to the first batch of the British troops to evacuate the country as a result of the Transfer of Power. The ship flying the tricolour and the union jack was packed to capacity with soldiers. It was a day for which India had been waiting for a hundred years, a fitting climax to Bombay's glorious celebrations. The governor general dressed in olive green took his place at the mole pier at 10.15 am as the first of the last batch of embarking troops came out of the customs shed.[61]

Gandhi was assassinated on 30 January 1948. The news of his death led to some violent outbursts in the city that were soon controlled. Three-hundred thousand people paid him a silent homage at the beach outside Bombay, dipping in the sea as the radio announced that Gandhi's funeral pyre had been lighted.[62]

The people of Bombay paid their last homage to their much loved leader, when the urn containing a portion of the Mahatma's ashes was kept on view in the Town Hall in February 1948. The place turned into one of pilgrimage. The brass pot containing the ashes was taken to the Town Hall by B.G. Kher and the BPCC president S.K. Patil, and placed on a four-tiered, khadi-draped pedestal erected in the centre of the hall. The decoration in white was simple and impressive. The armed forces and the government officials paid homage to Gandhi. Lamps were burnt and the fragrance of incense sticks filled the air as thousands came with flowers and hearts heavy with grief. Many occupied the steps and the road leading to the hall and listened to bhajans in the evening. More than 500,000 people formed a procession on 12 February for the immersion of Gandhi's ashes in the Arabian Sea at Chowpatty. At Chowpatty, the largest crowd ever seen on the sands had assembled; there was the chorus of Gandhi's favourite bhajans and recitations from the Gita, the Quran, and the Zend-Avesta. After the prayers, S.K. Patil carried the urn to a fire float of the Port Trust and the ashes were cast into the sea. The city observed a complete hartal. The flag

**Figure 9.8** The procession carrying the urn containing Gandhi's ashes for immersion at Chowpatty, Bombay, on 12 February 1948.
*Source*: Vithalbhai Jhaveri Collection/Dinodia Photos.

flew at half-mast. The public traffic services were suspended and all restaurants, cinemas, and places of entertainment were closed.[63]

Emotional and touching tributes were paid to the Mahatma all over the world. In Bombay, according to B.G. Kher's tribute, 'It is the duty of every Indian to head the path shown by him and foster brotherhood and harmony among all communities.' In the words of M.C. Chagla, 'He was not fighting for power, not for loaves and fishes of office but for the very soul of Nation. He made us rediscover our soul. He made us conscious of our great heritage;

he installed in us a sense of pride and dignity, and rekindled in us the burning flame of patriotism.'[64] A resolution passed by the cabinet of the Bombay government stated that 'Mahatma Gandhi dedicated his whole life to the service of humanity. He did not use the beaten track, but forged a new method and a new outlook for approaching problems of human life, whether religious, moral, social or economic. He thereby gave a new meaning to life.'[65]

The association of the Mahatma with Bombay has a long history. It contains pages from the life of the Mahatma and the people of the city. It provides glimpses seen in Bombay of his unconventional approach to politics, his innovative strategies, his ability to bring together and mobilize people of different ideological streams, his human qualities, and his ways of communication. The response of the people of Bombay to his call was no less important. He energized the city, and the city nurtured him.

## Notes and References

1. Home Department (Special), File 1110 (6)-A (2), 1942, MSA.
2. Home Department (Special), File 1110 (6)-A (2), 1942, MSA.
3. Dalal, *Gandhi*, p. 204.
4. *The Times of India* dated 6 March 1944 filed in Home Department (Special), File 1110 (3) (d) 1944, MSA.
5. *The Bombay Chronicle* dated 13 March 1944 filed in Home Department (Special), File 1110 (3) (d) 1944.
6. *The Bombay Chronicle* dated 17 March 1944 filed in Home Department (Special), File 1110 (3) (d) 1944.
7. *The Bombay Chronicle* dated 30 March 1944 filed in Home Department (Special), File 1110 (3) (d) 1944.
8. *The Bombay Chronicle* dated 7 October 1944 filed in Home Department (Special), File 1110 (3) (d) 1944.

9. D.G. Tendulkar, *Mahatma: Life of Mohandas Karamchand Gandhi*, illustrations collected and arranged by Vithalbhai K. Jhaveri, Vol. 6 (Bombay: Vithalbhai K. Jhaveri and D.G. Tendulkar, 1953), p. 312; Dalal, *Gandhijini Dinwari*, p. 509.

10. P.C.'s Office, Bombay, extract from File No. 3001/H/X, 2 Political quoted in Kunte, *Source Material for a History of the Freedom Movement in India*, Vol. III, Part VII, pp. 630–1.

11. *CWMG*, Vol. 77 (New Delhi: Publications Division, Ministry of Information and Broadcasting, Government of India, 1979), p. 488; Dalal, *Gandhi*, p. 145.

12. *CWMG*, Vol. 77, p. 275.

13. *CWMG*, Vol. 77, pp. 488–9.

14. Chief Commissioner's Office, Bombay, File No. 3001/HP cited in *CWMG*, Vol. 77, p. 433.

15. *The Hindu* dated 7 August 1944 cited in *CWMG*, Vol. 78 (New Delhi: Publications Division, Ministry of Information and Broadcasting, Government of India, 1979), p. 10.

16. Pyarelal, *Mahatma Gandhi*, Vol. 1, p. 48.

17. Dalal, *Gandhi*, p. 144.

18. Dalal, *Gandhi*, p. 145.

19. *CWMG*, Vol. 78, p. vi.

20. Tendulkar, *Mahatma*, Vol. 6, p. 333.

21. Tendulkar, *Mahatma*, Vol. 6, p. 341.

22. *The Hindu* dated 29 September 1944 cited in *CWMG*, Vol. 78, p. 103.

23. *CWMG*, Vol. 78, p. 87.

24. *The Hindu* dated 29 September 1944 cited in *CWMG*, Vol. 78, p. 117.

25. *The Hindu* dated 29 September 1944 cited in *CWMG*, Vol. 78, p. 123.

26. 'Gandhi–Jinnah Talks', in *CWMG*, Vol. 78, pp. 142–3.

27. 'Bombay Secret Abstract', 1944, p. 94, para 282 cited in Kunte, *Source Material for a History of the Freedom Movement in India*, Vol. IX, p. 286.

28. Dalal, *Gandhi*, p. 147.

29. 'Bombay Secret Abstract', 1945, p. 102, para 311 cited in Kunte, *Source Material for a History of the Freedom Movement in India*, Vol. IX, p. 287.

30. *The Bombay Chronicle* dated 4 April 1945 cited in *CWMG*, Vol. 79 (New Delhi: Publications Division, Ministry of Information and Broadcasting, Government of India, 1980), pp. 341–2.

31. *The Bombay Chronicle* dated 7 April 1945 cited in *CWMG*, Vol. 79, p. 349.

32. The meeting took place on 12 April as recorded in Dalal, *Gandhi*, p. 147.

33. 'Bombay Secret Abstract', 16 April 1945, p. 67, Bombay City, S.B., Congress Affairs cited in Kunte, *Source Material for a History of the Freedom Movement in India*, Vol. IX, p. 300.

34. 'Bombay Secret Abstract', 16 April 1945, p. 295, Bombay City, S.B. (I) cited in Kunte, *Source Material for a History of the Freedom Movement in India*, Vol. IX, p. 289.

35. *The Bombay Chronicle* dated 12 April 1945 cited in *CWMG*, Vol. 79, p. 358.

36. *CWMG*, Vol. 79, p. 359.

37. *CWMG*, Vol. 79, p. 361.

38. 'Bombay Secret Abstract', 16 April 1945, p. 67, Bombay City, S.B., Congress Affairs cited in Kunte, *Source Material for a History of the Freedom Movement in India*, Vol. IX, p. 300.

39. *The Bombay Chronicle* dated 13 April 1945 cited in *CWMG*, Vol. 79, pp. 364–7.

40. *CWMG*, Vol. 79, p. 384.

41. *The Bombay Chronicle* dated 18 April 1945 cited in *CWMG*, Vol. 79, pp. 389–91.

42. 'Bombay Secret Abstract', 1945, p. 116, para 353 cited in Kunte, *Source Material for a History of the Freedom Movement in India*, Vol. IX, p. 289.

43. Dalal, *Gandhi*, p. 148.

44. 'Bombay Secret Abstract', 1945, p. 291, para 876 cited in Kunte, *Source Material for a History of the Freedom Movement in India*, Vol. IX, p. 293.

45. *The Bombay Chronicle* dated 22 September 1945 cited in *CWMG*, Vol. 81 (New Delhi: Publications Division, Ministry of Information and Broadcasting, Government of India, 1980), p. 274.

46. Meena Menon, 2010, 'Chronicle of Communal Riots in Bombay Presidency (1893–1945)', *Economic & Political Weekly*, 45(47), p. 71.

47. 'Bombay Secret Abstract', 16 March 1945, p. 171, Bombay City, S.B. (I) cited in Kunte, *Source Material for a History of the Freedom Movement in India*, Vol. IX, p. 299.

48. Kanji Dwarkadas, *Ten Years to Freedom, 1938–1947: An Eyewitness Story* (Bombay: Popular Prakashan, 1968), pp. 155–6.

49. Nripendra Nath Mitra (ed.), *The Indian Annual Register: An Annual Digest of Public Affairs of India, January–June 1946*, Vol. I (Calcutta: Annual Register Office, 1946), p. 306.

50. *Amrita Bazar Patrika* dated 23 February 1946 quoted in Biswanath Bose, *RIN Mutiny, 1946: Reference and Guide for All* (New Delhi: Northern Book Centre, 1988), p. 126.

51. *Harijan* dated 3 March 1946 cited in *CWMG*, Vol. 83 (New Delhi: Publication Division, Ministry of Information and Broadcasting, Government of India, 1981), p. 175.

52. *Harijan* dated 7 April 1946 cited in *CWMG*, Vol. 83, pp. 241–3.

53. *The Hindu* dated 14 March 1946 cited in *CWMG*, Vol. 83, p. 245.

54. *Harijan* dated 31 March 1946 cited in *CWMG*, Vol. 83, pp. 245–6.

55. *Harijan* dated 7 April 1946 cited in *CWMG*, Vol. 83, pp. 256–9.

56. 'Bombay Secret Abstract', 1945, p. 109, para 246 cited in Kunte, *Source Material for a History of the Freedom Movement in India*, Vol. IX, pp. 298–9.

57. P.C.'s Office, Bombay, extract from File No. 3001/H/XIII, p. 197, Bombay, 1 April 1946 cited in Kunte, *Source Material for a History of the Freedom Movement in India*, Vol. III, Part VII, p. 673.

58. Dalal, *Gandhi*, p. 152.

59. *Harijan* dated 21 September 1947 cited in *CWMG*, Vol. 89 (New Delhi: Publications Division, Ministry of Information and Broadcasting, Government of India, 1983), p. 178.

60. *The Times of India*, 12 October 1947.

61. *The Free Press Journal*, 18 August 1947.

62. *The Sun*, 1 February 1948.

63. *The Times of India*, 10, 11, and 14 February 1948.

64. Kamalini Manmade (compiler), *World's Tributes to Mahatma Gandhi: The Father of the Nation, Our Beloved 'Bapu'* (Bombay: Lotus Publication, 1949), pp. 84–5.

65. *The Times of India*, 5 February 1948.

# CONCLUSION

BOMBAY VIBRATED WITH UNPRECEDENTED VITALITY AND ENERGY during the period of the freedom struggle. The Rowlatt Satyagraha, hartal on the deportation of Horniman, involvement in the Khilafat Movement, boycott of the Prince of Wales, protest against the Simon Commission, and participation in the Civil Disobedience and Quit India movements demonstrated tenacity and bravery, defiance and determination, and fearlessness and perseverance of the people of Bombay. Celebrations of 'Gandhi Day' or 'Flag Day' during the Gandhi Week were expressions of the city's nationalist spirit and its adoration for Gandhi. People's protests against the British rule transformed the city into a magnificent stage with Gandhi as the master director. Well-known leaders as well as little-known or unknown men and women played major roles.

They created history with their passion for the motherland and drive for freedom. Gandhi's leadership was charismatic, and their participation astounding. Although they had their moments of despair and desolation, they surpassed the obstacles of violent outbursts and repression by the British. Together they opened uncharted avenues to reach the destination of independence.

Processions, hartals, picketing against shops of foreign cloth and liquor, flag-salutation ceremonies, and political meetings engulfed various parts of the city. Meetings at different halls, such as the Muzaffarabad Hall or the Morarji Gokuldas Hall, or at the Chowpatty sands or the Esplanade Maidan were arranged with efficiency. In this context, the example of a call for a public meeting at the Esplanade Maidan is relevant. Issuing a note to the press on 28 August 1930, the Bombay Satyagraha Committee declared:

[It was] the inherent right of every citizen to use the Azad Maidan for purposes of congregation, exercise, drilling or such other purposes as are non-violent. In pursuance of this declaration it is the inherent right of the satyagraha committee to assert its right for the use of the Azad Maidan as will vindicate the public liberty. The satyagraha committee calls upon the citizens of Bombay to exercise their right undeterred by any order, or ordinances which are meant to throttle all expressions of freedom.[1]

The committee further stated, 'The satyagraha committee has decided to hold the monthly flag salutation ceremony on the Azad Maidan on the morning of Sunday the 31st August 1930 at 8 a.m.'[2] Such was the spirit that kept the city energized.

Prashant Kidambi aptly describes the situation.

Gandhian nationalism in Bombay produced an impressive array of political spectacles—*hartals*, flag salutations, dawn marches, sit-downs, pickets, parades and processions—that reinscribed the city's public arenas as nationalist space. In the campaign against the Rowlatt Act in choreographed rituals of resistance were usually enacted in the Gujarati and Maharashtrian localities of the Indian Town. Occasionally, too, very large nationalist gatherings were held at Chowpatty beach on the western foreshore of the island, which served as a 'point of intersection' between the European- and Indian-dominated parts of the city. However, during the Civil Disobedience movement a decade later, Gandhian nationalists began to lay claim to the spaces hitherto dominated by Bombay's colonial elite. In particular the Esplanade Maidan in South Bombay, a vast open space that was the physical and symbolic centre of the British political and business establishment within the city, was renamed Azad Maidan ('Freedom Park') and became the principal site for staging nationalist spectacles of collective defiance and protest.[3]

By the 1920s, nationalist sentiments had started influencing the portals of the BMC also. There were strong leaders in the corporation who were inclined towards Gandhi and the Congress. The Nationalist Municipal Party led by Vithalbhai Patel was close to Gandhi and the Congress. A fresh breeze blew in with the boycotting of the functions to bid farewell to the outgoing governor or welcome the incoming governor. Presenting of the addresses to Gandhi in 1924 and 1931 by the BMC was an echo of the nationalist spirit surging outside the civic institution.

Aloo Dastur had vivid memories of Bombay during the freedom struggle. Talking about the Civil Disobedience and Quit India movements, she said:

The traditional Indian attitude of passivity somehow vanished into thin air. This was truly something great accomplished by Gandhiji. Perhaps he himself was not aware of the forces he was unleashing but I believe that the greatest impact Gandhiji made was in making the Indian shed his innate fear. He restored to us Indians our erect posture. He made us look any foreigner in the face. He made us shed our fear of the lathi, the prison house, even the bullet. This was no mean achievement and since this was done, it was evident that freedom could not be delayed much longer. The Indian by 1930 had, so to say, found his soul. This came to be carried on a little further in the Quit India movement.[4]

Bombay had left an indelible mark on the history of the India of those times. According to Claude Markovits, during the first half of 1932 the developments in Bombay were particularly spectacular and the great metropolis of western India formed an increasing contrast to the rest of urban India. In most towns and cities, the repressive measures taken by the authorities, including the confiscation of property on a large scale, effectively deterred business people from participating in civil disobedience activities, and the campaign failed to make a great impact. Boycott activities took place on a much reduced scale, particularly in Calcutta. Everywhere the Congress seemed to be short of funds. The major exception in this situation was Bombay (and, to a lesser extent, Ahmedabad). The governor of Bombay could rightly call the city 'the keep of Gandhism', for the disturbances in the cotton market there were greater than those in 1930.[5]

For Gandhi, politics was a sphere not merely for the elite and the educated; it belonged to all the people. Accordingly, he drew various people to nationalist politics—the people who were not yet politicized, who were so far on the periphery of politics. He could get support from different people, cutting across the divisions of community, caste, and gender. Many sacrificed all they had for the emancipation of the motherland. Inspired by Gandhi, they broke social taboos and political restrictions. Usha Mehta remembered the days of Quit India warmly. In her words:

It was my good fortune to have been able to contribute my humble mite to the Quit India struggle of 1942—our last struggle for freedom. The freedom for which we were fighting was not merely political freedom. It was freedom which had a moral basis. The struggle in 1942 was a spontaneous revolution. It was not a revolution which was engineered by any particular section or class in the society but was an uprising of the whole nation. When we were fighting for freedom we certainly had a picture of an independent India before us. Gandhiji taught us that we have to build a new India where there will be no high caste and no low caste, no rich and no poor. There will be no distinction between one community and another or between men and women.[6]

Insisting there were many young freedom fighters at that time, she said humbly, 'I just did what I had to. I just rendered my duty to my motherland.'[7]

However, the emergence of communal/caste identity politics and electoral politics also brought bitterness among various groups of the people. Feelings of separate interests were encouraged by the British among the Muslims and the depressed classes. Also, the working class in Bombay did not participate in the mainstream freedom struggle.

The participation of the Muslims was mainly tied up with the Khilafat issue and the leadership of the Ali brothers. Once the issues faded, so did their participation. Although some nationalist Muslims were with Gandhi and the Congress, by and large, the Muslims felt alienated after the upsurge of the Khilafat subsided. According to Rakhahari Chatterji, politics characterized by the passion for unity generated by the Khilafat and Non-Cooperation movements came to be replaced by politics of interest by the mid-1920s. Muslims largely came to rediscover that they had an identifiable political interest in India dictated by the concerns of their community and distinguishable from that of the Hindus.[8] Politics of separate identity, interest, and representation deepened the cleavages. The situation had changed drastically from the 1920s to the 1930s. Arundhati Virmani explains it in the context of the national flag. In 1923, the Muslims rallied in favour of Gandhi's 'Swaraj flag' when it was being defended in the Nagpur flag satyagraha as the symbol of Indian identity and nationhood. In the aftermath of 1923, the Muslim League's relationship with the Swaraj flag evolved from one of acceptance to a certain wariness, then to a more systematic opposition in the early 1930s, and finally to a massive rallying behind its own flag after 1937. According to the secretary of the All-India Khilafat Committee, at the height of the Civil Disobedience Movement the 50,000 Muslims assembled in the Esplanade Maidan of Bombay in 1931 to honour the Muslim flag mirrored this new political mood.[9]

Gandhi was painfully aware of the widening rifts among various groups and communities and, consequently, the emergence of a divided society where religious identities would encourage people to act with passion, pushing reason and solidarity to the margins. He wanted to promote and protect the dignity of the individual and the good of society as a whole. He did not favour reservations and urged for the inclusion of all. His constructive activities, his protests against injustice, and his efforts for dialogue at all levels with all communities as well as the government were aimed at securing this goal. His efforts to find a common ground with Ambedkar, however, were not successful; ultimately, the Poona Pact was agreed upon. There were scenes of protest against him by the members of the depressed classes and the communists on his return from the Round Table Conference on 28 December 1931.[10]

Although Bombay was the centre of the textile industry and throbbing with the working of the mills, the workers were not active in the non-violent struggle of Gandhi. Tilak was their undisputed leader, and Gandhi's non-violent discourse and plan of action did not make an impression on them. Gandhi was also cautious in dealing with their issues. The launch of the Non-Cooperation Movement coincided with Tilak's death on 1 August 1920, resulting in bringing huge numbers of workers out on the streets of Bombay. But the issues of the workers were not tied up with the movement.

There were huge strikes of workers in the city in 1919 and early 1920. The young Marxists had built up a powerful union in the textile industry—the Girni Kamgar Union. In 1928 and 1929, S.A. Dange and his associates led the textile workers of Bombay in massive strikes that paralysed the entire industry. There was an effort by some to identify the working-class movement with the activities of the Congress. Independent of the satyagraha at Vile Parle and Girgaum in 1930, the railway workers of Parel and Matunga were persuaded to associate their strike with the broader struggle about to be launched in the city. But the government of Bombay dealt with them harshly, resulting in violence and anarchy. Further, the Gandhi–Irwin Pact evoked strong opposition from the radical leaders of Bombay. Massive unemployment among the workers, partly due to the Congress-sponsored boycott of mills using foreign yarn, but mainly due to the economic recession, prevented an alliance between the working and middle classes.[11] The communists retained the grip over the mill workers for a long period.

The paths and methods of the Gandhian nationalists and the leftist workers were different. Such differences often burst out on the issue of the flag. According to a news report on 26 January 1930, around 300 communist mill workers rushed to the platform at Chowpatty Sea Face where a big meeting was being held for 'Independence Day'. They pulled down independence flags and sought to hoist the red flag in its place.[12] Discontent against the Congress and Gandhi was also expressed by the display of red flags when Gandhi was departing for London to participate in the Round Table Conference.[13]

Despite such reservations in some sections of the people, Gandhi had a wide support. He had this amazing aura that could touch the lives of the rich and the poor, the educated and the uneducated, the men and the women in Bombay as everywhere else. Women constituted Gandhi's enormous and effective constituency. They supported him in all his activities, from satyagraha to constructive work, from processions to meetings, and from picketing to spinning. Describing the participation of women in breaking the salt law, Kamaladevi has written, 'Women turned every house into a sanctuary for the law breaker. They lent sanctity to their act by their purity of spirit. Even the mightiest military power cannot cope with a struggle that has its being in the sacred precincts of the home.'[14] The contribution of the members of the Desh Sevika Sangh in Bombay was amazing; they broke social taboos by leading the funeral procession of Babu Genu and setting torch to his pyre. They marched fearlessly in the city, produced 'illegal' salt, and even sold it. A report stated that Kamaladevi Chattopadhyaya paid a visit to the Share Bazar in the afternoon of 12 April 1930 and sold salt there at fancy prices. The highest bid for a packet of salt was Rs 500. She succeeded in collecting about Rs 4,000 in all. The *Bombay Chronicle* dated 13 April contained the list of the brokers who purchased salt from her.[15] Women such as Maniben Nanavati intuitively connected to Gandhi's constructive work. She remembered women from all castes and classes working together: 'We were busy with collective cooking, spinning and taking the message to the people … We ate food together and we were together while being beaten by the police too.'[16]

Gandhi drew huge supporters from among the small merchants and shopkeepers in Bombay. They closed their shops when hartals were called, went to the meetings of Gandhi and other leaders, and contributed to the Congress funds. Organizations such as the Cotton Brokers' Association, the Grain Merchants' Association, the Bombay Shroffs' Association, the Indian Merchants' Chamber,

and the Bombay Native Piece Goods Merchants' Association
supported Gandhi and his movement. According to B.R. Nanda,
Gandhi never expected much from the Indian capitalists and
preferred the Congress funds to come from its supporters at the
grassroots.[17] The established industrialists and capitalists were
cautious in their support of Gandhi, although they respected him
and, at times, contributed to his calls for funds. The people at the
middle and lower-middle levels, by and large, had contributed
a lot by their energetic and spontaneous participation in the
movement and constructive work, giving whatever little money
they had and sacrificing opportunities for a secured future.

Gandhi was aware of the potential of the young, and he got
good support from the students in Bombay. His lieutenants
were busy with the work from the early days of the satyagraha.
Shankarlal Banker, an active member himself, had noted that the
students were very enthusiastic about the boycott of educational
institutions. Sarojini Naidu, Vithalbhai Patel, Gangadharrao
Deshpande, Khadilkar, and Jamnadas Mehta used to address the
students in an effective way. Professor Gidwani also used to come
frequently from Ahmedabad to address the students in Bombay.[18]

The Quit India Movement filled the young generation with
new energy. Vasant Pradhan, a young student then, remembered
the days of Quit India vividly: 'Those were exciting days and
every event of that time was inspiring. We didn't think of
whether we would live to see an independent India, but we
kept on moving forward. We were steadfast in our resolution.'
Thousands of students had plunged into the movement. Pradhan
said that there were different groups of students in the city,
each following its own ways. Throwing stones at the locations
housing foreign companies or trying to ignite fire in the police
stations were prevalent activities for them. They did not bother
about the consequences. As Pradhan said, 'We were parts of

the movement and had to do everything to take the movement forward.' For them, 'it was important to be able to volunteer for any nationalist political activity'.[19] He was arrested three times. The students participated in activities such as distributing bulletins, picketing, teaching Hindustani, and carrying messages in different parts of the city such as Girgaum, Dadar, Prabhadevi, Wadala, and Vile Parle.

Bombay was special for Gandhi. The city enthusiastically supported his calls for satyagraha, constructive work, and the collection of funds for nationalist causes. He was happy with the positive responses of the city and equally pained when the city did not meet his expectations. He praised Bombay in endearing terms such as 'Bombay the Beautiful' when the city donated generously to the Tilak Swaraj Fund. But in 1925, the city's apathy to the causes of the sale of khadi, removal of untouchability, and the Hindu–Muslim unity troubled him and he wrote, 'Bombay, which is the first city of India, which was the capital of Pherozshah Mehta's empire, the field of Dadabhai's activity, the place where Ranade, Badruddin and others achieved fame, appears to be asleep today!'[20]

What is remarkable is the fact that Gandhi had faith in people's power right from the beginning of his struggles in South Africa—a faith that rarely found an echo in the government or in the minds of the then leaders and intellectuals of India. This was the faith that rattled the colonial rule in India and this was the faith that stirred nationalist spirit in Bombay.

Gandhi, like every original thinker and trendsetter, has had many critics—during and after his lifetime—ranging from political leaders to academics, including Annie Besant, Winston Churchill, M.N. Roy, Joseph Lelyveld, Ashwin Desai, and Goolam Vahed to name a few. He never claimed to know the absolute truth; he lived by the principle that truth is the end and non-violence the means. His journey took him from one truth to the other. Gandhi's power was not centralized but spread over a nonlinear layering. His ways to strengthen the people were neither intimidating nor contrived. His faith in the innate goodness of human beings and his endless love for all converted men and women of his generation into courageous people not daunted by a coercive state and its repression. Processions, marches, salt raids, picketing, and flag-hosting ceremonies involved many people from diverse backgrounds and provided them a new prism to visualize the independent India. The diversity of caste, class, religion, language, region, and locality during the struggle was not an obstacle; people developed the ability to understand each other and work together. The oppression of the British rule and an urge for independence evoked a spontaneous bonding among them and enabled them to shed all their fears and claim human dignity.

The relationship between Gandhi and Bombay is spread over the chronicles of meetings, protests, political actions, effective leadership, mass mobilization, different ways of communication, and people's aspirations—capturing powerful moments of unfolding nationalism at the local level. Innumerable individual and collective experiences are woven with the mega story where much has been told and yet much remains to be told. The telling and retelling of the story of the city and the leader is important. It gives a better understanding of our past, the city's past. The marching of khadi-clad men and women on the streets; the young and the old bearing the lathi blows and courting prison; women picketing fearlessly and spinning tirelessly; the leader calling for satyagraha, building his teams, and implementing his strategies; meetings swelling in thousands to have his darshan; non-violent battles undertaken by the people under their charismatic leader— these were all scenes of our story of struggles, sufferings, and sacrifices to achieve independence.

Mani Bhavan in Mumbai treasures memories of the Mahatma's association with Bombay. It is a modest two-storeyed building on Laburnum Road in the comparatively quiet locality of Mumbai called Gamdevi. Gandhi stayed here whenever he visited Bombay during the years 1917–34. It served for about those 17 eventful years as the nerve centre in the city for Gandhi's activities and movements. It belonged to Revashankar Jagjivan Jhaveri who was an ardent devotee of Gandhi and his affectionate host during that period. Today Mani Bhavan is a hallowed memorial to Gandhi, to his stay there, and to the activities he initiated from there. This heritage building of national importance is visited daily by a large number of visitors from India and abroad.

Mani Bhavan resonates with the memories of Gandhi's satyagrahas, his fasts, his spinning, his writings, his meetings, and

**Figure C.1** Rajendra Prasad, the then president of India, paying tribute to Gandhi at Mani Bhavan, Bombay, on 10 January 1959.
*Source*: Mani Bhavan Gandhi Sangrahalaya.

his arrest. It is the place where he interacted with his colleagues to mould the freedom movement in the image of the cherished ideals of truth and non-violence. It is a source of inspiration for the lovers of freedom and peace the world over. Revisiting Mani Bhavan on 11 March 1959, Pandit Jawaharlal Nehru observed: 'Mani Bhavan in Bombay will ever remain a precious memory to all those who visited it on many occasions when Gandhiji used to stay there. I am glad therefore, that this house is being converted into a Gandhi Memorial.'

**Figure C.2** Mani Bhavan, Bombay.
*Source*: Mani Bhavan Gandhi Sangrahalaya.

# References

1. 'Daily reports of the police commissioner of Bombay', Confidential No. 4493/H/3717, Head Police Office, Bombay, 28 August 1930 cited in Chaudhari, *Source Material for a History of the Freedom Movement in India*, Vol. XI, p. 451.

2. 'Daily reports of the police commissioner of Bombay', Confidential No. 4493/H/3717, Head Police Office, Bombay, 28 August 1930 cited in Chaudhari, *Source Material for a History of the Freedom Movement in India*, Vol. XI, p. 451.

3. Prashant Kidambi, 2012, *Nationalism and the City in Colonial India: Bombay, c. 1890–1940, Journal of Urban History*, 38, p. 959.

4. Centre of South Asian Studies, University of Cambridge, available at www.s-asian.cam.ac.uk/archive/audio/collection/a-dastur (accessed on 26 September 2016); personal interaction with Aloo Dastur.

5. Claude Markovits, *Indian Business and Nationalist Politics 1931–39: The Indigenous Capitalist Class and the Rise of the Congress Party* (Cambridge: Cambridge University Press, 1985), p. 82.

6. Usha Mehta, 'Reminiscences', in Nawaz B. Mody (ed.), *Women in India's Freedom Struggle* (Bombay: Allied Publishers, 2000), pp. 371–8.

7. Usha Mehta, 'Reminiscences', pp. 371–8; personal interaction with Mehta.

8. Chatterji, *Gandhi and the Ali Brothers*, p. 219.

9. Arundhati Virmani, *A National Flag for India: Rituals, Nationalism, and the Politics of Sentiment* (Ranikhet: Permanent Black, 2008), pp. 223–4.

10. 'Bombay Secret Abstract', 1932, p. 110, para 164 cited in B.G. Kunte (ed.), *Source Material for a History of the Freedom Movement in India: Mahatma Gandhi*, Vol. III, Part IV: 1931–1932 (Bombay: Directorate of Printing and Stationery, Maharashtra State, 1973), p. 71.

11. Kumar, 'From Swaraj to Purna Swaraj', pp. 260–73.

12. *The New York Times*, 27 January 1930.

13. Virmani, *A National Flag for India*, p. 108.

14. Kamaladevi Chattopadhyaya, 'The Struggle for Freedom in India', in Tara Ali Baig (ed.), *Women of India* (New Delhi: Government of India, 1958), p. 19.

15. 'Daily reports of the police commissioner of Bombay', Confidential No. 1682/H/3717, Head Police Office, Bombay, 14 April 1930 cited in Chaudhari, *Source Material for a History of the Freedom Movement in India*, Vol. XI, p. 19.

16. Usha Thakkar, 'Maniben Nanavati: Spinning the Yarn of Freedom', in *Women in India's Freedom Struggle*, p. 119.

17. B.R. Nanda, 'Gandhi and the Capitalists', in *In Search of Gandhi*, p. 127.

18. Shankerlal Ghelabhai Banker, *Gandhiji ane Rashtriya Pravritti (Sansmarano ane Anubhavo)* (in Gujarati) [Gandhiji's Nationalist Activities (Reminiscences and Experiences)] (Ahmedabad: Navjivan Prakashan Mandir, 1967), p. 81.

19. *Participation in the Quit India Movement (1942)*, available at https://www.youtube.com/watch?v=q0RwuH_TMLE (accessed on 26 September 2016); personal interaction with Pradhan.

20. *Navajivan* dated 29 March 1925 cited in *CWMG*, Vol. 26, p. 384.

## FURTHER READINGS

*1921 Movement: Reminiscences.* 1971. New Delhi: Publication Division, Ministry of Information and Broadcasting, Government of India.

Allen, Douglas. 2011. *Mahatma Gandhi.* London: Reaktion Books.

Anderson, Perry. 2013. *The Indian Ideology.* London: Verso.

Ali, Aruna Asaf. 1991. *Resurgence of Indian Women.* New Delhi: Radiant Publishers (under the auspices of Nehru Memorial Museum and Library). Written in collaboration with G.N.S. Raghavan.

Baig, Tara Ali (ed.). 1958. *Women of India.* New Delhi: Publications Division, Ministry of Information and Broadcasting, Government of India.

Bakshi, S.R. 1998. *Gandhi and Mass Movements.* New Delhi: Atlantic Publishers.

Bhattacharya, S. 1981. 'Capital and Labour in Bombay City, 1928–29', *Economic & Political Weekly*, Review of Political Economy, 16(42–3): PE 36–PE 44.

*Bombay to Mumbai: Changing Perspectives.* 1997. Bombay: Marg Publications.

Brown, Judith M. and Anthony Parel (eds). 2011. *The Cambridge Companion to Gandhi.* New Delhi: Cambridge University Press.

Chakrabarty, Bidyut. 2013. *Confluence of Thought: Mahatma Gandhi and Martin Luther King Jr.* New York: Oxford University Press.

Chandra, Bipan, Mridula Mukherjee, Aditya Mukherjee, K.N. Panikkar, and Sucheta Mahajan. 1997 [1988]. *India's Struggle for Independence,* eighteenth impression. New Delhi: Penguin Books.

Chandra, Bipan. 2012. *The Writings of Bipan Chandra: The Making of Modern India, From Marx to Gandhi.* Hyderabad: Orient Blackswan.

Chattopadhyay, Kamaladevi. 1986. *Inner Recesses, Outer Spaces: Memoirs.* New Delhi: Navrang.

Coward, Harold (ed.). 2003. *Indian Critiques of Gandhi.* Albany: State University of New York Press.

Dalton, Denise. 1998. *Gandhi's Power: Non-violence in Action.* New Delhi: Oxford University Press.

Desai, Ashwin and Goolam Vahed. 2015. *The South African Gandhi: Stretcher-Bearer of Empire.* New Delhi: Navayana.

Desai, Narayan. 2009. *My Life is My Message,* translated by Tridip Suhrud, vols I– IV. New Delhi: Orient Blackswan.

Devji, Faisal. 2012. *The Impossible Indian: Gandhi & the Temptation of Violence.* London: C. Hurst & Co.

Di Salvo, Charles. 2012. *The Man before the Mahatma: M.K. Gandhi, Attorney at Law.* Noida: Random House.

Dobbin, Christine. 1972. *Urban Leadership in Western India: Politics and Communities in Bombay City, 1840–1885,* Oxford Historical Monographs. Oxford: Oxford University Press.

Dossal, Mariam. 2010. *Theatre of Conflict, City of Hope: Mumbai, 1660 to Present Times.* New Delhi: Oxford University Press.

Dwarkadas, Jamnadas. 1969. *Political Memoirs.* Bombay: United Asia Publications.

Dwarkadas, Kanji. 1950. *Gandhiji through My Diary Leaves: 1915–1948.* Bombay: Kanji Dwarkadas.

Dwivedi, Sharada and Mehrotra Rahul. 1995. *Bombay: The Cities Within*. Bombay: India Book House.

———. 2004. *The Bombay High Court: The Story of the Building, 1878–2003*. Bombay: Eminence Designs.

Edwardes, S.M. 1909–10. *Gazetteer of Bombay City and Island*, vols 1 to 3. Bombay: Times Press.

Epstein, S.J.M. 1988. *The Earthy Soil: Bombay Peasants and the Indian Nationalist Movement, 1919–1947*. New Delhi: Oxford University Press.

Erikson, Erik H. 1969. *Gandhi's Truth: On the Origins of Militant Nonviolence*. London: Faber and Faber.

Fisher, Louis. 2007. *The Life of Mahatma Gandhi*. New Delhi: HarperCollins.

Gandhi, Gopalkrishna (com. and ed.). 2007. *A Frank Friendship—Gandhi and Bengal: A Descriptive Chronology*. London: Seagull Books.

Gandhi, Jagdish. 2010. *A Tale of Native Towns of Mumbai; Bhuleshwar, Girgaum & Malabar Hill*. Bombay: Jagdish Gandhi.

Gandhi, M.K. 1942. *Quit India*, Yusuf Meherally (ed.), Current Topic Series. Bombay: Padma Publications.

*Gandhiji in Ahmedabad*. 2011. Ahmedabad: Sabarmati Ashram Preservation and Memorial Trust.

Ganesh, Kamala, Usha Thakkar, and Gita Chadha (eds). 2008. *Zero Point Bombay: In & around Horniman Circle*. New Delhi: Roli Books.

Gordon, Johnson. 1973. *Provincial Politics and Indian Nationalism: Bombay and the Indian National Congress, 1880–1915*. London: Cambridge University Press.

Habib, Irfan. 2011. *The National Movement: Studies in Ideology and History*. New Delhi: Tulika Books.

Hardiman, David. 2003. *Gandhi in His Time and Ours*. Delhi: Permanent Black.

Herman, Arthur. 2008. *Gandhi and Churchill: The Epic Rivalry that Destroyed an Empire and Forged Our Age*. New York: Bantam Dell.

Hunt, James D. 1978. *Gandhi in London*. New Delhi: Promilla & Co.

*India's Struggle for Independence: Visuals and Documents.* 1986. New Delhi: National Council of Educational Research and Training.

Israel, Milton. 1994. *Communications and Power: Propaganda and the Press in the Indian Nationalist Struggle, 1920–1947.* New Delhi: Cambridge University Press. The Indian edition published by Foundation Books.

Jayakar, M.R. 1958. *The Story of My Life, 1873–1922,* Vol. 1. Bombay: Asia Publishing House.

———. 1959. The *Story of My Life, 1922–1925,* Vol. 2. Bombay: Asia Publishing House.

Kamat, Manjiri (ed.). 2013. *Mumbai Past and Present: Historical Perspectives and Contemporary Challenges.* Mumbai: India Source Books.

Kumar, R. (ed.). 1971. *Essays on Gandhian Politics: The Rowlatt Satyagraha of 1919.* Oxford: Clarendon Press.

Lelyveld, Joseph. 2011. *Great Soul: Mahatma Gandhi and His Struggle with India.* New Delhi: HarperCollins.

Low, D.A. (ed.). 1977. *Congress and the Raj: Facets of the Indian Struggle, 1917–47.* London: Heinemann.

*Mahatma Gandhi: Photo Album.* 1954. New Delhi: Publications Division, Ministry of Information and Broadcasting, Government of India.

Majumdar, R.C. 1963. *History of the Freedom Movement in India,* Vol. III. Calcutta: Firma K.L. Mukhopadhyay.

Mehta, Subhash. 2015. *M.K. Gandhi: Attorney at Law.* Bombay: Geeta Prakashan.

Menon, Meera and Adarkar Neera. 2004. *One Hundred Years, One Hundred Voices.* Calcutta: Seagull Books.

Nanda, B.R. 1985. 1958. *Mahatma Gandhi: A Biography.* London: George Allen & Unwin.

———. *Gandhi and His Critics.* New Delhi: Oxford University Press.

Narayan, Shriman. 1971. *Memoirs: Window on Gandhi and Nehru.* Bombay: Popular Prakashan.

Naik, J.V. 2005. *British Secret Official View Regarding Lokmanya Tilak and Gita-Rahasya (with Original Documents)*. Poona: Tilak Smarak Trust.

Pantham, Thomas. 1995. *Political Theories and Social Reconstruction: A Critical Survey of the Literature on India*. New Delhi: SAGE Publications.

Parekh, Bhikhu. 1995. *Gandhi's Political Philosophy: A Critical Examination*, Delhi: Ajanta Publication. By arrangement with Macmillan, London (first Indian edition).

———. 1999. *Colonialism, Tradition, and Reform: An Analysis of Gandhi's Political Discourse*, revised edition. New Delhi: SAGE Publications.

Pyarelal. 1958. *Mahatma Gandhi: The Last Phase*, Vol. II. Ahmedabad: Navajivan Publishing House.

Rudolph, Llyod I. and Sussane Hoeber Rudolph. 1967. *The Modernity of Tradition: Political Development in India*. Chicago: University of Chicago Press.

Sarkar, Sumit. 1983. *Modern India: 1885–1947*. New Delhi: Macmillan.

Shakir, Moin. 1983. *Khilafat to Partition: 1919–1947*. Delhi: Ajanta Publications.

Sharma, Radha Krishna. 1981. *Nationalism, Social Reform and Indian Women*. Patna: Janaki Prakashan.

Sheppard, Samuel Townsend. 1917. *Bombay Place-Names and Street-Names: An Excursion into the By-ways of the History of Bombay City*. Bombay: Times of India Press.

Shukla, Chandrashanker (ed.) 1951. *Reminiscences of Gandhiji* (in Gujarati). Bombay: Vora & Company Publishers.

———. (ed.). 1949. *Incidents in Gandhiji's Life*. Bombay: Vora & Company Publishers.

Sorabji, Richard. 2012. *Gandhi & the Stoics: Modern Experiments on Ancient Values*. Oxford: Oxford University Press.

Srinivasan, R., Usha Thakkar, Pam Rajput (eds). 1999. *Pusphpanjali: Essays on Gandhian Themes in Honour of Dr. Usha Mehta*. Delhi: Devika Publications.

'Taj and Swaraj', 1982. *Taj Magazine*, Bombay, 2(2).

Taneja, Anup. 2005. *Gandhi, Women, and the National Movement, 1920–47*. New Delhi: Har Anand Publications.

Terchek, Ronald. 2000. *Gandhi: Struggling for Autonomy*. New Delhi: Vistaar Publications.

Thapar-Bjorkert, Suruchi. 2006. *Women in the Indian National Movement: Unseen Faces and Unheard Voices, 1930–42*. New Delhi: SAGE Publications.

*The Gazetteer of Bombay, City and Island*. 1900. Vol. II, compiled under government order. Bombay: Times Press; Files, Maharashtra State Archives, Bombay.

Tidrick, Kathryn. 2006. *Gandhi: A Political and Spiritual Life*. London: I.B. Tauris.

Tindall, Gillian. 1992. *City of Gold: The Biography of Bombay*. London: Penguin.

Tope, T.K. 1986. *Bombay and Congress Movement*. Bombay: Maharashtra State Board for Literature and Culture.

Trivedi, Lisa N. 2007. *Clothing Gandhi's Nation: Homespun and Modern India*. Bloomington: Indiana University Press.

Weber, Thomas. 1997. *On the Salt March: The Historiography of Gandhi's March to Dandi*. New Delhi: HarperCollins.

Wolpert, Stanley. 2001. *Gandhi's Passion: The Life and Legacy of Mahatma Gandhi*. Oxford: Oxford University Press.

Zaidi, A. Moin. 1973. *The Way Out to Freedom: An Inquiry into the Quit India Movement Conducted by Participants*. New Delhi: Oriental India.

Zakaria, Rafiq (ed.). 1985. *100 Glorious Years, Indian National Congress 1885–1985*. Bombay: Reception Committee of the Congress Centenary Session.

# Glossary

| | |
|---|---|
| bhagini | Sister; woman |
| bhandar | Store |
| dhanushtakli | A particular type of spindle |
| duragraha | Pursuit in a manner unworthy of the cause |
| Ganapati | A Hindu god |
| Hindu Mahasabha ki jai | Hail Hindu Mahasabha (a Hindu organization) |
| hitwardhak | Promoting welfare |
| jhaveri | Jeweller |
| kcharapatti | Slum |
| Mahatma Gandhi ki jai | Hail Mahatma Gandhi |
| Pavitraekadashi | Auspicious eleventh day in the first half of the Shrawan month of the Hindu calendar |
| prabhat pheri | Morning march |
| Quaid-e-Azam | The great leader |

| | |
|---|---|
| Ramdhun | Chanting of prayers for Lord Rama |
| rasda | A form of Gujarati folk dance |
| sabha | Meeting |
| samaj | Society |
| sanad | Permit |
| sanatan | Eternal |
| sarghas | Procession |
| satyagrahi | One who practices satyagraha |
| segree | A stove that uses wood or coal as fuel |
| shraddha | Faith |
| shuddha | Pure |
| takli | An instrument for spinning; spindle |
| tola | A unit of weight used in the old Indian system. One tola is equal to 180 grams |
| vanar sena | Group of children; literal translation is an army of monkeys |
| Vaishnav | Follower of Vishnu |
| vastra | Cloth |
| wadi | A large compound surrounded by buildings. |

## Lines of Songs

| | |
|---|---|
| Vaishnav jan to tene kahiye je peer parai jane re | A devotee of Lord Vishnu is the one who understands the pain of others |
| Charkhe ke karaamat se lenge swarajya lenge | We shall win Swaraj with the strategy of charkha |

## INDEX

# About the Authors

Usha Thakkar is the president of the Mani Bhavan Gandhi Sangrahalaya, Mumbai, India. She retired as professor and head, Department of Political Science, SNDT Women's University, Mumbai, India. She has done postdoctoral research at the University of Chicago, USA, on a Fulbright Fellowship and at Cornell University, New York, USA, on a Sr Fulbright Fellowship and at York University, Toronto, Canada, and on a WID Fellowship from the Shastri Indo-Canadian Institute, New Delhi, India. She was also a visiting fellow at Sheffield City Polytechnic (now Sheffield Hallam University), UK. She has been the vice president of the Asiatic Society of Mumbai, India, and of Banasthali Vidyapith (deemed university for women), Rajasthan, India. Her research areas are Gandhian studies, women's studies, and Indian politics.

She has presented papers at many national and international conferences and has contributed to many prestigious journals. Her publications include *Understanding Gandhi: Gandhians in Conversation with Fred J Blum* (co-editor, 2011), *Women in Indian Society* (co-author, 2001), *Zero Point Bombay: In and Around Horniman Circle* (co-editor, 2008), *Culture and the Making of Identity in Contemporary India* (co-editor, 2005), *William Erskine* (a monograph in the series Founders and Guardians of the Asiatic Society of Mumbai, 2015), *Politics in Maharashtra* (co-editor, 1995), *Kautilya's Arthashastra* (co-author, 1980), and Women's Studies Series (in Gujarati, co-editor, 2000–3). She is associated with many educational institutions.

**Sandhya Mehta** is an independent researcher and the coordinator of the website www.gandhi-manibhavan.org of the Mani Bhavan Gandhi Sangrahalaya. Her publications include *Gandhiji on Religious Conversion* (compilation, 2002). She graduated from Jesus and Mary College, University of Delhi, India. Her interests include the history of the freedom movement of western India and local history. Currently, she is engaged in research on the revolutionary freedom fighters of Gujarat.